HOMEGROWN
GURUS

From Hinduism in America
to American Hinduism

Edited by

ANN GLEIG

and

LOLA WILLIAMSON

SUNY
PRESS

On cover from left to right: Gangaji (Photo courtesy of Gangaji Foundation); Sivaya Subramuniyaswami (Photo courtesy of Himalayan Academy); Ram Dass (Photo courtesy of Rameshwar Das); and Master Charles (Photo courtesy of Synchronicity Foundation)

Published by State University of New York Press, Albany

© 2013 State University of New York

For information, contact State University of New York Press, Albany, NY
www.sunypress.edu

Production by Ryan Morris
Marketing by Anne M. Valentine

Library of Congress Cataloging-in-Publication Data

Homegrown gurus : from Hinduism in America to American Hinduism /
    edited by Ann Gleig and Lola Williamson.
        pages cm
    Includes bibliographical references and index.
    ISBN 978-1-4384-4791-9 (alk. paper : hc)—978-1-4384-4792-6 (alk. paper : pb)
1. Hinduism—United States.   2. Gurus—United States.   I. Gleig, Ann, editor
of compilation.   II. Williamson, Lola, editor of compilation.

BL1168.U532H66 2013
294.50973—dc23   2012045699

10 9 8 7 6 5 4 3 2 1

We dedicate this volume, with loving memories, to our parents:
Lola Williamson's mother, Lola Washington,
her father, Richard Scott Washington,
and Ann Gleig's father, Michael "Spike" Gleig,
all of whom passed away during the preparation of this volume,
as well as to Ann's mother, Ann Gleig,
who resides in Liverpool, England.

Contents

Figures

Editors' Note

Regarding the transliteration of Sanskrit and Hindi terms, in order to accommodate nonspecialist readers, we have chosen to avoid diacritical marks, and instead transliterate words in as readable a fashion as possible. Thus, for example, we render the Hindu deity "Śiva" as "Shiva" and the word *ṛṣi* (sage) as *rishi*. We also break words that may appear as one word in Sanskrit, as, for example, *Bhagavad-Gita* rather than *Bhagavadgita*. However, we do employ the spelling preferred by the guru or movement in question, which may entail previous knowledge of pronunciation from the reader. For example, in chapter 5, rather than "Shaiva Siddhanta," we use "Saiva Siddhanta," and rather than "Subra-muni-ya-swami," we use "Subramuniyaswami."

Introduction

From Wave to Soil

Ann Gleig and Lola Williamson

Some would argue that the term "Hinduism" is woefully inadequate because it enforces a false uniformity on such a wide variety of practices, philosophies, and beliefs. Yet this English word identifying religious propensities of the Indian subcontinent, based on a much earlier Persian designation for the people who lived in the area of the Sindhu (Indus) River, has been in use since the late eighteenth century, and it is likely here to stay. Thus, we somewhat reluctantly continue to use the word "Hinduism." In this book, however, we move to a new problem: how does one characterize this vast array of beliefs and practices we call Hinduism after it has been removed from its original Indian context and begun to mingle with Western worldviews and customs in America?

Thomas Forsthoefel and Cynthia Humes employ the metaphor of waves in *Gurus in America* to chart the phenomenon of Hinduism in America.[1] The first wave began with nineteenth-century teachers such as Swami Vivekananda (1863–1902), and the second wave is dated to those Indian gurus who came in the wake of the lifting of the Asian immigration act in 1965.[2] This book might be viewed as a continuation of *Gurus in America*. It examines the challenges and changes that have occurred in response to the earlier two waves of Hindu gurus, as well as the legacies that have been carried forward from them.

In one sense, then, the gurus appearing here consist of what might be thought of as a third wave of gurus. Many of these gurus, for example, are students and successors of second-wave gurus and so historically represent a third manifestation of Hinduism in America. We employ the concept of a third manifestation, however, primarily as an analytical rather than chronological category in order to signify American-born gurus in Hindu lineages. For example, Helen Crovetto discusses the innovations of American guru Swami Rudrananda, or Rudi, that occur partially in opposition to his own second-wave guru, Muktananda. The American Rudi and the Indian Muktananda were acting in the capacity of guru at the same time. Muktananda's style, however, was decidedly Indian while Rudi's style conveyed his American roots.

After more than a century of experimentation during which Hindu gurus adjusted their teachings to accommodate their American milieu, a new stage in the development of Hinduism in America appears to be taking shape. It can now rightly be called its own tradition—"American Hinduism"—rather than an imported religion. As American-born gurus are increasing in number and their innovative styles reflect a distinctively American cultural and religious ethos, the metaphor of waves washing over the surface breaks down. Given that these gurus, teachers, retreat centers, and organizations come not from across the far shore but are produced from the ground up in America, we prefer to think of them as homegrown.

What happens when we replace "wave" with "soil" or "ground" as our fundamental metaphor? One consequence is the tilting of the balance between Indian and American cultural matrixes. To understand these homegrown gurus, we need to fully comprehend the cultural soil in which they have grown as well as the foreign traditions that have sustained them. Numerous studies have discussed the influence of Western Enlightenment, Romantic, and liberal Protestant discourses on the shaping of Hinduism between the eighteenth and twentieth centuries.[3] One Western lineage we want to draw particular attention to here is Western esotericism.[4] Elizabeth De Michelis's groundbreaking study of modern yoga, *A History of Modern Yoga: Patañjali and Western Esotericism*, brought attention to the role of modern esotericism in the construction and promotion of Hinduism in the West.[5] As De Michelis correctly notes, the seminal role of Western esotericism has been consistently overlooked and neglected in the study of modern and contemporary Hinduism.

Similarly, Catherine Albanese has drawn attention to the determinative role that she terms "American metaphysical traditions" has played in the assimilation of Asian religions in America.[6] In a lineage stretching from colonial New England to the Californian New Age, and incorporating traditions as diverse as Transcendentalism and the Human Potential Movement, Albanese shows how American metaphysical traditions express a distinct American religious ethos that is strongly flavored by American cultural values such as individualism, pluralism, antiauthoritarianism, egalitarianism, democracy, and pragmatism.

Albanese examines how early American metaphysical traditions such as the Theosophical Society and New Thought produced and promoted what she calls "metaphysical Asia," the refashioning of Asian religious and philosophical ideas through an American metaphysical filter. She discusses how, in late nineteenth-century America, the imagined otherness of Asia was channeled into culturally available templates liberal Protestantism, evolutionary theory, and metaphysical traditions provided. According to Albanese, Theosophical leader Madame Blavatsky's 1888 text, *The Secret Doctrine*, was central to providing a reading of Asia that met American metaphysical requirements.[7] Here Blavatsky weds Asian religious discourse with Western esotericism and Darwinian evolutionary theory to reveal the "secret doctrine" of Asia that, in turn, would provide the vocabulary for a generic metaphysical Asia discourse. In the metaphysical Asia Blavatsky produced, Asian historical particularity was erased and ideas such as karma and reincarnation were offered as universal concepts. Albanese convincingly argues that the general American metaphysical project of the late twentieth and twenty-first centuries would continue to sound themes and enact Asias that originated in the Blavatsky opus.

Indeed, many of these themes are present in the homegrown gurus documented here, from Ram Dass's erasure of the North Indian *bhakti* context of his guru to John Friend's reading of Tantra through a New Thought lens; from Andrew Cohen's refashioning of enlightenment through an evolutionary lens to Eckhart Tolle's nonsectarian, universal rendering of traditional Advaita. This book examines the results of this mixture of Hindu sources with American metaphysical traditions, as well as American values such as individualism, egalitarianism, democracy, and a Protestant work ethic. Classifying the different strains of American Hinduism that have been produced from this encounter is no simple task. A possible beginning would be to focus on practitioners and distinguish between immigrant-based Hinduism and forms of Hinduism that Euro-Americans practice. However, even this simple bifurcation lacks precision since some well-known groups, such as the International Society for Krishna Consciousness (ISKCON) and the Satya Sai Baba movement, originally consisted of Euro-Americans but are now populated primarily by Indian Americans. Furthermore, American-born Subramuniyaswami, founder of the Saiva Siddhanta Church in Hawaii and *Hinduism Today Magazine*, has 3 million Hindu followers from countries around the world. Another typology might look at presentation and distinguish between those forms of Hinduism that embrace Indian culture and customs and those that attempt to incorporate Western values and conventions with Hindu-derived practices. Once again, we tread in muddy waters since separating "Indian" from "Western" conventions with today's amalgamation of cultural values is difficult. The British colonization of India from the eighteenth to the mid-twentieth century began a process of enculturation that continues today with the globalization of ideas and cultures. A third possibility is to examine practices and attempt to differentiate between those that have a *bhakti,* or devotional, emphasis and those that stress meditation. Yet this distinction is not always clear. For example, some Hindu meditation-based traditions, such as Transcendental Meditation, are increasingly showing a renewed interest in devotional and ritual aspects that were initially neglected or discarded in the first two guru waves of Hindu teachers.

None of these ways of categorizing is ultimately satisfactory. Just as with Indian Hinduism, the complexity of American Hinduism belies simple classification. Yet one pattern that emerges across the case studies presented in this volume is the simultaneous appearance of an increasing decontextualization of Hindu traditions and a renewal of interest in traditional forms of Hinduism. These two seemingly contrary trends—innovation and preservation, radicalism and recovery—suggest the appearance of conditions more characteristic of postmodernity than modernity. Whereas the modern is characterized by an emphasis on the universal and the objective, the postmodern is defined by its reembrace of the local, the particular, and the subjective. The return to the particular within postmodernity includes a recovery of traditional elements initially discarded in the modernization process. Yet, alongside the revalorization of tradition, one also finds increasing modernization appearing within postmodernism, as well as various combinations of the modern and traditional. Approached this way, these chapters illuminate what might be articulated as the unfolding of postmodern trends, which began with the wave of Indian Hindu gurus who entered the United States in the 1960s in the Euro-American assimilation of Hinduism. Hence, the reader will find examples of American gurus who continue to modernize and universalize Hinduism, as well as examples of those who return to and embrace tradition. Yet other American gurus combine the traditional and the modern in innovative ways.

The emergence of postmodern trends needs to be located in relationship to the modernization of Hinduism. Numerous studies have shown that first- and many second-wave gurus presented what was essentially a modern rather than traditional form of Hinduism.[8] One of the first Hindu gurus to visit America, Swami Vivekananda, produced a modern form of Hinduism identified as "Neo-Vedanta." In order to make it more palatable to a Western audience, Vivekananda demythologized Hinduism and his teaching was markedly absent of the devotionalism that one finds in his guru, Ramakrishna Paramahamsa (1836–1886). Incorporating numerous Western values such as rationality, ethics, and tolerance, Vivekananda framed Hinduism as universal and scientific, and thus a viable choice for modern Western people.

Following Vivekananda, the majority of second-wave gurus also promoted an essentially modernized and Westernized vision of Hinduism, which placed a universal mystical experience at the core of all religions and offered meditation techniques as scientific tools for accessing higher states of consciousness. As Humes and Forsthoefel note, those Indian gurus who came to America after the lifting of the 1965 Asian immigration act rarely presented a traditional form of Hinduism but rather adapted it in various creative ways to make it more suitable for an American audience. Maharishi Mahesh Yogi, for example, the founder of the Transcendental Meditation movement, was skilled at accommodating Hinduism for his American audience, consciously marketing a spiritual movement not bound by culture or ethnicity. Humes shows how Maharishi creatively used the universalism implied by Advaita Vedanta to thrust Hinduism into the global marketplace of ideas. He taught Americans that classical practices of renunciation could be discarded and "cosmic consciousness" could be attained by the simple recital of a mantra.[9] Ramana Maharshi's perennial appeal to Americans was due to his paradigmatic experience of realization and his insistence that such experience is accessible to all, regardless of cultural or social conditioning.[10]

This modern privileging of experience in Asian religions, which scholars such as Robert Sharf have discussed, is a theme of several gurus featured here.[11] Yet some gurus discussed in this volume most decidedly are concerned with ritual or doctrine or both, and others have explicitly challenged the modern, decontextualized experiential focus. This variability presents a formidable challenge in organizing the case studies that follow. We have chosen a structure loosely based on chronology and modern/postmodern themes. Before proceeding to a more detailed consideration of individual chapters, a brief outline of the chapter progression will illuminate the variety of styles of American gurus and how they might be charted along the traditionalist/modernist spectrum of postmodernity.

The opening chapters explore two gurus, Ram Dass and Rudi, who influenced the hippie cohort of the 1960s and 1970s to exchange psychedelic drugs for Hindu-style practice. Although their styles and teachings were different, both maintained a primary modern emphasis on experience. Chapters 3 and 4, focusing respectively on the American legacies of two *shaktipat* (spiritual energy bestowing) gurus, Amrit Desai and Muktananda, exemplify a combination of traditional and innovative forms of religion characteristic of postmodernity. In Chapters 5 and 6, two American gurus are explored: Subramuniyaswami and Kirtanananda, both of whom initially continued the modernization process by decontextualizing and universalizing their respective traditions of Saiva Siddhanta and Hare Krishna (ISKCON), but, for different reasons, ended in reinstituting traditional forms. The final two chapters discuss Neo-Advaitins and Andrew Cohen—which, in their radical reframing of *advaita*, have extended the modernization process to such a degree that even to associate them with traditional Hinduism is questionable.

The homegrown gurus documented here then both reproduce and react against modern forms of Hinduism. Influenced by the Romantic defense of religion from its Enlightenment critics, one of the key characteristics of modern forms of Hinduism is its emphasis on experience rather than doctrine and belief. Ram Dass set the tone for American Hinduism's emphasis on personal experience. F. X. Charet describes in chapter 1, "Ram Dass: The Vicissitudes of Devotion and Ferocity of Grace," how he sought to create a universal message from his emotional encounter with Neem Karoli Baba, a guru from a North Indian *bhakti* tradition. This guru was particularly devoted to Hanuman, a mythical monkey who symbolizes devotion in the Hindu epic, the *Ramayana*. How could Ram Dass make this foreign mythology relevant for a Western audience? His answer, as Charet elucidates, was to simply ignore it and focus instead on his personal experience with a miracle-working guru. Glossing over the cultural context and specificities of Neem Karoli Baba, Ram Dass concentrated on the idea of the guru, presented as disconnected from religion, from culture, and even from his family. In this way, Ram Dass represents the universalizing tendency seen in modernism.

Charet's chapter provides an appropriate opening for the volume since Ram Dass was an influential herald of second-wave gurus, whom many viewed as an original American guru himself. The former Harvard professor's book, *Be Here Now*, became a bible for the hippie faction of the baby boomer generation. Charet's account of Ram Dass's life sheds light on his deeply conflicted personality. Plagued by guilt for what he perceived to be his human imperfections—primarily his homosexuality—Ram Dass's own journey is mirrored in the trajectory of American Hinduism as a whole. While leading a generation to "turn on" by turning East, Ram Dass sought an elusive enlightenment by denying his own humanity and attempting to appear holy in the eyes of others. Only after entering a deep depression did he come to accept himself. Like many others involved in the second-wave guru phenomenon, he suppressed his "shadow side" to his own detriment.[12] When he finally came out about his homosexuality, confusion ensued among many of his followers. Ram Dass's life and his followers' responses epitomize the struggle found in some American Hindu groups between the ideal of the perfected guru and the reality of the embodied person.

Although not as well-known as Ram Dass, Rudi, the subject of chapter 2, "Building Tantric Infrastructure in America: Rudi's Western Kashmir Shaivism," was a significant American Tantric guru. He died in a plane crash in 1973, but several of his American followers, now gurus, keep his legacy alive. Helen Crovetto describes how Rudi adapted the Shaiva Tantra of Kashmir to his American propensities for egalitarianism, a strong work ethic, and an unabashed eclecticism. Rudi was a disciple of Nityananda, Muktananda's guru, as well as of Muktananda himself, and of Adi Da, an American Tantric guru who was also once a disciple of Muktananda. Like these other guru's, Rudi conveyed spiritual energy to his disciples through *shaktipat*. Unlike them, however, Rudi maintained a normal worldly life, working as an art dealer and maintaining association with his relatives.

Rudi did not believe in organizations, and much of his teaching took place in informal settings such as his oriental art store in New York City. He spoke in simple, direct language and encouraged his students to maintain a "working, physical life." The focus on experience we saw with Ram Dass is evident in Rudi as well. However, it does not take the form of devotion to a guru, which Rudi discouraged. Rather experience was sought in practices that stimulated the movement of *prana* (subtle energy). Rudi emphasized these over any type of intellectual learning. He wanted his students to develop their intuition, not their intellects. Rudi preferred to work with individuals in small, local venues, as do American gurus who hail from his teaching today, which sets them apart from second-wave gurus, many of whom established large organizations. Although Rudi distinguished the guru from the disciple regarding the spiritual function of each, he was informal in his social interactions with disciples, reflective of an American egalitarian stance.

Chapter 3, Ellen Goldberg's chapter on Amrit Desai, "Amrit Desai and the Kripalu Center for Yoga and Health," reiterates some of the same conflicts found in chapter 1. With Desai's "fall from grace" due to sexual liaisons, we find a confused community of followers that needed to reassess its concept of the guru as a perfect being. Their response was to reject the guru concept altogether as they ousted Amrit Desai and formed a secular and eclectic retreat center that uses multiple visiting teachers. This blurring of lines between the secular and the spiritual evident in the Kripalu Center for Yoga and Health is a growing expression of postmodern religiosity. By following the paths of both Amrit Desai and the Kripalu Center, Goldberg's chapter provides examples of both a continuation of second-wave themes and an opposition to them.

Amrit Desai grew up in a small village in India, so we cannot call him American-born, and yet "homegrown" is an appropriate descriptor. He came to America at a young age to study art and quickly learned the lingo of what Robert Bellah and others in *Habits of the Heart* call the "American therapeutic character." Goldberg describes how his style of teaching has always incorporated "narratives from Western self-help, holistic health and healing, New Age and pop psychology" into a more traditionally Indian guru-disciple relationship and ashram living model. Goldberg describes Desai's growth as a guru using Weber's terminology of slowly attaining "charismatic legitimacy" that is dependent on a group of followers and the eventual building of an institution. What is unique about this case study is that the institution did not collapse upon the guru's loss of authority. Even with the drastically different styles of the Kripalu Center for Yoga and Holistic Health in Massachusetts and the Amrit Institute in Florida where Amrit Desai continues his work with disciples, an important similarity exists. Both employ holistic healing and pop psychology. Both also teach methods for discovering the unity of mind, body, and *prana* (breath or spirit). Given that the postmodern is associated with an embrace of embodiment and a move away from the transcendental Cartesian subject, this celebration of the body as part of spirituality marks these seemingly disparate teaching models as containing postmodern aspects.

In chapter 4, "Swamis, Scholars, and Gurus: Siddha Yoga's American Legacy," Lola Williamson explores ways in which Tantra is being disseminated to an American audience by gurus and teachers who were once linked to the second-wave guru, Muktananda, or to his successor, Gurumayi. She explores two gurus, Master Charles and Sandra Barnard, and then a network of teachers that had been part of a Teachers and Scholars Department in Gurumayi's ashrams. All of the spiritual teachers and gurus she discusses are concerned with both the preservation of traditional Tantric ideas and practices, as well as innovative ways of understanding them. Master Charles, for example, has developed a form of high-tech meditation using sonic waves that are fed into the meditator's ears through earphones. Even *shaktipat* (awakening of spiritual energy) is given through sonic vibrations delivered to the entire body with the help of a metallic grid. Master Charles continually researches and then employs the latest methods of therapeutic healing. At the same time, he supports a traditional idea of the guru-disciple relationship and engages with his disciples in traditional Hindu chanting. Shrines to

Hindu goddesses are situated throughout the grounds of the Synchronicity Sanctuary in Virginia. However, in the eclectic fashion that characterizes many Hindu-inspired movements in the West, statues and pictures of Mary, the mother of Jesus, and Kuan Yin, the Buddhist *bodhisattva* of compassion, can also be found.

The same tendency toward both innovation and recovery appears in Sandra Barnard. Meditation and traditional Hindu chanting is interspersed in her weekend workshops with forms of bioenergetics, which she learned from a Turkish healer. She feels that work on the psychological and personality levels must always accompany work on the spiritual level. The integration of body, mind, and spirit is also found in John Friend's Anusara Yoga. After he was well established as a Postural Yoga teacher, he invited some of the swamis and scholars he had come to know through his time in Gurumayi's ashrams to teach his students the more intellectual and scripture-based aspects of Tantra. This type of collaboration was rarely seen in second-wave gurus and marks an innovative turn. While Friend displays the second-wave tendency to reach a global audience, create organizations, and trademark terms, some of the teachers he associates with, such as Hareesh Wallis, prefer a less-structured environment. Sally Kempton, another teacher in this network, incorporates depth psychology into her work, yet she is careful to ground her teachings in traditional texts from Kashmir Shaivism, Vedanta, and Yoga.

Some contemporary Hindu gurus have called for a return to tradition or have developed a renewed interest in elements of traditional religion, such as scripture and ritual, which had earlier been discarded in the modernization process. Richard D. Mann, for example, in chapter 5, "A Life in Progress, the Biographies of Subramuniyaswami," explores how Sivaya Subramuniyaswami, the American-born founder of the Saiva Siddhanta Church, established himself as a guru within the South Indian Hindu tradition of Saiva Siddhanta and, through his guru lineage, became the *satguru* (true guru) of 2.5 million Tamil Sri Lankans. Mann analyzes how Subramuniyaswami's biography became an important tool Subramuniyaswami and his followers used to legitimate his status within the tradition of Saiva Siddhanta and validate his authority as representing an orthodox voice within Hinduism. An examination of Subramuniyaswami's biographies and the historical circumstances of their production demonstrate a steady shift in the image of Subramuniyaswami from the 1950s to his death in 2001. From the 1950s to the early 1970s, his teaching is firmly located in the American metaphysical lineage, with its eclectic mixture of psychological, Hindu, and Western esoteric thought. However, after the 1980s and 1990s witnessed a backlash against new religious movements as well as increased levels of South Asian immigration into the United States, Subramuniyaswami's biographies reframe and establish him as an orthodox Hindu guru. In tracing how Subramuniyaswami moved away from the American metaphysical lineage toward a more conservative image as an authentic Hindu guru who primarily addresses an Indian audience, Mann demonstrates the significant impact of diaspora communities on the practice and understanding of Hinduism in America.

The homegrown gurus who teach primarily to a South Asian audience might be expected to display an increasing embrace of traditional religious and cultural forms of Hinduism. The growing appetite for traditional forms of Hinduism in Euro-American practitioners, however, may be more surprising to some. E. Burke Rochford Jr. and Henry Doktorski explore the limits of innovation and the precariousness of noninstitutionalized charismatic authority in chapter 6, "Guru Authority, Religious Innovation, and the Decline of New Vrindaban": a study of the New Vrindaban community in West Virginia. New Vrindaban was led by American-born Kirtanananda Swami, one of the early disciples of A. C. Bhaktivedanta Swami Prabhupada, the founder of the International Society for Krishna Consciousness (ISKCON), more popularly known as the Hare Krishna movement. Following Prabhupada's death in 1977, Kirtanananda became one of ISKCON's eleven successor gurus. After he was violently attacked and subsequently charged with criminal activities and moral transgressions, Kirtanananda's authority and leadership began to waver. Expelled from ISKCON, he initiated several controversial religious innovations at New Vrindaban, including the integration of practices from Christianity and other religious traditions that were intended to Americanize Krishna Consciousness. Such radical changes in the community's core teachings, however, contributed to New Vrindaban's dramatic decline as a religious community.

The second trend toward innovation is clearly demonstrated in the last two essays, Philip Charles Lucas's "Neo-Advaita in America: Three Representative Teachers" and Ann Gleig's "From Being to Becoming, From Transcending to Transforming: Andrew Cohen and the Evolution of Enlightenment." The authors deal with gurus who have moved so far away from traditional forms of Hinduism that the question of whether the label of Hinduism is applicable to them is a legitimate one. These gurus raise questions about how much innovation is possible before the tradition becomes a fundamentally new one. They also point to differences and tensions within the innovative stream itself.

In his exploration of what he calls "the Ramana effect," Lucas highlights the increasing modernization of traditional Advaita Vedanta, asking how Ramana Maharshi, in spite of his disinterest in founding a spiritual movement, has inspired a host of spiritual teachers in America, who are grouped under the general rubric of Neo-Advaita. Traditional Advaita Vedanta is a conservative monastic institution, which holds the view that realization of ultimate reality can be attained only through correct scriptural interpretation. Furthermore, only male Brahmin renouncers are fully qualified to study scripture. In contrast, Maharshi claimed that direct experiential realization of *Brahman* is possible for all people, regardless of caste, gender, or culture, through the practice of self-inquiry. Drawing on Thomas Csordas, Lucas identifies two essential factors—portable practice and transposable message—that must be present for a religious tradition to move successfully into a new cultural setting. Lucas argues that Maharshi's influence is attributable to both the portability of his spiritual method and the universality of his teaching, which required no commitment to institution or ideology.

By deemphasizing the traditional Hindu elements of their teaching and repackaging them within the therapeutic climate of contemporary America, Lucas shows how three Neo-Advaita gurus—Eckhart Tolle, Gangaji, and Arunachala Ramana—have further radicalized Maharshi's experiential Advaita. Moreover, he notes that these Neo-Advaita gurus can be located within a distinctively American liberal spiritual lineage, which stretches from the Transcendentalists to the New Age, and which values characteristics such as interior awakening, a privileging of the experiential over the doctrinal dimensions of religion, a mistrust of religious institutions, open-ended spiritual seeking, and an appreciation of the unity of the world's spiritual traditions.

These Neo-Advaita gurus have been criticized by more traditional Advaita followers, who have lamented the decontextualization of a nondual metaphysics from its cultural matrix and its framing as an essentially universal experiential category. Whereas such voices have rallied against the experiential emphasis by calling for a return to a traditional Hindu institutional context, American guru Andrew Cohen has advocated the development of a new "post-traditional" cultural context that unites the premodern contemplative wisdom of the East with the modern scientific achievements of the West and thereby renders enlightenment relevant for the twenty-first century. Ann Gleig charts Cohen's career from his early period as a Neo-Advaita teacher to his present manifestation as a leading proponent of "evolutionary enlightenment," a teaching that places Eastern religious understandings of nonduality in an evolutionary context.

After a short period as a charismatic Neo-Advaita teacher, Cohen had an acrimonious split with H. L. Poonja, his Indian Advaita guru, and dismissed the "instant enlightenment" teachings of Neo-Advaita as both unethical and ineffective. Cohen insisted that enlightenment experiences must be expressed in impeccable behavior and set as the aim of his second teaching—impersonal enlightenment—the perfect expression of the absolute Self on the relative level. In his current teaching of evolutionary enlightenment, Cohen moves from ethics to evolution and posits a spiritual hermeneutic of evolution and an evolutionary interpretation of enlightenment. Framing his teaching as a shift "from Being to Becoming or from Transcending to Transforming," Cohen reconfigures enlightenment from a world-negating and transcendent state to a unique form of consciousness that furthers the evolution of the cosmos. In doing so, Gleig notes, Cohen has aligned and legitimated his teaching with a Tantric rather than Advaitin understanding of nonduality that affirms the material world as an expression and site of the Absolute.

This Tantric-aligned affirmation of the material also fits with the postmodern celebration of embodiment and its move away from the Cartesian mind-body dualism. As noted, many of the gurus documented here demonstrate an interest in nondual metaphysics and particularly Tantric world-affirming ones. From a purely socioeconomic perspective, a Tantric embrace has been dismissed as merely the inevitable infiltration of American materialism into Asian renunciate traditions.[13] A more generous hermeneutic, however, can appreciate it as an authentic attempt to develop more integrative forms of spirituality that include and transform rather than repress and deny embodiment and the everyday world.[14] For many, such an integrative move became ethically and pragmatically imperative after the now well-documented "fall of the guru," the series of financial and sexual scandals that rocked a number of North American Hindu and Buddhist communities in the 1980s and 1990s.[15] In the wake of these controversies, many of these communities were forced to question the efficacy of importing a traditional hierarchical Indian guru-disciple relationship into a contemporary Western society that values individualism and equality.

Many American gurus have attempted a democratic revision of the guru-disciple relationship as one response to the controversies. The absolute barrier between the "enlightened guru" and the "lost seeker" has softened. Another response is evident in American Hindus' hesitation to place complete trust in a single person. Thus, we see increased collaboration among American Hindu gurus and teachers, as well as a tendency from those on the Hindu path to learn from multiple teachers, either sequentially or simultaneously. On the other hand, the valorization of the guru-disciple relationship cultivated by first- and second-wave gurus has become deeply embedded in much of American Hinduism, and in some cases, the ideal of submission to a single guru over a lifetime is still upheld. A third response appears as a distrust of large organizations. Smaller and more personal venues are growing in number, which is a postmodern rather than modern trend.

The homegrown gurus appearing here, therefore, can be dotted along an arc from the modern to the postmodern. Interestingly, David McMahan and Jeff Wilson have uncovered similar trends in their respective studies of American Buddhism, revealing that the American adaptation of Buddhism is not a progressive linear movement away from traditional Asian elements toward modern phenomena; rather, it increasingly demonstrates an interest in more traditional elements that had been discarded in the initial modernization process.[16] In a survey of contemporary American Buddhism, McMahan notes that the practitioners are taking a variety of positions along the traditionalist-modernist spectrum. He sees this as a sign of the emergence of conditions associated with later-modernity or postmodernity, such as multiple interpretations of tradition, increasing pluralism, and a combining of various forms of modernism and traditionalism. Just as McMahan implies that these changes signal the development of postmodernist Buddhism, we suggest that with these homegrown gurus, we are witnessing the flourishing of a postmodern stage in the Euro-American assimilation of Hinduism.

Notes

1. Thomas A. Forsthoeffel and Cynthia Ann Humes, eds., *Gurus in America* (Albany, NY: SUNY Press, 2005).

2. For details of the first wave, see Polly Trout, *Eastern Seeds, Western Soil* (Palo Alto, CA: Mayfield Publishing, 2001); and Lola Williamson, *Transcendent in America* (New York: New York University Press, 2010).

3. Raymond Schwab, *The Oriental Renaissance: Europe's Re-Discovery of India and the East 1680–1880*. (New York: Columbia University Press, 1984); Carl Jackson, *The Oriental Religions and American Thought* (Westport, CT: Greenwood Press, 1981).

4. For definitions and discussions of Western Esotericism, see Wouter Hanegraaff, *New Age Religion and Western Culture: Esotericism in the Mirror of Secular Thought* (Albany, NY: SUNY Press, 1989) and Antione Faivre, *Access to Western Esotericism* (Albany, NY: SUNY Press, 1994).

5. Elizabeth De Michelis, *A History of Modern Yoga* (London: Continuum, 2004).

6. Catherine Albanese, *A Republic of Mind and Spirit: A Cultural History of American Metaphysical Religion* (New Haven, CT: Yale University Press, 2007).

7. H. P. Blavatsky, *The Secret Doctrine* (New York: Theosophical University Press, 1888; 2009).

8. De Michelis, *A History of Modern Yoga*; Thomas Forsthoefel and Cynthia Humes, eds., *Gurus in America*; Karen Pechilis, ed., *The Graceful Guru* (London: Oxford University Press, 2004); Lola Williamson, *Transcendent in America*.

9. Cynthia Anne Humes, "Maharshi Mahesh Yogi: Beyond the TM Technique," in *Gurus in America*, ed. Forsthoefel and Humes, 55–80.

10. Thomas Forsthoefel, "Weaving the Inward Thread to Awakening," in *Gurus in America*, ed. Forsthoefel and Humes, 37–54. See also Phillip Lucas in the present volume.

11. Robert Sharf, "Experience," in *Critical Terms for Religious Studies,* ed. Mark C. Taylor (Chicago: University of Chicago Press, 1998), 94–116.

12. See chaps 3, 4, and 5 in Williamson's *Transcendent in America* for examples of this tendency toward suppression of personal and organizational negativity in Self-Realization Fellowship, Transcendental Meditation, and Siddha Yoga.

13. See Hugh B. Urban, *Tantra: Sex, Secrecy, Politics and Power in the Study of Religion* (Berkeley: University of California Press, 2003); Jeremy Carrette and Richard King, *Selling Spirituality* (London: Routledge, 2005).

14. Jeffrey J. Kripal, *Esalen: America and the Religion of No Religion* (Chicago: University of Chicago Press, 2007).

15. Jeffrey J. Kripal, "Seeing Inside and Outside the Goddess: The Mystical and the Ethical in the Teachings of Ramakrishna and Vivekananda," in *Mapping Boundaries: Essays on the Ethical Status of Mysticism,* ed. Jeffrey J. Kripal and William G. Barnard, 230–264 (New York: Seven Bridges Press, 2002).

16. Jeff Wilson, *Mourning the Unborn Dead* (Oxford, Eng.: Oxford University Press, 2009), and David McMahan, *The Making of Buddhist Modernism* (Oxford, Eng.: Oxford University Press, 2008).

1

Ram Dass

The Vicissitudes of Devotion and Ferocity of Grace

F. X. Charet

The following focuses on one example of the influence of contemporary Indian gurus in the West by exploring the personal backgrounds and contexts of American-born Ram Dass and his Indian guru Neem Karoli Baba, as well as the transformation of ideas, beliefs, and practices that have occurred in the process of this particular transmission of Hinduism to America.[1] Ram Dass has been instrumental in bringing Indian spirituality and practices to America in what could be termed the second great awakening of Eastern spirituality in the 1960s and 1970s, the first being initiated by the presence of Vivekananda and others at the 1893 World Parliament of Religions in Chicago. The story of how Dr. Richard Alpert became Ram Dass, one of the foundational figures of the so-called New Age and a popular spokesperson for a range of Indian-inspired beliefs and practices, is a fascinating and largely unexamined one.[2] It also provides an example of how ideas and beliefs can be intimately connected with an individual's personal history and psychology and illustrates the considerable change that ideas undergo as they are transplanted from one cultural context into another.[3]

This chapter examines the encounter between Neem Karoli Baba and Ram Dass, the background out of which this encounter arose, and the results it had on the loosely knit *satsang* (spiritual community) of Western devotees and fellow travelers. The chapter demonstrates how the *bhakti* (devotional) Hinduism that Neem Karoli Baba practiced, advocated, and embodied, with its sources in the emerging Hanuman tradition in India, its mix of sectarian *Vaishnava* and *Shaiva* belief, practice,

15

and iconography, has considerably morphed and transformed under Ram Dass's tutelage as it found its way into the West. The *satsang* under Ram Dass's direction, following the publication of *Be Here Now* (1971), produced its foundational literature in the subsequent gospel text, *Miracle of Love: Stories about Neem Karoli Baba* (1979), while also establishing several organizations and programs such as the Hanuman and Seva foundations and the prison and hospice projects.

This first generation, still in existence and clearly influential, is now beginning to give way to a subsequent generation whose ties to its putative leader and inspiration, Neem Karoli Baba, are largely created through media, including a number of publications, stories, films, and photographs.[4] The new generation is also, in part, anchored in the one full-fledged center in the West, the Neem Karoli Baba Ashram in Taos, New Mexico.[5] This, in turn, is supported by the distant living presence of Neem Karoli's much-beloved successor and keeper of his memory,

Figure 1.1. Ram Dass playing the tamboura (Photo courtesy of Love Serve Remember Foundation)

the aged Siddhi Ma of Kainchi Ashram, Uttarakhand, where the first generation of the Western *satsang* encountered Neem Karoli Baba. This chapter's main focus, though, will be on the journey of Richard Alpert—from his early experiments with psychoactives and his troubling sexuality, to his encounter with the living spirituality of contemporary Hinduism, to the unmaking of his potential status as guru and the making of his identity as Ram Dass, the devotee and, finally, the remaking of him into an American guru.

Richard Alpert: Sex, Drugs, and Spirituality

Ram Dass has briefly sketched his own background and what led him to his fateful encounter with Neem Karoli Baba in *Be Here Now* and repeated it numerous times in his many presentations. In these accounts he offers little detail about his early life, but does say he was inordinately attached to his mother, somewhat removed from his distant and successful father, and stemmed from an affluent New England "Jewish anxiety-ridden high-achieving tradition."[6] His undergraduate and graduate schooling at Tufts and Wesleyan was conventional and his athletic and academic accomplishments were undistinguished. Nevertheless, following his doctoral studies at Stanford, more due to his skills as a lecturer and connections than research and scholarship, his rise in the world of academic psychology was swift and successful. He served in various roles at Stanford and finally at Harvard, where he secured a position that would lead to tenure. Outwardly, he was in an enviable position and a paragon of success. Inwardly, he was neurotic, sexually troubled, and deeply unhappy.[7]

The early 1960s witnessed the beginning of experimentation with various substances, from street-available marijuana and psilocybin to laboratory produced LSD. This countercultural phenomenon attracted the attention of several professionals in psychiatry and psychology, including Ram Dass, then Dr. Richard Alpert, who was later joined at Harvard by another psychologist, Timothy Leary, who eventually achieved considerable notoriety. The common version of what happened is that Leary and Alpert became heavily involved in experimenting with these substances, especially the psychedelics, and encouraged their students and others to do likewise. They saw themselves as pioneers in the mapping of the mind and in exploring the further reaches of consciousness, but they encountered opposition from conservative forces at Harvard and elsewhere. This inevitably led to their 1963 dismissal from their positions at Harvard. The media portrayed them as radical promoters of dangerous mind-altering substances. The reality is that this picture, oft repeated and largely mirrored in the media, is only partially true. The full truth is more complex and hides dark forces in Alpert's life.

In fact, as a teenager Alpert had ongoing difficulties in school and not only felt oppressed by his successful lawyer father's ambitions for him, but also experienced a deep sense of inadequacy intellectually, emotionally, and sexually. He had unsuccessfully tried to enter Harvard and resisted his father's influence that would have allowed him to be admitted to medical school at Tufts, the other profession to which a young Jew of his background should aspire. Instead, he headed for Stanford to study psychology and succeeded in obtaining his doctorate with a dissertation that focused on academic anxiety. Between the more liberal atmosphere of San Francisco and staid Boston, he lived something of a double life, a subject that has not surfaced in his accounts of these years until more recent times. While on occasion he admitted in passing his bisexuality, he did not disclose his early teenage struggles with his emerging homosexuality, as well as how sexually active he was when at Stanford and later at Harvard, until he gave numerous interviews for gay publications in the 1990s. As he confessed, "I'm sure I've had thousands of sexual encounters. It was often two a night."[8] In fact, this behavior figured prominently in the circumstances surrounding his dismissal from Harvard.

Just before the Harvard debacle, Alpert, Leary, and several of their followers moved into a residence Alpert purchased in Newton, a town outside Boston. The house in Newton was renovated to accommodate Leary's eccentric ideas on maintaining a self-contained, closed space to enhance the many psychedelic sessions they were conducting. Neighbors were so displeased by the comings and goings, loud music, and behavior that they tried to have the many occupants evicted. Alpert's father appeared before the board of zoning appeals and successfully argued for the rights of the occupants to be considered "a family," thereby staving off eviction. Various members of "the family" shared tasks, and gender differences and traditional roles became blurred, as did boundaries of sexual intimacy.[9] In addition to experimenting with mind-altering substances, Alpert wanted to "turn on" the many young men with whom he was having relations. Medical student Andrew Weil influenced an editor of *The Crimson*, the Harvard school newspaper, to print an exposé of the dubious scientific value of the experimenting that was occurring and that eventually resulted in Alpert's termination.[10] As Alpert stated more candidly than ever before in an interview with Mark Thompson published in 1994:

Tim Leary and I and a lot of friends had one of these big community houses. We got into a situation where Harvard started to get so freaked about the drugs we were using that they asked us to stop doing our research using any undergraduates. We could use graduate students, or outside populace, but we couldn't use undergraduates because it was too risky. But I had all these relationships with young men whom I really wanted to turn on with. And it had nothing to do with our research; it was my personal life, so I went ahead. It turned out there was another student who was very jealous of this, an editor of the campus newspaper, and he created a huge exposé.

[Thompson:] So it was gay eros and not LSD that got you thrown out of Harvard?

[Alpert:] It was a combination of all those things. In a way, LSD had given me the license to be what I am. It looked at me inside and out and said what you are is okay. And that gave me a license to start to say I didn't want to hide anymore.[11]

But much as drug-induced states may have enhanced Alpert's sexual proclivities, they also deeply divided him. For a time he even entertained the possibility of ridding himself of his homosexuality with the aid of psychedelics by going deep enough to uncover its roots and alter his sexual orientation.[12] Moreover, in the depths of his mind-altering experiences, a transpersonal and spiritual dimension surfaced that had a significant impact on him. In the summer of 1961, at the Fourteenth International Congress for Applied Psychology held in Copenhagen, Alpert surprised everyone, including Leary, by announcing from the podium during Leary's presentation that drug-induced altered states had religious implications and led to a mystical end that resulted in love and peace.[13] The famous "Good Friday Experiment" undertaken in Marsh Chapel at Boston University the following year further enhanced this view when several theological students were administered psilocybin, the majority of whom reported extraordinary experiences of being in the presence of the divine.[14]

Added to this were the extensive associations Alpert and Leary made openly with various spiritual practices and experiences. In particular, Eastern religions, rituals, and practices, along with available textual sources became of considerable interest. They eventually wrote a book, *The Psychedelic Experience: A Manual Based on the Tibetan Book of the Dead* (1964), coauthored with Ralph Metzner. Parallels and connections were made between the altered states induced by the ingestion of psychedelics and *bardo* states reported in *The Tibetan Book of the Dead*, as well as of the raising of the *kundalini* through the *chakras* discussed in Tantric texts and the extensive commentary by Sir John Woodroffe called *The*

Serpent Power. These two works in the coming decades would obtain a status among a generation of Western seekers out of proportion to their relative native obscurity.[15]

The fame that resulted from the dismissal of Alpert and Leary from Harvard and the latter's charismatic and promotional skills extolling the self-developmental virtues of mind-expanding substances, drew the interest and support of heirs of the Andrew Mellon fortune, who would be Alpert's and Leary's chief benefactors for the next few years. This resulted in Alpert, Leary, and others taking up residence in a large mansion in Millbrook, New York, after being forced out of various places from Mexico to the Caribbean.[16] Millbrook turned into an experimental playground in the expansion of consciousness for those who came through its doors.

Along with the mind-altering substances there was also sexual experimentation, and Alpert indulged himself accordingly, largely with young men—so much so that Leary, after a trip to India, grew suspicious and accused Alpert of having seduced his fifteen-year-old son, Jack, whom he had left in his care. Leary's libertarian ideas were not sufficiently broad to include the practice of homosexuality, something he saw as "evil" and potentially curable through the use of psychedelics.[17] Ralph Metzner, who had also returned from India and was present when the accusation was made, recalled Alpert's sexual proclivities and the proclamations of his male lovers: "Oh. He's my guru now. Tim's not my guru anymore."[18] In the end, Alpert's behavior created a rift between the two of them, and he was forced to leave Millbrook. The grand experiment and self-indulgence of Millbrook began winding down. Alpert settled temporarily in California and, seemingly in a bid to alter his sexual orientation and maintain a relationship of intimacy with a woman, he took up with Caroline Forrest with whom he lived for a while, but the relationship did not endure.[19] In the end, while Alpert and Leary agreed on many things, they would go their separate ways: Leary to infamous grandstanding and reckless proclamations of "turn on, tune in, drop out," and Alpert to the feet of his beloved guru, Neem Karoli Baba, and a new identity as Baba Ram Dass with a message to "be here now."

Encountering Neem Karoli Baba

Of Neem Karoli Baba's earlier life, we have only an outline that is increasingly but inadequately being filled by details that are not always consistent as he revealed little to his followers. He was born Lakshmi

Narayan Sharma of Brahmin descent in the village of Akbarpur, Firoz-abad, Uttar Pradesh, and though the date of his birth is unclear, it was probably early twentieth century. He left home sometime in his youth and travelled to Gujarat to undertake *tapas* (ascetic practices), and then returned nearer to his home. Known by different names and a host of miraculous deeds, he came to be named after the town of Neeb Karori. This morphed into Neem Karoli, as he is known by his Western devo-tees. While he travelled widely across northern India, his chief ashrams when Alpert encountered him in 1967 were near Nainital in the Kumaon district of Uttarakhand and soon to be in one established in Vrindaban, Uttar Pradesh.[20]

The direct influences on Neem Karoli's own religious development are unclear and though a *Vaishnava bhakta* in the *Ram Nam* tradition and a devotee of the monkey deity, Hanuman, he seems neither to have belonged to a formally established *sampradaya* (tradition or school) nor any evident *parampara* (lineage of succession). The written sources of inspiration were less the *shruti* of the canonical *Vedas* than the broad *smriti* literature, especially the Hindi vernacular *Ramayana*, the *Ramacha-ritamanasa* of Tulsidas (1532–1623), the *Mahabharata*, the *Bhagavad-Gita*, the *Anugita*, and other disparate sources such as the sayings of Kabir (1440–1518). Nevertheless, like Tulsidas, a *sarwariya* Brahmin *Vaishnava*, Neem Karoli's devotion to Rama did not preclude, but in fact assured, his acknowledgement of the Vedas and dedication to Shiva and the God-dess, the latter two prominent in his ashrams and temples. Moreover, the distinctly non-Vedic monkey god, Hanuman, was Neem Karoli's pre-ferred deity. One of Neem Karoli's elderly Indian devotees expressed to me in the Neem Karoli Baba ashram in Virbhadra near Rishikesh, presided over by a forty-foot-tall Hanuman in full regalia, "Hanuman is the servant of Rama and is Shiva in his devotional form."[21] Increas-ingly, many of Neem Karoli's followers in India consider him to be an incarnation of Hanuman, a *premavatar* (incarnation of love) as one recent publication put it.[22] The rumor of this was already developing on that fateful day in 1967 when Alpert arrived with Bhagwan Das at the Bhumiandar Ashram and Hanuman Mandir near Nainital in search of "Maharaji," as Neem Karoli was called. A few days later he crossed the footbridge over the nearby valley river, which Neem Karoli had named Uttar Vahini Ganga (the north flowing Ganges) and entered the Himalayan ashram at Kainchi to begin his *sadhana* (spiritual practice) that would change the course of his life and, through him, the lives of many others who followed him.

The story of Alpert's encounter with Neem Karoli has been told and retold by both Alpert and those close to him.[23] What is central to the telling is the fact that Alpert was not prepared for what awaited him, namely someone who could see right into him, including his problematic and guilt-ridden sexuality, and yet embrace him in love, compassion, and acceptance. In fact, as he recounts in *Be Here Now*, Neem Karoli emerges as the omniscient and miracle-working *mahasiddha* of the Kumaon district of Uttarakhand, as he was known then in northern India, and even more so now. The ashram, Kainchi Dham, sequestered in a lush Himalayan valley and built over the cave the legendary but little-known Sombhari Baba, Premi Baba, and other *sadhus* once occupied was the ideal spot for Alpert to escape from the world he had left behind and to establish a new identity. Filled with Hindu temples and *murtis* of Rama, Sita, Hanuman, Durga, and other deities to whom daily ritual offerings and prayers were made, it was a pilgrimage center for *sadhus* and other devotees. Here they stopped to have *darshan* (be in the presence of the guru); listen to the recitation of Tulsidas's *Ramacharitamanasa* or the chanting of the *Hanuman Chalisa*; receive advice, a blessing; partake of *prasadam* (food offerings) and *chai* (tea); and be sent on their way.

For Alpert the breaking point came when Neem Karoli deciphered he had been thinking of his recently departed mother, to whom he was inordinately attached, which he later would publically identify as instrumental in his not being able to develop satisfactory intimate relations with women.[24] He describes it this way in *Be Here Now*:

> Some time later we were back with the Maharaji and he said to me, "Come here. Sit." So I sat down and he looked at me and he said,
> "You were out under the stars last night."
> "Um-hum."
> "You were thinking about your mother."
> "Yes." ("Wow," I thought, "that's pretty good. I never mentioned that to anybody.")
> "She died last year."
> "Um-hum."
> "She got very big in the stomach before she died."
> . . . Pause. . . . "Yes."
> He leaned back and closed his eyes and said, "Spleen. She died of spleen."
> Well, what happened to me at that moment, I can't put into words.[25]

Alpert was incredulous that Neem Karoli could know his thoughts and feelings about his mother and her illness and death:

There just wasn't any place I could hide in my head about this. And at the same moment, I felt this extremely violent pain in my chest and a tremendous wrenching feeling and I started to cry. And I cried and I cried and I cried. And I wasn't happy and I wasn't sad. It was not that kind of crying. The only thing I could say was it felt like I was home. Like the journey was over. Like I had finished.[26]

He went on to add there were other experiences such as watching Neem Karoli ingest 915 micrograms of LSD and "nothing—nothing happens!"[27] As he later commented:

Now the impact of these experiences was very profound. . . . I had been through many years of psychoanalysis and I had still managed to keep private places in my head—I wouldn't say they were big, labeled categories, but they were certain attitudes or feelings that were still very private. And suddenly I realized that he knew everything that was going on in my head, all the time, and he still loved me. Because who we are is behind all that.[28]

Richard Alpert had become Baba Ram Dass (servant of Ram), a name Neem Karoli conferred on him, and was put under the tutelage of his appointed teacher at the ashram, Hari Dass Baba. He absorbed what he could of *bhakti* Hinduism in its oral form and practice, learned some yoga, and pursued his own eclectic spiritual reading, all of which forms the "Cookbook for a Sacred Life" and "Painted Cakes: Books," later parts of *Be Here Now*.

The Making of Baba Ram Dass in America

Arriving back in America, long haired, bearded, barefooted, and dressed as a Hindu swami, Baba Ram Dass launched his second career as a New Age teacher of neo-Hinduism, drawn from his experience in India and culled from his eclectic reading. This centered on the teachings of *karma, atman* (inner self), rebirth, yoga, *moksha* (enlightenment), and his devotion to Neem Karoli Baba as guru. A gifted storyteller, and casting himself as a disciple, he peppered his accounts with Sanskrit terms and represented Neem Karoli's teaching in a language and style that fit his American audience. Much of the Hindu context, ritual, practices, and literature that formed Neem Karoli's religious setting was left behind

Figure 1.2. Neem Karoli Baba with a copy of *Be Here Now* (Photo courtesy of Love Serve Remember Foundation)

or only selectively drawn on to enhance his presentation to a growing number of young people who were personally and spiritually adrift in uncertainty, depression, and meaninglessness.[29] Neem Karoli's North Indian *Vaishnava* background, devotion to Rama and Hanuman, the temple-based setting and liturgy of his ashrams, and the canonical and vernacular scriptural tradition from which he drew were peripheral to his status as a guru and an enlightened being par excellence. In fact, Neem Karoli was represented, then as now, as having transcended cult and caste, without specific teaching other than *sub eck* (all is one) and what could be gleaned by basking in his presence. The classic prosaic description was later rendered by a Western devotee, Anjani:

There can be no biography of him. Facts are few, stories many. He seems to have been known by different names in many parts of India, appearing and disappearing through the years. His western devotees of recent years knew him as Neem Karoli Baba, but mostly as "Maharajji"—a nickname so commonplace in India that one can often hear a tea vendor addressed thus. Just as he said, he was "nobody." He gave no discourses; the briefest, simplest stories were his teachings. Usually he sat or lay on a wooden bench wrapped in a plaid blanket while a few devotees sat around him. Visitors came and went; they were given food, a few words, a nod, a slap on the head or back, and they were sent away. There was gossip and laughter for he loved to joke. Orders for running the ashram were given, usually in a piercing yell across the compound. Sometimes he sat in silence, absorbed in another world to which we could not follow, but bliss and peace poured down on us. Who he was was no more than the experience of him, the nectar of his presence, the totality of his absence—enveloping us now like his plaid blanket.[30]

In classic *bhakti* style, Neem Karoli is identified and revered as a manifestation of the divine. In fact, the contemporary guru tradition in India and its exported varieties in the West are thought to be indebted to the *bhakti* tradition and to its personalized forms. As Joel Mlecko has commented in his judicious survey of the subject:

Within the *bhakti* tradition, Hinduism's *Vedic* roots, though not extracted, have been violently pruned. The charismatic, self-realized teacher triumphed over the hereditary priest-teacher just as devotion and *puja* (rites of offering) triumphed over *Vedic homa* (sacrifice in fire) and *Upanishadic* speculation, meditation, and *tapas* (austerities). Emphasis switched from the ritualism, intellectualism, and legalism of *Brahmanism* to the devotionalism, theism, and personalism of "Hinduism." *Bhakti* became a path of liberation open to seekers regardless of intellectual sophistication or social rank. To some degree this development undermined caste position and gave a decisive impetus to the development of the contemporary position of the guru. The guru is now revered not because he was born a priest or because of academic knowledge but because of existential and inspirational qualities rooted in his personal realization. Salvation centers not on textual authority or logical argument but on experience of founders and teachers who are exemplars of what others can achieve. In this context, the guru often assumes the role of deity.[31]

Whether these characterizations of the impact of the *bhakti* tradition and the assumptions underpinning them are reflective of an actual historical development has been the subject of some debate.[32] Nevertheless, they offer a reading that is congenial to the assimilation of the figure of the guru into modern Western interest in Indian spirituality. For Ram Dass, what became central and remains is the personal and potentially transformative experience of an encounter with a living spirituality, somewhat exoticized and with mystical overtones, but rendered accessible for those who had ventured into the mind-expanding regions of psychedelic-induced experiences. Now, Ram Dass reiterated, those altered states may be accessed through a distilled spiritual practice that focuses the mind and renders them permanent in the form of an enlightened state. The "spiritual props" of rituals, beliefs, traditions, and practices may offer some ways and means to the supreme state of unity with the divine, but the state itself is of signal importance. This is best accessed through those who have attained it, and India has more than its measure of such personages. The task of the *bhakta* (devotee) is *bhakti* (devotion) to the *ishtadevata* (selected deity), or the guru (the human embodiment of the divine), or both. This is the means to *moksha* (attainment of liberation).[33]

Footage from this early period, some included in the recent film biography of Ram Dass, *Fierce Grace,* shows numerous young people gathering on his family's estate in Franklin, New Hampshire, and tapes survive of the many talks he gave. The crowds were taken in by his manner and style and, in spite of the fact that Neem Karoli Baba had instructed him not to speak of him, the word inevitably got out and others began to trek to Kainchi and Vrindaban to see his guru. Over the next few years, and in the midst of his proclamations about overcoming the ego and sensual pleasures, Ram Dass struggled to conquer his narcissism and sexual predilections. Considerably troubled by his lack of success, and having cast himself in the role of spiritual teacher, in the fall of 1970 he returned to India and informed his guru: "Well, I am not pure enough to do whatever it is I am supposed to be doing—I don't even know what it is but I am not pure enough to do it." In response, Neem Karoli slapped him on the head, pulled his beard, and said, "You will be."[34]

Ram Dass's struggle with his sexuality was not so easily laid aside, and he tried again and again to overcome his desires through various means. In the end, he resorted to ritual. At the completion of the nine-day annual Hindu *navaratri/Durga puja* (celebration of the Great Goddess), participants are invited to unburden themselves of desires and other troubles and place them in the fire to be consumed. As Ram Dass describes his own motivation, actions, and the outcome:

> They were going to burn a huge straw effigy to Ravanna. Ravanna's the bad guy in the *Ramayana*; he was a huge ego and had ten heads, all filled with desire. You could throw into the effigy whatever within you was Ravanna-like. I figured, "Well, I'll be doubly safe and throw my lust into Ravanna." They took the torch and they lit Ravanna—he was sitting, on a huge chair—and they lit him right between the legs. Very symbolic.[35]

The Western Satsang

In addition to Ram Dass's personal struggles, he became what Neem Karoli humorously called "commander-in-chief" of a growing flock of followers from the West. Inspired by Ram Dass's account of his own experiences, the original group consisted of a motley crew of wannabe rock stars and yogis, drug dealers, anthropologists, psychologists, and others hailing mainly from America. All shared the spiritual malaise of the times and many, like Ram Dass, the taste of another world induced by the ingestion of psychedelics. Few knew much more of Eastern religion and practice than what they had come across in works such as the ubiquitous *Autobiography of a Yogi, The Gospel of Sri Ramakrishna, The Serpent Power,* cursory readings of the *Bhagavad-Gita, Upanishads, The Tibetan Book of the Dead,* Reps' *Zen Flesh, Zen Bones,* and the writings of D. T. Suzuki and Alan Watts, as well as the Chinese texts, *Tao Te Ching* and the *I Ching.* Nevertheless, the direct contact they had with India and the living embodiment of spirituality, Neem Karoli Baba, inspired them. Eventually with the publication of *Be Here Now* in 1971, the trickle became a modest flow from Europe, as well as New Zealand and Australia. Those whom Neem Karoli welcomed, and not all were, received illustrious Indian names such as Krishna, Draupadi, Kabir, Sita, Dasaratha, and so on, most figures drawn from the great Hindu epics and *bhakti* tradition.

Wide-eyed and deeply moved by the spiritual presence and love that Neem Karoli exuded, the experience became for many a high point of their lives. Most kept their newly minted names and held dear the experience of their encounter with Maharaji, as well as the many stories that circulated of his miraculous deeds. They, too, would return to their respective countries with a new and somewhat eclectic spirituality, language dressed up with Sanskrit terms, and memories that would last a lifetime. Several would take to the road as well, promoting their books and other products or offering upscale and Westernized *kirtan* (chanting) and storytelling. Following Ram Dass's example, few would develop any proficient degree of literacy in the languages or traditions of Hinduism, in its classical or contemporary form. Nor was any established practice ever formally instituted.

In Taos, New Mexico, the Neem Karoli Baba ashram has attracted a new generation of devotees who maintain some semblance of a Hindu liturgical cycle and who finally installed a controversial *murti* (statue) of Hanuman that Ram Dass had transported from India. The ashram celebrates such festivals as *Shivratri, guru purnima, Hanuman Jayanti*, and *navaratri/Durga puja*. An annual September *bhandhara* (celebration) of Neem Karoli's *mahasamadhi* (passing) is a well-attended event, but only sporadically attracts members of the original *satsang*.[36] This lack of organization, coherence, and a set of common Hindu principles and practices among Ram Dass's fellow travelers is often explained in terms of an openness to the spiritual currents rather than the result of a lack of grounding and leadership on his part.

The Unmaking of Baba Ram Dass

Neem Karoli's sudden death on September 11, 1973, while on his way from Kainchi to Vrindaban, where he passed away, was a traumatic event for many devotees and left an enormous gap in the role and place of authority for both his Indian and Western followers. Moreover, following his death, information surfaced that he had been married and, indeed, had three children still living and with whom he was in contact. At first, this seemed to many so inconsistent with the stories that had circulated and his early renunciation and ascetic practices in Gujarat, Uttar Pradesh, and Uttarakhand, as well as the longevity ascribed to him. Nevertheless, so great was his impact on his followers, Indian and Westerner alike, that this information was gradually absorbed into a larger, more complex story of his life and miraculous deeds that it became acceptable as a part of his earthly *lila* (pastime).[37]

Ram Dass's reaction to Neem Karoli's death appears to have been mixed, although he claimed to feel his presence, reasoning that he was guiding him as he had promised. Yet he also continued to take psychedelics because he wanted to maintain contact with the enlightened state that he believed Neem Karoli was in.[38] In spite of Ram Dass's charisma, empathetic communication skills, and his continued reference to things Hindu, he shied away from being cast as a guru figure. Though he spoke with the authority of his own experience and the seeming leadership position that Neem Karoli conferred on him, he repeatedly represented himself as a spiritual seeker and not as an enlightened being in the true sense. While ostensibly an indication of a degree of realism and even modesty, it also suggests a recognition of his own weaknesses, both as one susceptible to "lust," as he put it, and as insecure about assuming a leadership role. He wanted to remain the elder brother, a guru *bhai,* to the others in the *satsang.* This role was both easy and seemingly called for while Neem Karoli was still alive.

In 1974 the Tibetan teacher Chogyam Trungpa Rinpoche invited Ram Dass to deliver a series of lectures on the *Bhagavad-Gita* for the summer session that would inaugurate the founding of Naropa, the Buddhist University in Boulder, Colorado. Ram Dass's lectures were offered as an alternative to Trungpa's own lectures on Buddhist meditation and emptiness. It was an eclectic series attended by more than 1,000 people. The dual offerings created a division among the students attending between a course offered on "the heart" and another on "the mind" as organs of spiritual practice.[39] Apart from the humorous designation of this as "Holy Wars," Ram Dass was beginning to understand how rootless and eclectic his own spiritual foundation was. As he put it:

> I found myself floundering a little bit because my own tradition was so amorphous compared to the tightness of the Tibetan tradition. Trungpa and I did a few television shows together. We did one about lineages and I felt bankrupt. I had Maharaj-ji's transmission of love and service but I knew nothing about his history. I didn't know how to talk about what came through to me in terms of a formal lineage. I was also getting caught in more worldly play, and I felt more and more depressed and hypocritical. So by the end of the summer I decided to return to India. I didn't know what I'd find, but I would go anyway.[40]

Following the lectures, driving though Pennsylvania, he stopped for the night and had an unexpected vision of Neem Karoli. While in India his guru spoke in Hindi, a language that Ram Dass could not understand very well; in the vision he spoke in English, saying, "You don't have to go to India. Your teachings will be right here."[41]

Reassured by this, Ram Dass decided to forgo a planned trip to India and the search to uncover and reconstruct his Hindu lineage and instead returned to New Hampshire to meditate and clear his head. On his way through New York, he received yet another sign—a woman who claimed Neem Karoli had made an appearance in her basement. Such began his encounter with Joya, a Jewish housewife in Brooklyn who persuaded Ram Dass that she could channel Neem Karoli. In a brief time, dazzled by her intensity and penetrating insights, he came under Joya's spell and publicly declared her to be an enlightened being and a manifestation of the Divine Goddess.[42] Many of the *satsang* followed suit and gatherings took place in Brooklyn, Queens, and Long Island with Joya holding court. Brash and berating, she stripped bare those who chose to come within her reach. Moreover, in his interactions with Joya, Ram Dass's own sexual difficulties surfaced and became the focus of her punishing teachings and alleged curative practices. Prior to meeting Joya, he had been pessimistic about freeing himself from his sexual attachments:

> In view of how many years I had been trying to get free of these sexual clingings, including offering my lust into the sacrificial fires of India, I had given up hope of ever knowing freedom in this lifetime. The sexual karma just seemed too heavy.[43]

With Joya things were to change:

> And now I was presented with a woman teacher, who within a few months after commencement of the training began to focus on my sexuality. As I opened more and more, assured by her of her perfect non-attachment to any desire system, I felt a new hope that my dream for purification was finally manifesting through teaching. I plunged headlong into the tornado, casting caution and doubt to the wind.[44]

Ram Dass rationalized that because of Neem Karoli's devotion to the Goddess as Mother, he needed to work on this, and Joya was the instrument by which this could be accomplished. If LSD sessions could not root out his homosexual orientation and sexual addiction, perhaps an encounter with the Divine Mother could.

Yet this was not to be, and Ram Dass's devotion started to unravel as he saw through the elaborate drama and games Joya orchestrated for his benefit. Doubts and boredom grew and the so-called Tantric practices became as empty as most of the other sexual encounters he had had with women.[45] Along with this came the need to understand why he had been duped. His answer pointed to his longing and his doubt: "The fact that Joya continually spoke about Maharaj-ji and implied his presence . . . fed into my longing and somewhat shaky faith that, though Maharaj-ji had left his body, he was still around to guide my spiritual journey."[46]

The teaching came to an end, as did Ram Dass's hope of finding a living embodiment of the divine such as he had found in Neem Karoli. He had led many of the *satsang* into believing and trusting in Joya, and they were now left feeling deeply hurt, betrayed, and disappointed. So, too, ended his hubris that he was being prepared to be a world-class teacher with a large entourage of followers whom he would lead into the promised land of the New Age. He had been deceived and, as he put it, came away with "egg on my beard."[47]

Ram Dass the Devotee

Ram Dass struggled with why he had gone astray and where to locate himself with respect to his eclectic beliefs and relationship to Neem Karoli Baba. In the end, he attempted to resolve this by offering a reinterpretation of the place and significance of lineage in spiritual life. On this, he reasoned as follows:

> So at the beginning of the journey, you are very eclectic. That's what *Be Here Now* was. . . . But there comes the point where the pull in you starts to draw you in the direction of what is called one lineage or another. . . . The particular path, which is my lineage, is what might be called Devotional Tantra. In addition to my Guru, there are two things . . . the Mother, and the other is God. . . . I am consuming the Mother and I am taking all that energy and using it in order to stay with God. I make love to the mother. I make love to the universe. In truth, I am the bride of God . . . it is intercourse with God. You become both the lingam, the phallus, and the yoni, the vagina; you become both that which thrusts forth into God and that which opens to receive God. . . . Your Guru or guide represents a unique and specific lineage . . . designed to take you through itself and free you at the other end. A less pure teaching of a lineage traps you in the lineage, makes you a Buddhist or a Christian or a Hindu, not a free being. . . . A true master in the perfected sense, is someone who is a statement of the culmination of all ways, even though the form in which he or she manifests may be a vehicle for the transmission of

a certain lineage. Ramakrishna, ultimately, was a vehicle for the path of devotion to the Mother. But when he completed his work, though he remained in the path of devotion to the Mother, he was totally in the advait[a], non-dual state way beyond the Mother. So at the beginning is eclecticism, at the end is universality, and in the middle is lineage.[48]

Ram Dass's reinterpretation of the place of lineage absolved him of the need to submerse himself in the tradition of North Indian *bhakti* Hinduism. Once again, like Vivekananda's re-visioning of Ramakrishna and his significance in the context of neo-Hindu nondualist Advaita Vedanta, he offers a similar reading in which to place Neem Karoli and accommodate his own thinly disguised homoeroticism and mother complex with which it is entangled in what he termed "Tantric Devotionalism."[49] This representation of Neem Karoli, distanced from his own North Indian *bhakti* context, cast him as a miracle-performing guru whose lineage and all that came with it had long been transcended in an all-embracing universality. As a Western devotee, there was no need to revisit it.

Ram Dass's next project was to honor the memory of his guru and this took the form of a collection of Indian and Western accounts, offered in a lovingly crafted work of devotion entitled *Miracle of Love: Stories about Neem Karoli Baba* (1979). In invoking the memories of earlier encounters with their guru, the Indian setting is more evident as well as the typical popular Indian piety that takes more the form of hagiography than biography. This work, different from Ram Dass's hip and fluid rendition of a more personally focused, palatable, and less pious eclecticism, attracted a smaller audience than his other publications. Interestingly, he writes in his preface to the most recent edition:

> Though this book has thus far sold the fewest in number of any of the books with which I have been connected, nevertheless the impact has been among the greatest. For an incredible number of people, just through reading these stories with a receptive heart, have found themselves on this journey of *darshan* (being in the presence) of the Guru. And then they, as with me, find daily life transformed through this connection of heart.[50]

Moreover, in keeping with what Agehananda Bharati termed "the pizza effect," this work has found its way back to India and into a Hindi translation that is admired by certain Indian followers as a "veritable inspired gospel."[51] Stripped to its bare bones, the message of *Miracle of*

Love was stunningly simple and clear: "Love, Serve, Remember. Love everyone, serve or feed everyone, remember God."[52]

Over the next few years Ram Dass, following the example of his guru, moved around, engaging in various activities and yet practicing detachment. In fact, assuming the role of a *sadhu*, he tried to obliterate remnants of his past, destroying memorabilia of it by burning boxes of what he had stored and carted around, albeit all captured on film.[53] Nevertheless, though wanting to honor Neem Karoli's example, he felt estranged and a sense that the role he was playing put him at odds with himself. As he put it later:

> You smile a lot, you're very benevolent—its' [sic] the holy man role. I took all the parts of me that didn't fit into that role and shoved them under the rug so that I could be who everybody wanted me to be. I wanted to be that, too. I really wanted to be Ram Dass. . . . Psychologically there were whole parts of my being that I was afraid of and didn't accept. I had a justification for getting rid of them by becoming holy, and I was using my spiritual journey psychodynamically in order to get free of things that I couldn't acknowledge in myself.[54]

In fact, he found himself sliding into a depression when he was alone and losing a direct connection with Neem Karoli, at least to the degree to which this allowed him to seek other sources of inspiration and support.[55] This came in the form of a being named Emmanuel, channeled through Pat Rodegast, whom he had first heard on a New York radio station.[56] Shortly afterward, Ram Dass established an ongoing dialog with Emmanuel who, like an older uncle, advised him on various matters and whose presence and manner evoked an old world atmosphere.[57] His message fit with what Ram Dass apparently needed to hear:

> Each lifetime is a wonderful opportunity to expand your consciousness and to move closer, ever closer, to your oneness with God. This happens in very small stages. First oneness with self, oneness with the human community, then oneness with God. It cannot be done in one blinding flash. It would be too incomprehensible . . . too confusing. So be patient.[58]

And on human weaknesses, Emmanuel advised Ram Dass:

> So accept the distortions in you. Because when you accept them you can transform them. That's what life is about. You're

here to find these areas of imperfection, to understand them, to love them, and to educate them into reality which is truth, light, love.[59]

And on Ram Dass's role as urban *sadhu*, he said, "You took a human birth. You're so busy being holy, . . . why don't you try being human?"[60]

For Ram Dass the road to being human proved difficult and involved a good deal of pain and regression, and for a time he underwent psychotherapy, all in the service of coming to terms with his own humanity. As he put it, "No longer am I trying to imitate anyone else. I'm Dick Alpert and I'm a perfect Dick Alpert."[61] The universal that Ram Dass was now seeing come into view was more the essentially human and less the much sought after otherworldly enlightenment, framed in exclusively Eastern spiritual terms. An important move, and a controversial part of his reconciliation with his own humanity, involved his disclosures about his homosexuality. In several interviews for gay publications that I have already alluded to, Ram Dass tried to come out. As he stated it: "My life and my work have been about truth. All my life has been about teaching the truth. My homosexuality is the one thing I have not been truthful about. Now it is important to be honest."[62]

But such honesty came at a price and this took the form of criticism for explicitly disclosing his sexual orientation and making reference to an intimate homosexual relationship he had been involved in for some years. For many members of the *satsang*, both Western and Indian, such disclosures produced embarrassment and discomfort, and they maintained a distance from publically acknowledging Ram Dass's sexual orientation. In fact, mention of it in the recent film biography, *Fierce Grace,* ended up, as Ram Dass put it, "on the cutting-room floor."[63] His attempt to honestly and publicly come to terms with this part of his humanity met with resistance as it had for him in his own internalized guilt in the course of his life.

Nevertheless, Ram Dass's most dramatic encounter with his humanity came in the form of a near fatal stroke, a large bleed in the left hemisphere of his brain, which he suffered on Wednesday, February 19, 1997. It paralyzed his right side and resulted in expressive aphasia, the inability to speak fluently. He met this debilitating condition with a considerable amount of regret for having neglected his body and with a loss of faith in his guru and in God. Much of his world, both physically and spiritually, appeared to have been shattered and it seemed that he would sink into gloom, depression, and anger. Yet in the anger a redeeming teaching came through the gloom and depression. As he describes it in the book he was working on at the time of the stroke: "There was a surge of anger—the feeling, 'How could you let this happen to me?!' And then as I turned on Maharajji with all my fury, I felt his love just pouring into me, and I felt closer to him than ever. I was learning the lessons of fierce grace."[64] In the end, Ram Dass came to understand:

> The stroke was Maharajji's lightning bolt to jolt me into a new place in my consciousness. The ferocity of the method tested my faith, but in the end my faith held. My bond with Maharajji was strong enough to withstand the doubts. His love and his presence were strong enough to outweigh everything else.[65]

In 2004 once again Ram Dass became near fatally ill as the result of an infection that he developed when he returned from India and en route to Hawaii. After being hospitalized, he recovered, decided he would no longer travel, and took up residence in Maui, where he intends to spend his remaining days. With the help of supporters, he remains there and, along with other members of the *satsang*, established the *Love Serve Remember Foundation*. Its mission is to "disseminate and sustain the teachings of Neem Karoli Baba and Ram Dass on service and devotion."[66] In an interview with Sara Davidson for *Tufts Magazine* conducted in Maui in 2006, Ram Dass reflected on his life. Davidson writes:

> I ask what he thinks his life has been about. "Learning about suffering and compassion. I had to learn to be compassionate," he says. "And bringing people to God." . . . When people tell him he's their guru, he responds, "You've never met a real guru, like Maharaji, or you wouldn't say that. I'm not a realized being at this moment." . . . "Besides being lovable, the guru is God-realized and clear. He has no attachments, and nothing in his personality gets in the way." Would you like to become realized in this life? I ask. He shuts his eyes, letting the question sink in. "Yes," he says, opening his eyes and nodding. "Then I would help people so much. So much."[67]

Yet, more was to come. By a certain twist of fate or divine irony, having seemingly reconciled himself with his homosexuality, in 2009 he discovered that he had fathered a son in his earlier life and, in fact, is a grandfather.[68] Looking back over his long life and spiritual journey, rather than transcending the world as he had tried but failed to do, he realized that the vicissitudes of devotion and ferocity of grace can break a heart open in unconditional love, and he has enshrined this teaching in his most recent work *Be Love Now: The Path of the Heart*.[69] Yet in it, his struggle with homosexuality is passed over in favor of recasting the story of his personal journey as a spiritual one, replete with predictable accounts of his encounters with Neem Karoli, somewhat amplified and accompanied by additional vignettes of a roster of spiritual teachers, Indian gurus familiar and unfamiliar. In many ways it is an updated *Be Here Now* and serves to bring the final chapter of Ram Dass's life to a gracious close by returning to his initial spiritual awakening in India and casting himself as a devotee of Neem Karoli Baba. The spiritual landscape is painted with a somewhat broader brush but the story is essentially the same, the universal message that "all is one." If this appears to be the final chapter coauthored by Ram Dass, there also seems to be another in the making.

With the establishment by his close followers of the *Love Serve Remember Foundation* and the so-called online *satsang*, also called *Be Here Now*, Ram Dass appears to be poised to assume an additional role, one he lifelong denied himself, but which is now being created for him. Taking a leaf from Ram Dass's own life whereby Neem Karoli was transformed from being a Hindu *bhakta* and *guru* into a spiritual commodity for Western consumption he, too, is being presented as something more than a devotee. This is being done with media savvy, the marketing of Hawaiian retreats, lotteries, private consultations for a fee, and appearances with *kirtan* rock stars and other luminaries of the spiritual market place. Online broadcasts on the afterlife and such matters and the recently published *Remarkable Encounters with Ram* Dass,[70] echoing the format of *Miracle of Love,* indicate that he is emerging as more than an elder of the New Age and embodiment of the spiritual journey. He has become an American guru.

Notes

1. Some have argued that the influence of contemporary Indian gurus is undervalued. Robert Baird's editor preface to the collection *Religion in Modern India*, 4th ed. (New Delhi: Monohar, 2001), states, "Much more remains to be done for contemporary India. Guru cults continue to be inadequately represented, and cult has been virtually ignored." Philip Lutgendorf, *The Life of a Text: Performing the Ramcaritmanas of Tulsidas* (Berkeley: University of California Press, 1991), 360–362, also refers to a neglect of more traditional *sadhus* and gurus and the vernacular writings that they draw on and the languages they communicate in.

2. Some have even suggested that the publication of Ram Dass's *Be Here Now* (San Cristobal, NM: Lama Foundation, 1971) was a useful marker for the commencement of the New Age. This claim was later tempered to the impact it

had on the U.S. counterculture. See James R. Lewis, "Approaches to the Study of the New Age Movement," in *Perspectives on the New Age*, eds. James R. Lewis and J. Gordon Melton, 1–12 (Albany, NY: SUNY Press, 1992), 291 n. 3; and Wouter J. Hanegraaff, *New Age Religion and Western Culture* (Albany, NY: SUNY Press, 1998), 375.

3. The connection between a person's personal history and beliefs has been explored in the case of Vivekananda. See Thomas J. Hopkins and Brian A. Hatcher, "Vivekananda," and Narasingha P. Sil, "Vivekananda [Further Considerations]," in *Encyclopedia of Religion*, 2nd ed., ed. Lindsay Jones, 10089–10091 (Detroit, MI: Thomson Gale, 2005). The latter article is in the appendix in the final volume.

4. Numerous publications in English and Hindi as well as websites and photo galleries exist. Helpful, though more devotional in content than works of scholarship, are: Ram Dass, *Miracle of Love: Stories of Neem Karoli Baba. Compiled by Ram Dass* (1979) 3rd ed. (Santa Fe, NM: Hanuman Foundation, 1995); a follow-up drawing from the original collection of gathered stories is *Barefoot in the Heart: Remembering Neem Karoli Baba*, ed. Keshav Das (n.p.: NYONY Books, 2012). Also see Ravi Prakash Pande "Rajida," *The Divine Reality of Sri Baba Neeb Karori Ji Maharaj*, 2nd ed. (Kainchi, Uttarakhand: Sri Kainchi Hanuman Mandir and Ashram, 2005), which includes a section on Siddhi Ma and various temples; Dada Mukerjee, *By His Grace: A Devotee's Story* (Santa Fe, NM: Hanuman Foundation, 1990), and *The Near and the Dear: Stories of Neem Karoli Baba and His Devotees* (Santa Fe, NM: Hanuman Foundation, 1996) are from the hand of one of the most beloved of Indian devotees. Another recent work is Rabboo Joshi, *I and My Father Are One: The Grand Unification* (New Delhi: Rabindra Kumar Joshi, 2009). There are several web sites but the best serves as a portal to others as well: http://www.neebkaroribaba.com/index.htm. The most extensive site of photos galleries is: http://imageevent.com/neemkarolibabaphotos.

5. The ashram maintains a website: http://www.nkbashram.org/.

6. From part 1, "Journey: The Transformation: Dr. Richard Alpert Ph.D. into Baba Ram Dass," in *Be Here Now*, no pagination.

7. Don Lattin, *The Harvard Psychedelic Club* (New York: Harper One, 2010), 5–13, covers most of the ground for this and what follows.

8. Mark Thompson, "Ram Dass: A Life beyond Labels," in *Gay Soul*, ed. Mark Thompson (San Francisco, CA: HarperSanFrancisco, 1994), 153.

9. Lattin, *Harvard*, 100–102.

10. Lattin, *Harvard*, 85–96. The article in *The Crimson* can be found at: http://www.thecrimson.com/article/1973/1/24/the-crimson-takes-leary-alpert-to/ (accessed May 5, 2012).

11. Thompson, *Gay Soul*, 154.

12. Thompson, *Gay Soul*, 155; Ram Dass and Ralph Metzner with Gary Bravo, *Birth of a Psychedelic Culture* (Santa Fe, NM: Synergetic Press, 2010), 115.

13. Robert Greenfield, *Timothy Leary: A Biography* (Orlando, FL: Harcourt, 2006), 158–160.

14. For this see Huston Smith, *Cleansing the Doors of Perception* (New York: Jeremy P. Tarcher/Putnam, 2000).

15. See Bryan J. Cuevas, *The Hidden History of the Tibetan Book of the Dead* (New York: Oxford University Press, 2003), and Kathleen Taylor, *Sir John Woodroffe, Tantra and Bengal* (Richmond, Surrey: Curzon, 2001).

16. Lattin, *Harvard*, 111–113.

17. Ibid., 116–118, 124.

18. Ibid., 117.

19. Ibid., 126–137. Alpert wrote an interesting article on the subject, "LSD and Sexuality," *Psychedelic Review*, 10 (1969): 21–24, that reads like a thinly veiled account of his own experiments with LSD to free himself of his homosexuality and of his time with Caroline Forrest.

20. Most of the sketchy details can be gleaned from the sources already cited. Additional though also contradictory details are offered in B. D. Tripathi, *Indian Sadhus*, rev. ed. (Varanasi, Uttar Pradesh: Pilgrims Publishing, 2004), 250–252. He calls him a householder *sadhu* (*sanjogi sadhu*).

21. Ganesh Prasad Jhaldiyal, conversation with author, Neem Karoli Baba Ashram, Virbhadra, India, Sept. 2008.

22. P. C. Josi "Mukunda," *Premavatar: Baba Neem Karoli Maharaj* (Chennai, Tamil Nadu: Baba Neem Karoli Maharaj Prakashan, 2006). Another, reputedly endorsed by Siddhi Ma herself, is S. D. Ganda, *Hanuman Vistas* (New Delhi: S. D. Ganda, 2002). The author sets up the entire work by stating inside the front cover "tum ho saksat Hanumanta. . . ." "You are Hanuman incarnate." Philip Lutgendorf, *Hanuman's Tale: The Message of a Divine Monkey* (New York: Oxford University Press, 2007), 294–295, mentions this identification as well.

23. Bhagavan Das, *It's Here Now (Are You?)* (New York: Broadway Books, 1997).

24. Ram Dass, *Be Here Now*, pt. 1; Thompson, *Gay Soul*, 155.

25. Ram Dass, *Be Here Now*, pt. 1.

26. Ibid.

27. Ibid.

28. Ibid.

29. Krishna Das paints a picture of this aimlessness in his *Chants of a Lifetime* (Carlsbad, CA: Hay House, 2010).

30. From the back cover of Ram Dass, *Miracle of Love.*

31. Joel D. Mlecko, "The Guru in Hindu Tradition," *Numen* XXIX, no. 1 (1982): 57–58.

32. See the material surveyed in Philip Lutgendorf, "Medieval Devotional Traditions: An Annotated Survey of Recent Scholarship," in *The Study of Hinduism*, ed. Arvind Sharma (Columbia: University of South Carolina Press, 2003), 200–260.

33. I have set aside any discussion of the issues around cultural appropriation, exoticization, and the commodification of Eastern religious beliefs and practices. For a critical overview of the issues see Jeremy Carrette and Richard King, *Selling Spirituality* (New York: Routledge, 2005). Clearly, Ram Dass and other members of the *satsang* have engaged to some degree in the commercialization of "Eastern spirituality" in their books, music, and so forth, but also see the more positive assessment in Lutgendorf, *Hanuman's Tale*, 270–276.

34. Ram Dass in collaboration with Stephen Levine, *Grist for the Mill* (Santa Cruz, CA: Unity Press, 1977), 59–60.

35. Ram Dass, *Grist*, 61.

36. See the link to festivals on: http://www.nkbashram.org/. Not all members of the *satsang* and others were as receptive to having a *murti* of Hanuman and there were differing opinions. On this see Lutgendorf, *Hanuman's Tale*, 270–276. It has also been mockingly satirized in the novel by John Nichols, *The Nirvana Blues* (New York: Henry Holt, 1981).

37. Ram Dass, *Miracle of Love*, 370–373 gives an account of his death. Neem Karoli's family residence in Akbarpur has been turned into a pilgrim site along with other projects in his honor. His son, Dharm Narayan Sharma, now presides over the ashram in Vrindaban and other members of the family regularly attend the events that mark the celebration of his life and passing.

38. Ram Dass, *Grist*, 63.

39. See Ram Dass, *Paths to God: Living the Bhagavad Gita* (New York: Harmony Books, 2004), xiv–xv.

40. Ram Dass, *Grist*, 63.

41. Ibid., 63.

42. Ibid., 67.

43. Ibid., 67.

44. Ibid., 67.

45. Ibid., 68.

46. Ibid., 68.

47. Ram Dass, *Grist*, 68–70. A slightly different account is Ram Dass, "Egg on My Beard," *Yoga Journal* 104 (2009): 440.

48. Ram Dass, *Grist*, 75–77, 81–83, condensed.

49. Much has been written about the transformation of Ramakrishna in Vivekananda's hands from a Kali worshipping *bhakta* to an adherent of Advaita Vedanta. The *locus classicus* for this received tradition is *The Gospel of Ramakrishna*, translated with an introduction by Swami Nikhilananda (New York: Ramakrishna-Vivekananda Center, 1942). Readers should also note that there are traditions of *bhakti* Hinduism that conceive the divine as with form (*saguni*) or formless (*nirguni*); see David N. Lorenzen, "The Lives of the *Nirguni* Saints," in *Bhakti Religion in North India*, ed. David N. Lorenzen (Albany, NY: SUNY Press, 1995), 181–211.

50. Ram Dass, preface to *Miracle of Love*, xix.

51. Agehananda Bharati's term "the pizza effect" refers to the transformation the modest Calabrian and Sicilian staple went through when it arrived in America and got "all dressed" and then exported back to Italy. See his "The Hindu Renaissance and Its Apologetic Patterns," *Journal of Asian Studies* 29/2 (1970): 273–274. The comment on the Hindi edition comes from a conversation with longtime Indian devotee, K. K. Sah, in Nainital, Sept. 2008.

52. Ram Dass, *Grist*, 116.

53. Richard Alpert/Ram Dass, "A Ten-Year Perspective," *Journal of Transpersonal Psychology* 14, 2 (1982): 172.

54. Ibid., 173.

55. Ibid., 173.

56. Pat Rodegast's channeling of Emmanuel was triggered by a meditation practice she began in 1972. A brief sketch of her appears in Jon Klimo, *Channeling* (Los Angeles: Jeremy P. Tarcher, 1987), 136–138.

57. Ram Dass wrote effusive introductions to *Emmanuel's Book,* compiled by Pat Rodegast and Judith Stanton (New York: Friends of Emmanuel, 1985), and *Emmanuel's Book II,* compiled by Pat Rodegast and Judith Stanton (New York: Bantam, 1989). There is also a film about his experiences entitled *A Meeting with Emmanuel* by Valerie Mylonas and Clifford Pia.

58. Richard Alpert/Ram Dass, "A Ten-Year Perspective," 174.

59. Ibid., 174.

60. Ibid., 174.

61. Ibid., 182.

62. Alan Davidson, "Holy Man Sighted at Gay Porn House Talking with Ram Dass about Being Gay, Being Soul Friends, and Just Being . . . Ram Dass," *Outsmart*, Apr. 2001, http://outsmartmagazine.com/issue/i04-01/ramdass.html (accessed May 28, 2010).

63. Don Lattin, "Four Decades Later, Ram Dass Still Relaying Messages," Feb. 17, 2002, http://articles.sfgate.com/2002-02-17/living/17532944_1_richard-alpert-timothy-leary-film-biography (accessed Sept. 23, 2010).

64. Ram Dass, *Still Here* (New York: Riverhead Books, 2000), 200.

65. Ibid., 203.

66. http://www.ramdass.org (accessed Sept. 15, 2012).

67. Sara Davidson, "The Ultimate Trip For Baba Ram Dass, Spiritual Guide to a Generation of Seekers, the Road that Passed through Psychedelia—and Sheer Misery—Will End in Paradise," *Tufts Magazine*, Fall 2006, http://www.tufts.edu/alumni/magazine/fall2006/features/ultimate-trip.html (accessed Sept. 23, 2010).

68. Sara Davidson, "Ram Dass Has a Son! But Has This Revelation Changed His Conception of Love?" *Huffpost Living*, Nov. 3, 2010, http://www.huffington-post.com/sara-davidson/ram-dass-has-a- son_b_777452.html (accessed May 16, 2011).

69. Ram Dass, with Rameshwar Das, *Be Love Now: The Path of the Heart* (New York: Harper One, 2010).

70. *Remarkable Encounters with Ram Dass.* Compiled by Raghu Markus. (N.p.: Love Serve Remember Foundation, 2012).These can be found at http://www.ramdass.org (accessed on Sept. 15, 2012).

2

Building Tantric Infrastructure in America

Rudi's Western Kashmir Shaivism

Helen Crovetto

You must understand that what I say is not, in any sense, intellectual. I don't pass on ideas. I try to give you the raw flesh of my own experience. It may be slightly messy at times, but the blood is still warm.

—Swami Rudrananda, *Rudi: 14 Years with My Teacher*

Swami Rudrananda, also known simply as Rudi, was born in New York City in 1928 as Albert Rudolph. He was the eldest son of a Great Depression–era family who became one of the first American gurus to teach Hindu-inspired Tantric spirituality in the West. As David Gordon White's classical definition states:

Tantra is the Asian body of beliefs and practices that works from the principle that the universe we experience is nothing other than the concrete manifestation of the divine energy of the godhead that creates and maintains that universe, seeks to ritually appropriate and channel that energy within the human microcosm, in creative and emancipatory ways.[1]

Rudi referred to the type of Tantra that he taught as Kundalini Yoga. This spiritual system based on medieval Tantric practices is called "Kashmir Shaivism," a philosophical tradition that developed in the area of Kashmir between the eighth and twelfth centuries CE. Rudi reinterpreted Kashmir Shaivism for a twentieth-century American audience. He taught the construction of a basic internal spiritual structure designed to transfigure its practitioners and effect union with the ultimate nature of reality, nondual consciousness. At the time of his death in a plane crash in 1973, Rudi had thousands of students and had engendered a group of teachers with eclectic approaches to spiritual development.

Under Rudi's guidance, the branch of Tantrism known as Kashmir Shaivism underwent a metamorphosis, especially in its social approach, to adjust to the inclinations of people in America. The relationship between guru and disciple was made more informal and esoteric teachings were made accessible to the public, with most Sanskrit terminology having been eliminated from his teachings. Furthermore, he instituted what he considered a more egalitarian and democratic system for the distribution of spiritual knowledge. Some aspects of Rudi's lineage, such as manner of dress and ashram decoration, exhibit traditional South Asian cultural elements. Other aspects are esoteric and mystical in character. The latter includes ritual activity called *shaktipat*, the transfer of spiritual energy from guru to student. In Rudi's system, the construction of spiritual infrastructure is thought to be the result of concrete exercises that produce tangible results. Rudi and his lineage believe that success in the spiritual realm is measured by an individual's ability to "form soul" and to simultaneously access "other dimensions of energy" as a result of the accretion of consciousness through performing specific exercises.[2]

After describing Rudi and the spiritual influences that contributed to his system of practice, I discuss how he presented those practices in a way that proved to be very attractive for Americans. Then I examine the aspects of Kashmir Shaivism that Rudi incorporated into his Kundalini Yoga. I end with a consideration of the practices and teachings unique to Rudi and show how those who followed him carry these forward.

Rudi's Spiritual Eclecticism

Rudi was a successful oriental art dealer who had regular interactions with the public and maintained close relationships with blood relatives. Narratives of his early life describe his family as very poor. Rudi claims to have engaged in spiritual practices from age six, when he says that the

Heads of the Red and Yellow Hat sects of Tibetan Buddhism visited him in a visionary experience and placed two large knowledge-jars within his abdomen.[3] His spiritual search brought him in contact with a Gurdjieff study group in New York. George I. Gurdjieff (c. 1866–1949) was a Russian who founded an esoteric spiritual system called the "Fourth Way." He believed that human beings go through life as if asleep and that individuals should perform spiritual practices to develop themselves and become more conscious. The term "Fourth Way" was coined by Gurdjieff's students and refers to their belief that Gurdjieff combined techniques from three spiritual schools that emphasized the body, the emotions, and the mind to produce a fourth distinct approach. Rudi studied with the New York group for five years, and Gurdjieff's philosophy had a lasting impact on Rudi's teachings. Following Gurdjieff, Rudi taught that not all individuals may qualify for rebirth, but only those who made a conscious effort to build soul.[4]

Rudi also practiced Subud, a spiritual system from Indonesia that purports to develop surrender to the divine and effect subtle cleansing through exercises known as *latihan*.[5] This system does not rely on the intellectual capacity of the mind. Rather *latihan* requires the cultivation of an attitude of surrender to the divine. The Subud spiritual teacher is referred to as a "helper," but is not revered in the manner that Tantric gurus often are. The practices are said to be enabled through a spiritual transmission from "helper" to student. The Subud system does not refer to the transmission as *shaktipat* the way that some Indian Tantric systems do, but a strong similarity exists between the two as they both rely on a transmission of spiritual energy.

The spiritual cleansing techniques that John Mann describes in his biography of Rudi may have had their origins in Subud or have been influenced by it. However, Rudi could have had contact with these ideas through the Shankaracharya of Puri, Jagadguru Shankaracharya Sri Bharati Krishna Tirtha, a Hindu teacher in the Advaita Vedanta lineage. The Shankaracharya was visiting New York in 1958 at a time when Rudi said that he reached a block in his spiritual work. Rudi believed the problem was caused by an accumulation of spiritual refuse that had been produced within him as a result of his rapid spiritual progress. The Shankaracharya gave Rudi instructions to help with his purification process, which Rudi claimed saved his life.[6]

The beginning of Rudi's Tantric spiritual lineage should probably be dated from 1960, the time he first met his guru, Nityananda of Ganeshpuri. Rudi was on a business trip to India when he had a seemingly random but dramatic encounter with the famous saint, which had a deep impact on him. The stories told about Nityananda are fascinating. He is described as having been completely uninterested in maintaining public appearances or in spearheading any kind of organization. His hagiography includes stories of his living in a tree and throwing stones at people whenever they would come anywhere near. He is considered to be the first or root guru in Rudi's spiritual lineage.[7] When Nityananda died in 1961, Swami Muktananda, who was one of his disciples and one of the first Tantric teachers in America, served as a guru to Rudi.

Muktananda was not recognized as Nityananda's sole successor in India, but in the United States he became the de facto "lineage holder" or representative of Nityananda's spiritual line.[8] From 1970 through 1981, Muktananda toured the world three times, bestowing *shaktipat* and teaching a type of Guru Yoga (viewing guru as divine).[9] Guru Yoga is rooted in medieval Tantric lineages and can also be found among several contemporary Tantric groups.[10] However, the status of gurus has become a contentious issue in America, not only within the public arena but also among the members of contemporary Tantric schools. Some of the debates that arise consider whether the guru is actually divine, is only divine when in particular psychospiritual states, or is simply an access point to the realm of divinity.[11]

Eventually Rudi severed ties with Muktananda over what appears to have been differences in their teaching styles and protocols. Muktananda did not teach specific techniques as much as Rudi did, instead relying on his ability to transmit powerful states of awareness to his students. He was also much more formal in his dealings with his community. However, both teachers emphasized receiving the *shakti* experience (*shaktipat*).[12] The break between the two occurred in 1971 after Rudi had worked with Muktananda for more than ten years and organized a speaking tour that brought him to America. At the end of their collaboration, Rudi explained that he left Muktananda for what he termed "a higher and more merciful approach."[13] Their separation appears to have been both painful and rancorous. *Spiritual Cannibalism*, the only book that Rudi wrote, has a pointed reference to a former teacher who appears to be Muktananda. It accuses him of losing perspective with regard to his divine status. Rudi wrote, "A teacher in no way is a replacement for God and I found that the person with whom I had studied was so obsessed with his being God, or more than God, that I could not respect and sustain the relationship."[14] At the same time, however, Rudi recognized that though his relationship with Muktananda was not always easy, its difficult aspects provided him with an opportunity for rapid spiritual growth.[15]

An American Approach

As an American, Rudi had his own way of interpreting and presenting spiritual truths that were tinged by the culture in which he grew up. His approaches to his students must have seemed unorthodox compared to Indian teachers, but Americans appreciate a greater informality and transparency in the relationship between gurus or teachers and their students. Rudi expressed the American values of egalitarianism and democracy by emphasizing informal, loving relationships with his students and American pluralism by forming an eclectic spiritual tradition. He realized that taking a formal and authoritarian stance toward American spiritual seekers would just as likely repel them from the spiritual path as create a sense of awe and reverence. So he let his students approach him for guidance wherever they found him, which was usually in his New York City oriental art store. Rather than require guru *dakshina*, a period of service and attitude of submission to the instructor-guru, as a prerequisite, he taught them on the spot.

Rudi transmitted *shaktipat* in a number of ways. For example, he would sit them down in a chair opposite his and stare intently at them while sending spiritual energy.[16] At other times he transmitted *shaktipat* by hugging his students. As evidenced by the *Rudi Movie*, which contains footage from 1970, Rudi was perhaps the first guru in America to practice hugging students as a technique to effect spiritual elevation. This occurred almost twenty years before Mata Amritanandamayi, the so-called "hugging guru" from Kerala, came to the United States and turned the hugging of students into a spiritual tradition.[17] The *Rudi Movie* documents rare *shaktipat* interactions between Rudi and his students, including footage of students falling into ecstatic states and exhibiting dramatic *kriyas* (spontaneous energy manifestations). Sometimes Rudi applied *shaktipat* directly by pressing their *chakras* with his fingers. One student who experienced this reported that the energy he received from Rudi in 1970 created a consciousness of multilevel realms that was still with him thirty-seven years later.[18]

The character of Rudi's linguistic interaction with his students also expressed his accessibility and egalitarianism. He spoke to his students in a very straightforward manner and used images Westerners would easily understand. For example, he told them that trying to progress spiritually by serving others the equivalent of a cold, "leftover piece of pizza-pie" would not work well.[19] On another occasion, he described the human mind's time-bound response and unfolding to its own spiritual efforts as "a Contac cold capsule."[20] Another time, he said that trying to explain the activity of spiritual surrender to those who had never done it before was like "trying to squeeze a greased pig."[21] Apart from the humorous aspect of these descriptions, there can be little doubt that Rudi made himself understood to his target audience and that his intention was to convey what he saw as the essence of spirituality without an overdependence on Indian cultural images or languages.

Yet another way in which Rudi expressed his egalitarianism was the manner in which he made spiritual knowledge available. Rudi believed that a teacher should "drop the seeds of his teaching without selectivity" so that anyone who could take advantage of them would be able to.[22] One of his complaints about spiritual teachers from India was that they tended to be unnecessarily restrictive with their students. Rudi said, "Most Indians don't believe an American can be spiritual; if you weren't born Indian, you've had it as far as they're concerned."[23] He argued that no matter what was made available, each spiritual aspirant would receive according to his or her capacity and needs.[24]

Rudi's egalitarian teaching style is apparent in the *dhyana* photos of Rudi posed in various *mudras*—particular body and hand postures—as found in the *Rudi Movie*. Photographs of contemporary Tantric gurus in *mudras* such as *Varabhaya* (blessings and fearlessness) and *Janusparsha* (touching the knees) are often restricted to a limited number of individuals within their lineages. It is certainly uncommon to make them available to the public.[25] Rudi also worked with photographer Barry Kaplan to take "teaching photos" in which he documented physical changes he underwent as a result of his psychospiritual progress. He believed these should be preserved so that they might be of practical use to others who were engaged in spiritual work.[26]

Swami Chetanananda, one of the teachers in Rudi's lineage, summarized Rudi's attitude on cultural issues in the introduction to *Rudi: In His Own Words*. He said Rudi pointed out that "it is the substance of Eastern spiritual teaching that interests us, not the form" and that we are not here to realize any particular culture, but to transcend all of them.[27] The hallmark of contemporary Tantric spirituality is its universalism, or monistic theism. It recognizes all individuals and cultures as part of the cosmic creation and holds that the divine has not bestowed approval and love on only certain peoples and cultures to the exclusion of others.[28] Because of this and due to the individual spiritual need for a liberated psyche, Rudi said that it was a basic requirement for spiritual aspirants to accept themselves and their cultural heritage with all its religious, racial, and national implications.[29]

Rudi connected these beliefs to the need for his students to fulfill their responsibilities in the material world by creating a solid foundation

Figure 2.1. Rudi in Varabhaya mudra, blessings and fearlessness (Photo courtesy of Barry Kaplan © 2000)

Figure 2.2. Rudi: Janusparsha mudra, touching the knees (Photo courtesy of Barry Kaplan © 2000)

for themselves, including a "working, physical life" that would support them financially.[30] For Rudi, life and work in the world *was* spiritual life, and there was no attempt to evade hard social realities. This solid work ethic, attitude of responsibility, and commitment to immersion in one's natal culture highlight the social aspect of Rudi's quintessentially American form of Tantrism. Rudi's system can also be seen as a convergence of American Protestant values and a Tantric hermeneutic that embraces the spiritual potentials of the material world.

Furthermore, Rudi's Western Kashmiri Shaivites or Kundalini yogis do not belong to a large, overarching organization with a national presence. Rudi was of the opinion that spiritual systems and their organizations were of limited value because they "all become rigid and dogmatic in time, more a prison than a refuge."[31] As Kundalini yogis participate in local groups under the guidance of different gurus within Rudi's lineage, it is unlikely that tension would be generated between any one of their groups and the major or minor religious denominations in the United States due to the comparatively small size of the Kundanlini yoga groups as well as their decentralization.

Kashmir Shaivism in Rudi's System

The ideology and practice of Kashmir Shaivism, as summarized by scholar Navjivan Rastogi, has several aspects. It recognizes the self as divine, accepts the *svatantrya* (free will) of the individual, and believes that the universe is a unified whole.[32] It is the responsibility of a spiritual aspirant to do spiritual practices and realize his or her essential nature by merging into nondual consciousness. While Kashmir Shaivism's flowering occurred in the seventh through eleventh centuries, its intellectual aspect was not fully elaborated until the ninth century by Utpaladeva in his *Isvara-pratyabhijna-karika-s* and the end of the tenth century by Abhinavagupta in his *Trika* texts.[33] Therefore, the intellectual and aesthetic theories with which Kashmir Shaivism tends to be associated do not represent the totality of its practices and ideas.

In the twentieth century, considering changes in venue and culture, Rudi employed some aspects of Kashmir Shaivism that are action-oriented. His became a practice lineage almost exclusively. Sanskrit terminology was minimized and the intellectual emphasis was eliminated. The traditional forms and culturally oriented rituals were not mentioned.[34] Throughout his discourses, Rudi employed the single word "God" as well as phrases such as "higher creative energy" and "higher creativity." He explained the need for the proper use of free will, but did not use the Sanskrit word for it. Kashmir Shaivism's elegant theory of *spanda* (pulsation or vibration), which explains how the universe functions, is absent. However, vibrational theory resurfaces, albeit in a limited way, in the writings of Chetanananda, one of Rudi's students.[35]

Rudi once said, "I am not very interested in logic. I want results."[36] He was so deeply anti-intellectual and experientially oriented that citing even another student of his who compares with him regarding anti-intellectualism is difficult. Perhaps the teacher who comes closest to him regarding this point is Swami Shambhavananda, who neither lectures nor has directly authored any books.[37] "A hack uses his mind." Rudi asserted, "A really talented man uses intuition."[38] Rudi was truly uncompromising in his opposition to intellectualism: "You don't have to think to have a spiritual experience. Thinking is designed to steal reality from us." He pointed out that it requires "great inner strength and a very firm sense of reality to let go of thinking."[39] Chetanananda recalled Rudi saying that "we are not here to think about living; we are here simply to live. We are not here to try to figure out life; we are here to open ourselves to it. We do not grow strong by trying to protect ourselves; we grow strong by exposing ourselves."[40]

Rudi was of the opinion that books on spiritual topics often do more harm than good by inadvertently reinforcing people's illusions or undermining their energy and chemistry.[41] He probably inherited these ideas from Muktananda and Nityananda of Ganeshpuri. Muktananda had once been very interested in books until Nityananda told him they had no value.[42] Therefore, Rudi wrote only one book, *Spiritual Cannibalism*. Its title refers to the ways students take advantage of a guru's elevating energy while he transforms their negative karma into energy that, at least in part, becomes spiritually useful for him.[43] He likened this to eating one another's energy. The assertion here is that everything in the manifested universe is only the energy of divine consciousness and that a guru knows how to use all types of energy by modifying them for beneficial, spiritual purposes. After his death, Rudi's students compiled collections of his talks into two other books.[44]

Rudi was just as opposed to the idea of people indulging their emotions while on the spiritual path as he was to the overexercising of their intellects. He believed that emotions are blocks to spiritual growth and that emotions should only be expressed by those who had control over them.[45] He found devotional sentiments expressed toward himself to be particularly disturbing. Rudi thought that devotion toward the guru implied that students were in some ways unwilling to engage in their own spiritual work and that they were depending on the guru to do their spiritual work for them.[46] He was very clear that he thought each individual was responsible for his or her own spiritual development.[47] That said, Rudi recognized that a guru took on some of the karma of his students as well as made sacrifices for them. Rudi's suspicion of the dependent relation between guru and disciple can be seen as reflecting American Protestant values of independence and self-determination.

In order to understand how Rudi's practices qualify as Kashmir Shaivism, we must look to a particular division of Kashmir Shaivism or Trika that Utpaladeva and Abhinavagupta described during the Middle Ages. That division is called *anava* yoga, within which is a body of practices termed *uccara* yoga.[48] *Uccara* yoga deals with the functions of *prana* (energy): the absorption and elimination of things in the waking, dreaming, or other states through "breathing, speaking, thinking, working, [and] understanding."[49] This is a system believed to produce liberation in this lifetime through the activation of *kundalini*.[50] Rudi referred to it simply as Kundalini Yoga, which emphasizes action or effort (*kriya*).

One of the most prominent aspects of historical Kashmir Shaivism within Rudi's tradition was the practice of *shaktipat*. In chapter 13 of the *Tantraloka*, Abhinavagupta described nine types of *shaktipat*.[51] The guru might send *shaktipat* through a glance, verbal communication, touch, or thought.[52] In the twenty-first century the techniques include imparting *shaktipat* over the phone, through letters, and over the Internet as well as via *mudras* while a person is in a guru's physical presence.

Rudi raised the profile of *shaktipat* to such an extent that it can almost be said that energy transfer, combined with energy manipulation through *pranayama*, were the hallmarks of his interpretation of the tradition. Rudi was much more interested in using *shaktipat* than in discussing it. His students said that he took every opportunity to transfer elevating energy to them, whether he was working with them individually or in group settings.[53]

Navjivan Rastogi believes that the essence of Kashmir Shaivism was preserved satisfactorily in Rudi's lineage through its value system and basic philosophical ideas.[54] He asserted that he heard echoes of Abhinavagupta's *Anuttarastika* in Rudi's statements that all experiences must be absorbed, digested, and used in one's spiritual development.[55] While Rudi's lineage qualifies as a Kashmiri Shaivite lineage, it should be understood as an American branch of that lineage with a commitment to spiritual exercises that manipulate energy.

Rudi's Unique Practices and Beliefs

The uniqueness of Rudi's spiritual techniques and his personality made a strong impression on those he encountered. One of the American teachers in the lineage who followed Rudi described him as "very unusual," in addition to recognizing him as a powerful *siddha*, or perfected master of occult powers.[56] The students who Rudi attracted were similarly distinctive. Those who appeared in the *Rudi Movie* were, for the most part, young people from the American hippie culture of the 1960s. Swami Shambhavananda was one of Rudi's students who became an established spiritual teacher. He characterized both the teachers and the students of his lineage as individuals who "didn't color within the lines."[57] For spiritual practitioners in Tantric lineages antinomian demographics are standard. In a broader context, the Tantric traditions in South Asia and America have both been described as having countercultural functions.[58]

Rudi taught that a human being is a microcosm of the universe.[59] His cosmology consisted of three dimensions: the physical horizontal, the spiritual horizontal, and the level of Time and Space.[60] These were connected by threads of consciousness and energy sometimes referred to as the vertical line of infinity and described as "a descending expression of sound."[61] Classical Kashmir Shaivism contains the similar, but more complex idea termed *visarga-shakti*: the fifty phonemes of the Sanskrit alphabet as manifestations of consciousness that concretize into the form of the universe.[62]

To build soul, Rudi believed an individual had to reach from the physical horizontal, through the vertical line of infinity to the spiritual horizontal, where soul could start to form,[63] which necessitated both surrender to the divine and regular spiritual practices. Rudi's spiritual language was sprinkled with images of building and surrendering and ascending. He said, "You are building a structure. It can be a great structure that stretches from earth to heaven, but the higher it goes, the sounder the foundation must be."[64] On other occasions he said, "It is all material for surrender. You build to give away."[65]

Building and ascent were accomplished by creating an occult weaving. In that fabric Rudi said the "layers," the horizontal threads, or weft, were formed as a result of spiritual practices.[66] The warp was composed of sound threads, the vertical line or lines of infinity that stretched into "paradise" and higher realms.[67] One of the etymologies of the word "Tantra" comes from the *Rig* and *Atharva Vedas* (ca. 1500–1000 BCE) where the word signifies "weaving," from the root "tan," meaning to stretch or to weave.[68] John Mann continued the lineage's use of weaving imagery when he described his kundalini awakening experience as "crossing a woven suspension bridge across an abyss."[69]

Rudi's mystical infrastructure has some similarities to contemporary as well as historic Tantric groups who believe that the universe is structured in *lokas*, or levels. Among these groups are the Kashmiri Shaivites, who describe seven levels of universal existence as seven substances.[70] In comparison to them, Rudi's cosmology and images of infrastructure have an exceptionally strong sense of solidity because his spiritual aspirants must play an active role in the construction of both the weft in the weaving (upon which they can ascend spiritually) and the soul that they believe is subsequently being formed at the spiritual horizontal level.

The idea that concrete psychophysical and psychospiritual actions such as the practices of *pranayama* and meditation might translate into specific psychospiritual gains is common in Tantrism. It is the assumption on which most spiritual practice is based. According to some Tantric *sannyasis* from Bengal, this reciprocity is sometimes represented by the single Sanskrit word *"kripa." Kripa* translates as "grace," but implies that those who expect to be graced by the divine (the phoneme *"pa"* means to absorb or get) must first do something (*"kri"* means do): *kri+pa* = do and get.[71] This is consistent with Rudi's ideology. However, the belief that spiritual practices will produce esoteric psychophysical or psychospiritual structures in the form of a weaving or net on the one hand and an accumulation of consciousness that could be termed soul on the other is a specialty of Rudi's system. "The purpose of spiritual work is to get you off the Earth!" Rudi said.[72] Considering the extent to which he encouraged a sense of responsibility in his students, he clearly did not mean to foster escapism. He wanted his students to go to places in the cosmos where he believed the energy, or *prana,* was superior and absorb that energy before returning to the Earth.[73]

The techniques that Rudi used to absorb and control *prana* were varied and included one that could be practiced while sleeping.[74] The latter, called "astral flight," is mentioned only briefly in his lineage's publications. Rudi is best known for a *pranayama* exercise called double-breathing. In it a single round of the exercise requires holding the breath inside the body two times. Rudi described it in the following way, "You breathe into your heart to the count of ten. Hold for the count of ten, begin to breathe out, but immediately shift your attention to the lower belly and after having expelled a small amount of air, begin to breathe in again for the count of ten; hold for ten and out for ten."[75]

A significant portion of *Spiritual Cannibalism* is devoted to an explanation of what Rudi called the psychic digestive system. This is a form of the subtle nervous system and its *chakras* that characterize systems of Tantra and Tantra yoga. He described it as having eight major chakras and half a dozen secondary *chakras* that are activated by energy circulation.[76] The first *chakra* is the third eye, the second is located at the throat, the third is the heart *chakra* in the middle of the chest, the fourth is at the solar plexus, the fifth is two inches below the navel, the sixth is the sex center, the seventh is at the tip of the spine, and the eighth is at the top and back of the head. Rudi explained the function of the psychic digestive system as similar to that of physical eating: the intake, transformation, and utilization of *prana* in the human body. But the psychic digestive system transformed internal and external energies into nourishment for higher functions.[77] In *Spiritual Cannibalism* Rudi asserted that "everything is part of perfection and must be taken in in a state of surrender; it must be digested and transcended."[78] Therefore negative psychic energy stored in the unconscious mind or the body's *chakras* was simply considered "fuel."[79] The double-breathing exercises that Rudi taught were believed to provide tremendous energy that vitalized this system.

In the psychic digestive system, the "third eye" functions as a mouth in which energy enters the body and is circulated down to the sex organs. At the sex center, an alchemical reaction occurs transforming the "base metal of natural sex energy" into the "gold of transmuted sex energy."[80] From the sex center, the transmuted energy flows to the base of the spine and up the spinal cord to the top of the head.[81] There it forms a reservoir that eventually overflows and provides subtle nourishment to the brain and kundalini.[82] This nourishment is considered a natural activator and release for *kundalini*. Rudi did not believe in celibacy per se, but he acknowledged that control over sexual energy and fluids is necessary, especially during certain periods of a spiritual aspirant's development.[83] Rudi observed that spiritual feeding and growth are incremental processes and that just like the muscular system, the psychic digestive system is strengthened "through gradual and consistent use."[84]

With regard to eliminating the negative *prana* that Rudi called "negative psychic tensions," he recommended four psychic cleansing exercises.[85] Rudi used the word "tensions" as a substitute for the Hindu concept of karma that has been formed over many lifetimes. Simply put, negative psychic tensions are his equivalent of bad karma. Various Sanskrit words have richer nuances than Rudi's English phrase, which pertains to how karmic impressions are formed. These include *samskaras* (mental residue or mental reactions), *sanchita karma* (accumulated karma), and *prarabdha karma* (karma set in motion).[86] The problem is that even when these terms are translated into English, they require elaboration to such an extent that we can easily understand why the anti-intellectual Rudi chose to avoid them. The full significance of the term "tensions" for Rudi's lineage is adequately described in *Spiritual Cannibalism* and in Shambhavananda's *A Seat by the Fire*.[87]

If practitioners were able to successfully manage their energy, Rudi's lineage believed they would be able to start building their soul.[88]

The belief that soul is not an innate property within each human being and that it must be created over time as a result of individual effort is an idea that Rudi appears to have inherited from Gurdjieff.[89] In an extension of the idea of building soul, Rudi mentioned that an individual may not qualify for rebirth depending on whether he or she has been able to create soul.[90]

Rudi believed that success on the spiritual path required an almost infinite appetite for disciplined work, the ability to assume responsibility in all areas of a person's life, and spiritual detachment born of continuous, total surrender.[91] His sense of responsibility did not extend to becoming involved in social causes.[92] He emphasized that in spiritual work there was neither a simple way nor a shortcut.[93] He sounded a note of realism when he said, "The process of growing will take much longer and be much more costly than you think.[94]

Rudi had quite a lot to say about the special chemistry of the guru-student relationship. His attitude was typically Tantric in insisting that a guru was absolutely necessary for an aspirant because the spiritual force had already awoken within the guru.[95] He said, "You can't just listen to your own ideas and expect to get anywhere."[96] For Rudi, the guru is simply a channel for supreme consciousness to manifest whatever it thinks is necessary.[97] Like many other Tantric gurus and disciples, he was of the opinion that the guru created a living force that did not diminish with the guru's death and that this enabled students to continue to access the divine through a guru who had taken up residence in another realm of consciousness.[98] Rudi was rare in discussing the fact that the guru would eventually have to be abandoned in order for students to establish their own relationship with the divine.[99] He said that "to be filled with anything less than God is a limitation."[100]

Rudi's Lineage

Rudi initiated a series of American-born teachers who either became part of his lineage or who launched spiritual schools of their own. Swamis Shambhavananda and Chetanananda are two of the better-known teachers within Rudi's lineage. Rishi Maha Mandaleshwar Sri Shambhavananda, whose name means "bliss of the natural state of being," founded the Shambhava School of Yoga in 1975. The title "Maha Mandaleshwar" means the "Head of a Circle (Mandala) of Swamis" and was bestowed by Ma Yoga Shakti Saraswati of Niranjani Akhara of India. Shambhavananda operates a residential ashram in Eldorado Springs, Colorado; a rural retreat center, called Shoshoni Yoga Center, in the Rocky Mountains near Rollinsville, Colorado; and an ashram called Konalani Yoga Ashram on the Big Island of Hawaii. His community has centers in various U.S. cities, Great Britain, Japan, and Australia.

Swami Chetanananda, whose name means "bliss of conscious-ness," founded the Nityananda Institute in Cambridge, Massachusetts, in 1982, renaming it the Movement Center when he and his community moved to Portland, Oregon, in 1993.[101] Chetanananda claims that Rudi designated him as his successor.[102] After Rudi's death, Chetanananda studied with Kashmiri Shaivite scholar Alexis Sanderson at Oxford and became a lineage holder in the Buddhist Tantric tradition of Pha Dampa Sangye.[103] He is the author of ten books and has meditation centers in several U.S. cities.[104]

Some of the other teachers Rudi initiated include Stuart Perrin, who is based in New York City; Lama Lars, of Taos, New Mexico; John Mann, who resides at Big Indian, New York, in the summer and Lummis Island, Washington, in the winter; Silver Ra Baker of Denton, Texas; and Swami Khecaranatha of Berkeley, California.[105] Stuart Perrin is the author of six books about the spiritual path and has meditation centers in the United States, Israel, and Brazil.[106] When I watched one of his videos I was struck by how much he sounds like Rudi in the *Rudi Movie*.[107] While Perrin's teaching focuses on what Rudi taught him, he also says that he was influenced by Kalu Rimpoche of the Tibetan Buddhist Karma Kagyu school, as well as numerous other spiritual personalities.

Lama Lars founded an organization called Grace Essence Mandala and is the author of four books.[108] At Rudi's direction he developed a practice that integrates techniques of Tibetan Buddhism (Nyingma) into those of Kashmir Shaivism.[109] He also received initiations in Rinzai Zen, Shugendo, and Shingon. John Mann founded the Center of Divine Androgyny and is the author of at least ten books, including the insight-ful *Rudi: 14 Years with My Teacher*.[110] Mann also received initiation in the Nyingma school of Tibetan Buddhism.

The work of Silva Ra Baker, an architect and visionary artist, is especially noteworthy because Rudi encouraged him to establish a "spir-itual university," where people could venerate the many paths that lead to cosmic consciousness. Baker was initiated into Tibetan Buddhism's Karma Kagyu school and studied with several contemporary shamans from the Americas.[111] He and Stuart Perrin established the Rudra Center for Enlightened Awareness, where these techniques are taught. Swami Kecharanatha founded Sacred Space Yoga Sanctuary in Berkeley, Califor-nia, and has written two books.[112] He was one of the individuals primarily responsible for the formation of the Nityananda Institute in Cambridge and has students teaching at his Berkeley center.[113] Kecharanatha does some teaching from the Tibetan Buddhist tradition. Currently, Rudi's initiates have begun to create a new generation of spiritual teachers, such as Bruce Rubin, one of the coproducers of the *Rudi Movie*.

Adi Da was a famous teacher who studied with Rudi for five years and established a completely separate organization.[114] The title of Adi Da's (Bubba Free John's) most popular book, *Garbage and the Goddess*, refers to the "garbage" of emotional blocks like guilt, self-pity, and fear that Rudi said a person must overcome on the spiritual path.[115] While Rudi wrote only one book, many of the other teachers mentioned above became prolific writers with many books to their credit.

Rudi not only permitted spiritual eclecticism in his teachers, but he also encouraged it. Four of them were initiated by masters of Tibetan Buddhism, one of those also practiced esoteric forms of Japanese Buddhism, and another studied with contemporary shamans. Although Rudi never explained his approval of eclecticism, his emphasis on practical results allows one to conclude that whatever spiritual system produced those results was considered legitimate. Rudi has undoubtedly contributed to the formation of a new American Hinduism that is richly eclectic.

Conclusion

Indian Tantra has been subject to both preservation and innovation since reaching the shores of America. One of several contemporary Tantric groups in which this is apparent is Rudi's lineage, which did not change the basic tenets of Tantric mysticism when it began operating on this continent. It did, however, revamp its social approach to allow the tradition to be comprehended with greater facility. The relationship to the guru was redefined in a way that permitted less formality and greater interaction among the teacher, his students, and the public. Rudi presented Tantra in a more accessible way than customary in South Asia. Some Indian cultural elements, such as the use of the Sanskrit language, were de-emphasized or abandoned and culturally relevant language and metaphors were introduced. Rudi believed that spiritual practitioners should be able to be productive members of society while, at the same time, not permitting the material world to become the primary focus of their lives.

Rudi's lineage can be distinguished from other forms of Tantra by its emphasis on *kriya* exercises and its belief in the idea that concrete exercises translate directly into equally manifest, though occult, spiritual indicators of success, including the formation of soul and mystical infrastructure. It is one strand in a widely varying group of Tantric ideologies and practices that are world-affirming. That the practice of Tantrism does not require renunciation and is suitable for most people who must simultaneously deal with constantly changing social and socioeconomic pressures as well as family and community responsibilities is certainly part of its appeal in America.[116] Rudi believed that "complete happiness and contentment are the best environment in which to [do spiritual] work."[117]

Notes

1. David Gordon White, ed., *Tantra in Practice* (Princeton, NJ: Princeton University Press, 2000), 9.

2. Swami Rudrananda, *Spiritual Cannibalism* (New York: Links Books, 1973), 17; and Swami Rudrananda, *Rudi: In His Own Words* (Cambridge, MA: Rudra Press, 1990), 21, 24.

3. John Mann, *Rudi: 14 Years with My Teacher* (Cambridge, MA: Rudra Press, 1987), 74.

4. Bruce Rubin and Beau Buchanan, *Rudi: The Teachings of Swami Rudrananda/Rudi Movie*, directed by Bruce Rubin and Beau Buchanan (rudimovie.org, 2007), DVD.

5. From http://www.subud.com/Introduction_to_Subud.pdf (accessed Dec. 28, 2010); and Mann, *Rudi*, 6.

6. Mann, *Rudi*, 77.

7. Nityananda's philosophy is nicely encapsulated in the following saying attributed to him: "The heart is the hub of all sacred places. Go there and roam in it." Swami Shambhavananda, *Spontaneous Recognition: Discussions with Swami Shambhavananda*, ed. Ashok N. Srivastava (1995; rpt. Eldorado Springs, CO: SGRY, 1998), xiv.

8. Lola Williamson, *Transcendent in America: Hindu-Inspired Meditation Movements as New Religion* (New York: New York University Press, 2010), 109.

9. Ibid., 108–109.

10. Helen Crovetto, "Embodied Knowledge and Divinity: The Hohm Community as Western-Style Bauls," *Nova Religio: The Journal of Alternative and Emergent Religions* 10, no. 1 (Aug. 2006), 79.

11. Helen Crovetto, "Channeling a Tantric Guru: The Ananda Seva Reformation." *Nova Religio: The Journal of Alternative and Emergent Religions* 15, no. 2 (Nov. 2011), 70–92.

12. Lola Williamson, personal communication to author, Oct. 24, 2010.

13. Mann, *Rudi*, 218–119.

14. Rudrananda, *Spiritual Cannibalism*, 139.

15. Mann, *Rudi*, 97.

16. Ibid., 9.

17. Selva J. Raj, "Passage to America: Ammachi on American Soil," in *Gurus in America*, ed. Thomas A. Forsthoefel and Cynthia Ann Humes (Albany, NY: SUNY Press, 2005), 128–129.

18. Stuart Perrin, Rubin and Buchanan, *Rudi Movie.*
19. Ibid.
20. Rudrananda, *Rudi: In His Own Words,* 37.
21. Rudrananda, *Spiritual Cannibalism,* 148.
22. Ibid., 47.
23. Mann, *Rudi,* 95.
24. Ibid., 110.
25. These assertions are based on the author's research into and interaction with contemporary Tantric spiritual schools in India and America between 1970 and 2005.
26. Mann, *Rudi,* 223.
27. Rudrananda, *Rudi: In His Own Words,* 11.
28. This may be contrasted with some medieval Tantric schools whose engagement in spiritual practices had personal power as their goal. (My assertion is based on research conducted from 1985 through the present.)
29. Rudrananda, *Rudi: In His Own Words,* 11.
30. Rudrananda, *Rudi: In His Own Words,* 39–40; Rubin and Buchanan, *Rudi Movie*; and Mann, *Rudi,* 227. Rudi's teachers have worked at various professions in addition to being spiritual teachers. Stuart Perrin is an author. Bruce Rubin is a screenwriter. John Mann has worked as a college professor and author. Silva Ra Baker is an artist and architect. Swami Shambhavananda has worked in the restaurant and natural foods production businesses as well as in real estate.
31. Mann, *Rudi,* 147.
32. Swami Chetanananda, *Dynamic Stillness. Part One: The Practice of Trika Yoga* (Cambridge, MA: Rudra Press, 1990), xiii.
33. The word *"trika,"* or three, is a name for Kashmir Shaivism. See Paul Muller-Ortega, *The Triadic Heart of Siva: Kaula Tantricism of Abhinavagupta in the Non-Dual Shaivism of Kashmir* (Albany, NY: SUNY Press, 1989), 46; and B. N. Pandit, *Specific Principles of Kashmir Saivism* (New Delhi: Munshiram Manoharlal, 1997), 91–92.
34. For the traditional forms see André Padoux, "Mandalas in Abhinavagupta's Tantraloka," in *Mandalas and Yantras in the Hindu Traditions,* ed. Gudrun Bühnemann, 238–250 (Leiden, Netherlands: Brill, 2003), 238.
35. Chetanananda, *Dynamic Stillness,* 27–28, 34, 56, 134, 145, and 162.
36. Mann, *Rudi,* 182.
37. Two books attributed to him are based on his answers to his student's questions and were compiled with his permission. These are *Spontaneous Recognition* (n. 9) and Swami Shambhavananda, *A Seat by the Fire: Spiritual Discussions with Sri Shambhavananda,* ed. Ashok N. Srivastava (Rollinsville, CO: SGRY/Prakasha Press, 2005). See *A Seat by the Fire,* 187 and 200, on the value of spiritual practice versus philosophical discussion.
38. Mann, *Rudi,* 119. See also Rudrananda, *Spiritual Cannibalism,* 45, on the mind as an enemy of spiritual development.
39. Mann, *Rudi,* 119.
40. Rudrananda, *Rudi: In His Own Words,* 14.

41. Rudrananda, *Spiritual Cannibalism*, 32–33, 37, 40, 55, 72; and Mann, *Rudi*, 139.

42. Williamson, personal communication.

43. Rudrananda, *Spiritual Cannibalism*, 3–4, 25; Mann, *Rudi*, 25; and Rudrananda, *Rudi: In His Own Words*, 31.

44. These are John Mann, ed., *Behind the Cosmic Curtain: The Further Writings of Swami Rudrananda* (Arlington, MA: Neolog Publishing, 1984), and Rudrananda, *Rudi: In His Own Words*, n. 2.

45. Rudrananda, *Spiritual Cannibalism*, 35, 44, 48, 77.

46. Rudrananda, *Rudi: In His Own Words*, 65.

47. Rudrananda, *Spiritual Cannibalism*, 24; Rudrananda, *Rudi: In His Own Words*, 37; and Mann, *Rudi*, 47.

48. Pandit, *Specific Principles of Kashmir Saivism*, 109. See also Shambhavananda, *Seat by the Fire*, 188–189, on the divisions or *upayas* (paths) within Kashmir Shaivism. Shambhavananda commented that higher divisions of Trika, such as *shambhava* yoga, are taught depending on the capacity of the student. Swami Shambhavananda, spiritual presentation, longhand notes, Boulder, CO, Jan. 12, 2009.

49. Pandit, *Specific Principles*, 109.

50. Pandit, *Specific Principles*, 111, 186. Rudi said that one of the results of the activation of *kundalini* is the production of *kriyas*, jerky or uncharacteristic movements within the physical body that eliminate an individual's residual karma (Rudrananda, *Spiritual Cannibalism*, 8). I observed the expression of *kriyas* in Shambhavananda's students on several occasions.

51. Those are intense or swift (*tivra*), moderate (*madhya*), and slow (*manda*), each of which could be expressed rapidly, at an even pace, or gradually; Pandit, *Specific Principles*, 86.

52. Ibid., 88.

53. Rubin and Buchanan, *Rudi Movie*.

54. Chetanananda, *Dynamic Stillness*, pt. 1, xiii, xv.

55. Ibid., xv.

56. Shambhavananda, *Seat by the Fire*, 126.

57. Ibid., 120.

58. Jeffrey J. Kripal, "Remembering Ourselves: On Some Countercultural Echoes of Contemporary Tantric Studies," *Religions of South Asia* 1 no. 1 (2007): 15–18, 23–26.

59. Rudrananda, *Spiritual Cannibalism*, 109.

60. Ibid., 116.

61. Ibid., 109.

62. Muller-Ortega, *Triadic Heart*, 132–133, 172.

63. Rudrananda, *Spiritual Cannibalism*, 113. Rudi also said that the psychic muscle system or psychic digestive system only existed on the horizontal spiritual dimension (15).

64. Mann, *Rudi*, 227.

65. Ibid., 101.

66. Rubin and Buchanan, *Rudi Movie*.

67. Rudrananda, *Spiritual Cannibalism*, 123; and Rubin and Buchanan, *Rudi Movie*.

68. Hugh B. Urban, *Tantra: Sex, Secrecy, Politics, and Power in the Study of Religion* (Berkeley: University of California Press, 2003), 25–26.

69. Mann, *Rudi*, 68.

70. In descending order the substances are referred to as Siva, Sakti, Sadasiva, Isvara, Vidya, Sadvidya, and Maya. Pandit, *Specific Principles*, 183. Though Shambhavananda speaks about the astral and devic levels, as well as Siddhaloka, none of these correspond with the classical names of the Kashmiri Shaivite's *lokas* (Shambhavananda, *Seat by the Fire*, 70, 123, 180–181).

71. This interpretation of the word *"kripa"* came up repeatedly during author interviews of sannyasis in Calcutta, India, during the 1980s.

72. Mann, *Rudi*, 230.

73. Rudrananda, *Rudi: In His Own Words*, 39; and Mann, *Rudi*, 229.

74. Ibid., 229.

75. Ibid., 146.

76. Ibid., 143.

77. Ibid., 46.

78. Rudrananda, *Spiritual Cannibalism*, 150.

79. Mann, *Rudi*, 47.

80. Ibid., 49.

81. Ibid., 142.

82. Rudrananda, *Rudi: In His Own Words*, 19; and Mann, *Rudi*, 49.

83. Mann, *Rudi*, 213.

84. Ibid., 111.

85. Ibid., 263.

86. See Christopher Chapple, *Karma and Creativity* (Albany, NY: SUNY Press, 1986), 37; and Robert E. Svoboda, *Aghora III: The Law of Karma* (Albuquerque, NM: Brotherhood of Life, 1997), 17–18, 321.

87. Rudrananda, *Spiritual Cannibalism*, 3; and Shambhavananda, *Seat by the Fire*, 97.

88. Rubin and Buchanan, *Rudi Movie*.

89. Commenting on the philosophy of Gurdjieff, see Lee Lozowick, *The Alchemy of Love and Sex* (Prescott, AZ: Hohm Press, 1996), 206.

90. Rubin and Buchanan, *Rudi Movie*.

91. Rudrananda, *Spiritual Cannibalism*, 22–23, 35, 40, 67, 72, 74, 97, 119.

92. Ibid., 46.

93. Mann, *Rudi*, 261; and Rudrananda, *Rudi: In His Own Words*, 48.

94. Rudrananda, *Rudi: In His Own Words*, 37.

95. Ibid., 64.

96. Mann, *Rudi*, 165.

97. Rudrananda, *Spiritual Cannibalism*, 20, 122; and Mann, *Rudi*, 200, 236.

98. Mann, *Rudi*, 20, 88, 97; and Rubin and Buchanan, *Rudi Movie*.

99. Mann, *Rudi*, 235; Rudrananda, *Spiritual Cannibalism*, 43.

100. Rubin and Buchanan, *Rudi Movie*.

101. From http://www.chetanananda.org/about.htm (accessed Aug. 6, 2010).

102. From http://www.chetanananda.org/#page_id=2&heading_id=11 (accessed Jan. 5, 2011).

103. From http://www.chetanananda.org/#page_id=2&heading_id=8 (accessed Jan. 5, 2011).

104. Some of his publications are *Will I Be the Hero of My Own Life* (Cambridge, MA: Rudra Press, 2001), *Dynamic Stillness. Part Two: The Fulfillment of Trika Yoga* (Cambridge, MA: Rudra Press, 2001); *Choose to Be Happy: The Craft and the Art of Living Beyond Anxiety* (Cambridge, MA: Rudra Press, 1996); *Songs from the Center of the Well* (Cambridge, MA: Rudra Press, 1995); and *The Breath of God* (Cambridge, MA: Rudra Press, 1988).

105. From <http://www.rudranandalineage.com/thelineage.php> (accessed Mar. 24, 2010). Rudi had one Norwegian disciple named Swami Ganeshananda who established the Rudra Meditation Center with various hubs in Europe. Ganeshananda was also initiated in Chod, Phowa, and other Tibetan Buddhist practices, which he teaches in addition to what he learned from Rudi, <http://www.rudranandalineage.com/thelineage_teachers.php?teacher=swamiganesha>).

106. Some of his publications are *Rudi: The Final Moments* (New York: Perrin Press, 2011); *Moving On: Finding Happiness in a Changed World* (Charlottesville, VA: Hampton Roads, 2004); and *A Deeper Surrender: Notes on a Spiritual Life* (Charlottesville, VA: Hampton Roads, 2001).

107. From http://www.stuartperrin.com/ (accessed Dec. 29, 2010).

108. Some of his publications are Lar Short (Lama Lars) with Martin Lowenthal, *Opening the Heart of Compassion: Transform Suffering through Buddhist Psychology and Practice* (Rutland, VT: Charles Tuttle, 1993); Lar Short with John Mann, *The Body of Light* (Rutland, VT: Charles Tuttle, 1990), and Lar Short, *The Way of Radiance* (New York: We Are Publishing, 1986).

109. From http://www.rudranandalineage.com/thelineage_teachers.php?teacher=lamalars> (accessed Mar. 26, 2010).

110. Other publications are *Students of the Light: An Educational Odyssey* (New York: Grossman, 1973); *Encounter: A Weekend with Intimate Strangers* (New York: Grossman, 1970); John Mann and H. Otto, *Ways of Growth: Approaches to Expanding Awareness* (New York: Grossman, 1968); and *Frontiers of Psychology* (New York: Macmillan, 1963).

111. They include Don Augustin from Peru and Naqual Shaman Thunder Strikes. From http://www.rudranandalineage. com/thelineage_teachers. php?teacher=rabaker (accessed Mar. 26, 2010).

112. These publications are *Merging with the Divine: One Day at a Time* (Springfield, OR: Prasad Press, 2011), and *Depth over Time: Kundalini MahaYoga: A Path of Transformation and Liberation* (Bloomington, IN: Author House, 2010).

113. From http://www.rudranandalineage.com/thelineage_teachers.php?teacher=swamikhecara> (accessed Mar. 24, 2010).

114. For an account of Adi Da see Jeffrey J. Kripal, "Riding the Dawn Horse: Adi Da and the Eros of Nonduality," in *Gurus in America*, ed. Thomas A. Forsthoefel and Cynthia Ann Humes, 193–217 (Albany, NY: SUNY Press, 2005), 195, 199.

115. Rudrananda, *Spiritual Cannibalism*, 6; Bubba Free John, *Garbage and the Goddess* (Middletown, CA: Dawn Horse Press, 1974).

116. Urban, *Tantra*, 207.

117. Rudrananda, *Spiritual Cannibalism*, 11.

3

Amrit Desai and the Kripalu Center for Yoga and Health

Ellen Goldberg

This chapter has three specific goals: first, to understand the Kripalu Center's initial growth based on Amrit Desai's (1932–) adaptation and innovation of the Hindu-inspired[1] ashram model, with emphasis on the guru-disciple relationship and the overwhelming popularity of the Kripalu approach to modern yoga; second, to document briefly the near collapse of the Kripalu community based on open allegations of Desai's sexual impropriety and the perceived betrayal of Desai's spiritual and moral authority; and third, to capture both Desai and Kripalu's remarkable resilience. Under the strong leadership and capable management of its current board of directors along with their ecumenical vision and educational insights, Kripalu has become one of the most successful spiritual retreat centers in North America today, with 2008 revenues estimated at $27.3 million. Kripalu's formula for financial success did not ultimately reside in Desai as guru, but rather in the innovative community he established—the American-born or "homegrown" Kripalu Center. As an alternative community, its structure provided the organizational stability and support needed as the devotees and disciples experienced the darkest period of Kripalu's history. Desai too has risen from the debacle stronger and more resilient. As the spiritual director of the Amrit Institute in Salt Springs, Florida,[2] Desai is currently teaching and training a new generation of yoga teachers and devotees using his deeply spiritual approach to yoga practice. Thus we see two distinctly different models at play. At the Amrit Institute, Desai as "Gurudev" continues to provide what Lola Williamson refers to as the "center of charismatic authority"—a role

Kripalu replaced after Desai's resignation by a roster of guest teachers and in-house programs. Consequently, the two models provide an ideal opportunity for comparison. Weber's model of charismatic leadership provides a thematic lens and informs the overall discussion.

Weber's Definition of Charisma

One of the hallmarks of Max Weber's contribution to sociology is his reference to and use of "ideal types" as a method of interpretive analysis and as an explanatory framework for understanding the interplay between individual and institutional social behavioral patterns. However, Weber's ideal types are psychosocial abstractions and largely represent a simplified reality. As Camic, Gorshi, and Trubek point out, Weber's ideal types do not reflect "reality-as-such" but rather provide a useful analytical tool for thinking about "recurring features of the sociohistorical world."[3] Philip Smith argues more specifically that Weber's "charismatic type" has been used rather "indiscriminately" and that at best it is an ambiguous model in contemporary studies of culture.[4] Nonetheless, Weber's model offers a clear definition of charisma as well as a sharp heuristic tool for understanding the dynamics of institution building that we see operating within the life and work of Amrit Desai and the Kripalu Center for Yoga and Holistic Health. Thus Weber's understanding of charisma provides a central theme throughout this chapter.

In his classic work *Economy and Society*, Weber defines charisma as "a certain quality of an individual's personality by virtue of which he is set apart from ordinary men and treated as endowed with supernatural, superhuman, or at least specifically exceptional powers or qualities."[5] Based on this definition, essentially meaning the "gift of grace," we see how a symbiotic relationship ensues between the charismatic leader and his or her organization.[6] Weber states clearly, "social or political systems based on charismatic legitimacy exhibit certain characteristics which reflect the intense and personal nature of the response to charisma."[7] Consequently, charismatic leadership reflects a mode of authority that is ultimately driven by its dependence on group recognition and subsequent institution building.[8] In other words, charisma requires reciprocity in social relationship—it cannot operate in a vacuum. Or, as Weber puts it:

> It is the recognition on the part of those subject to authority, which is decisive for the validity of charisma. This is freely given and guaranteed by what is held to be a "sign" or proof,

originally always a miracle, and consists in devotion to the corresponding revelation, hero worship, or absolute trust in the leader.[9]

For Weber the charismatic personality remains unconditionally dependent on the validation and recognition of others for his or her status as community leader.[10] This is an important point that we return to later in the chapter when Desai's moral authority is called into question.

So, too, the institution depends on the leader's ability, as Barnes points out, to summon "deference, devotion and awe" toward himself or herself.[11] Weber accredits this devotional affect to the charismatic's ability to draw on and use salvation narratives successfully within the community.[12] We will see further on how Desai embraces enlightenment themes specifically from Indian religion (for example, hatha yoga) rather than dualistic idioms (for example, good and evil) typically used in Western salvation narratives, and fuses them with narratives from Western self-help, holistic health and healing, New Age, and pop psychology. This confirms Weber's theory that various "local ways" of articulating the "universal quest for salvation" are central to the charismatic leader's success.[13] Although Desai is Indian born, most members of the Kripalu community are "homegrown"; thus we see the strategic use and integration of East-West narratives in his teachings. What is unmistakable in Desai's approach and in his charismatic style is the integration of local narrative set in the context of the guru-*shisya* (guru-disciple) relationship and the Hindu-inspired ashram model. This provides the institutional setting to generate his message of modern yoga.

Desai and the Kripalu Center for Yoga and Holistic Health: Phase One

Desai's role as charismatic leader and founder of the Kripalu Center is central to understanding its initial success. Although Desai has not received scholarly attention, he has arguably been one of the most influential and sought-after figures in the development of hatha yoga in America in the last forty years, and the Kripalu Center was an innovative vehicle whereby he could transmit his charismatic leadership.[14] Desai's and the Kripalu Center's history has three distinct chronological phases. The first and longest phase begins in 1960 when Desai arrives in America from the small village of Halol in Gujarat, India, to study at the Philadelphia College of Art.[15] As a student, Desai was selected to represent India at an International Day celebration. In front of nearly 2,000 people, Desai demonstrated various yoga *asanas* (postures). This event launched his career as a yoga teacher in America. With the growing success of his teaching, Desai founded the Yoga Society of Pennsylvania in 1966 as a nonprofit, tax-exempt organization. It offered 150 classes per week, as well as a teacher-training program.[16] Desai, his wife Urmila, his brother Shanti, and their newly trained yoga teachers taught more than 2,500 students per ten-week semester—a remarkable accomplishment given the formative period of yoga in America at the time. More important, there is no indication whatsoever in this period of his life that Desai had the attributes of a charismatic leader nor is there any nascent evidence in his youth, however talented he might have been both as an artist and as a yoga practitioner.

However, in 1969 Desai went to see his guru Swami Kripalvananda (better known as Kripalu or Bapuji,[17] 1913–1981) at his ashram in Malav, India.[18] Desai explains how Kripalvananda (hereafter referred to as Kripalu) taught him about the higher practices of yoga during three

Figure 3.1. Amrit Desai with his guru, Kripalu (Photo courtesy of Amrit Desai)

intensive two-hour sessions per day for three months. This guru-disciple exchange represents a critical turning point in Desai's early spiritual life and marks the period when his charismatic appeal is initiated, although it was not until he, his wife Urmila, and two of his students were practicing *asana* (yoga) together in 1972 that Desai truly understood the blessing or transmission Kripalu bestowed on him. Desai explains how he suddenly became "absorbed" and "entered a deep meditative state" during a routine yoga practice.[19] He writes, "I was flooded with bliss throughout my entire being, and I felt myself being irresistibly drawn into another level of consciousness."[20] He says, "I was no longer the performer of the exercises: they were being performed through me."[21] At the peak of this experience, Desai claims, "my body spontaneously began to twist and turn on its own, flowing smoothly from one posture to the next. The movements were effortless and free, extraordinarily elastic and stretched smoothly and easily beyond its previous limits; I was not aware of giving any direction to the movements."[22] In fact, Desai admits many of the postures he manifested spontaneously during this meditation experience were completely new to him. In a passage Desai recounts frequently, he writes:

> One after another, the postures flowed. Some of them were traditional yoga exercises; others were movements which I had never felt before. At the end of this flow of postures, my body naturally entered the lotus position, and an intense stillness, so deep that it penetrated every level of my being, emanated from within me. Suddenly, an explosion of ecstasy spread through me, and I became engulfed, overwhelmed, by a state of complete inner bliss.[23]

According to Desai's autobiographical account, his wife and his two students, Barbara and John, were deeply affected by the meditation experience. Barbara said, "I felt as if I were doing the postures with you."[24] John told Desai, "I felt some new force take over you and begin to move your body."[25] But it was Urmila's comment that rang most true. She said the postures appeared "automatic"—a term Desai continues to use as the basis of his approach to Kripalu yoga. This communal experience is pivotal for two reasons: first, it provides a sign or proof of Desai's charisma and, second, it launches Desai as a spiritual leader or guru in America. In Weberian terms, it marks the moment when Desai is set apart from others.

Some further explanatory remarks are necessary to understand this critical period in Desai's life. In 1950, when Desai was a young boy living in India, he observed his guru spontaneously and effortlessly performing *asana* (postures) and *mudras* (advanced postures and hand gestures) during meditation. At the time, Kripalu told Desai that the movements he was witnessing him performing were the result of *prana* (energy or *shakti*)—what we could call charisma or the gift of grace. In 1970 Desai remembered this incident and wrote Kripalu asking for an explanation of the spontaneous movements he himself had performed during his own meditation. Kripalu informed Desai that he had experienced a partial release or an awakening of prana, referred to by yogis as *pranotthana*.

More precisely, Kripalu gave Desai *shaktipat diksha* (initiation) during his visit to India with the hope that it would help him in his work as a yoga teacher in America, and in his progress on the yogic path.[26] *Shaktipat* initiation defines a profound moment of spiritual transformation in Desai's life, as it does in the lives of many of Desai's devotees. Douglas Brooks draws on a similar experience of *shaktipat* within the Siddha Yoga meditation movement of Swami Muktananda and Gurumayi Chidvilasananda. He defines *shaktipat* as the *shakti* (energy) unleashed by the guru or as the guru's "grace-bestowing power" (*anugraha shakti*).[27] Paul Muller-Ortega writes about *shaktipat* as a "deeply secret and mystical notion of spiritual awakening" considered "the highest form of spiritual initiation, an initiation that bestows immediate and spontaneous entry into spiritual life."[28] June McDaniel notes that the Kularnava Tantra[29] (the Ocean of the Kula, circa ninth through thirteenth century CE) refers to *shaktipat* initiation by the earlier name *"vedha diksha"* meaning "initiation by piercing," and describes five basic types of initiation including *vak diksha* (initiation by word or mantra), *sparsha diksha* (initiation by touch), and *draksanjana diksha* (initiation by sight or gaze).[30]

Within the Kripalu *parampara* (lineage), *shaktipat* is perceived as a profoundly embodied psychophysical experience marking a partial awakening of *prana*, or energy, of *kundalini shakti*. After receiving *shaktipat* the yogi or yogini typically experiences an array of automatic movements and preliminary manifestations called *kriyas* that could include shaking, crying, dancing, chanting, visions, and spontaneous or automatic *asanas* (postures) and *mudras* (advanced postures or hand gestures) such as the yoga experiences Desai described above. For Kripalu, Desai's guru, these manifestations, or *kriyas*, serve as an intrinsic part of the initial or preliminary stages of *shodhana* (body-mind purification) required on the yogic path. This is an important point that is often overlooked in various schools of modern, transnational, or Anglophone yoga, particularly ones that focus on asana only and rarely discuss or are even aware of yogic teachings on *prana*. It is important to bear in mind that although *shaktipat* initiation does not indicate the full awakening of *kundalini* and is considered only a preliminary experience, in the case of Desai, it marks a fundamental shift in his role as charismatic leader and the beginning of the development of the Kripalu ashram organization.

In the Kripalu lineage, *shaktipat* identifies the beginning life of the spiritual virtuosi and distinguishes them from ordinary seekers. As Andrew Cohen correctly points out, after *shaktipat* Desai "went from being a successful yoga teacher to a true guru in his own right."[31] There are three specific reasons to account for this. First, after *shaktipat* Desai develops a systematic approach to modern yoga called "Kripalu Yoga" in honor of his guru. Second, Kripalu gave Desai permission to give *shaktipat* to a few deserving disciples. Third, Desai's charisma was so apparent that disciples and devotees receptive to his message received or experienced *shaktipat* merely by being in his presence. Charismatic leaders openly demonstrate some kind of intimate connection with a transcendent or immanent divine source—in the Kripalu lineage this implies *shakti* or *prana*.

We can attribute Desai's emerging role as an "American" guru to two critical factors: (1) the systematization, adaptation, and innovation of the yoga teachings of his guru as an effective training protocol to awaken *prana* in his own students; and (2) with Kripalu's permission and his own motivation and ability to give *shaktipat* initiation to disciples and devotees in his growing yoga community, Desai places himself firmly in the Kripalu lineage or, to borrow a phrase from Weber, the "charismatic aristocracy."[32] This is a role that is typically reserved in Indian tradition for *sannyasins* (renunciates).[33] In America, no such rule applies. Thus, these two critical factors were instrumental in setting Desai apart from and conferring his charismatic spiritual authority over others.

Growth of the Kripalu Community

By all accounts, members of the growing Kripalu community could tangibly feel Desai's charisma, and were profoundly transformed by his presence and his ability to transmit *shakti* or *prana*. In 1972 Desai purchased property in Sumneytown, Pennsylvania, hoping to delve deeper into his own spiritual *sadhana* (practice). However, many of his yoga students who recognized this deep change within him wanted to live with him on the new property. Consequently, the first Kripalu Yoga Ashram based on a guru-disciple relationship and the Hindu-inspired ashram model opened and eventually grew to become the largest residential yoga community in America. Thus we see how Desai's charisma is community-directed, and his public presence generates conversion, change, and unity within the emerging organization.[34]

The American-based, Hindu-inspired Kripalu ashram began with five male residents who were subsequently joined by five women advocating gender equity. In response to their proposed coed residency, Desai adopted the yogic model of *brahmacarya* (celibacy) for nonmarried residents. By 1974, the ashram grew from five to twenty-five members. Its subsequent expansion to a new residence at Summit Station provides further evidence of Weber's theory that, by and large, community members have a strong desire to participate in the "charismatic act." By 1984, the Kripalu Yoga Fellowship had incorporated as a nonprofit, tax-exempt, educational public trust, and it expanded to a 350-acre property with residential facilities at Shadowbrook, a former Jesuit seminary in the New England countryside that they purchased for just in excess of $3 million. By 1994, Kripalu became the largest and most widely respected residential yoga center of its kind in America.

It also is important to consider that Desai started his career as a yoga teacher in the United States in the mid-1960s to 1970s—a time when the counterculture movement had a profound sense of rebellion and disenchantment with the world and emphasized alternative lifestyles advocating spiritual growth and holistic health. For more than two decades, Desai attracted a diverse group of young hippies experimenting with alternative lifestyles. He also attracted an international group of high-profile professionals, including prominent thinkers in the fields of academia, art, sports, psychology, politics, and business. The Kripalu website advertises that yoga teachers from all over the world came to Kripalu to learn from Desai a style of yoga that he refers to as "the yoga of self-discovery." The systematization and adaptation of his guru's teachings, as we will see, clearly appealed to the needs of the American lifestyle. At Kripalu, Desai created what Stephen Cope refers to as "a transformational environment" particularly suited to students exploring or looking to find a more "authentic" and "slightly more monastic" approach to the yoga lifestyle.[35]

Thus, Kripalu, under Desai's charismatic spiritual directorship, initially operated as an *ashram* (religious order) where residents took formal vows of simplicity, obedience, and *brahmacarya*—that is, residents lived either as monks and nuns or followed the married residents program of sexual moderation. For fifteen years, the Kripalu Center sustained 350 full-time residents under a model Weber refers to as "charismatic education."[36] Residents were essentially isolated, by choice of course, from familiar familial environments. After being initiated and given Sanskrit names, they dressed in white Indian clothes, ate in silence, followed a strict vegetarian diet with weekly fasts, and cultivated various physical exercises (that is, yoga) to awaken and stimulate their pranic capacity. A typical day at Kripalu started in the early morning with group *asana* (postures), *pranayama* (breathing exercises), and meditation classes. *Seva* (selfless service) projects began after breakfast and might include maintenance of the property, cooking, teaching courses to lay community members, counseling, administration, and so on. In the evening, the Kripalu community gathered for *satsang*—a deeply spiritual practice that involves chanting, dance, and inspirational talks by Desai. A typical discourse embraced an eclectic blend of traditional yoga philosophy fused with contemporary teachings in holistic healing and self-help or growth psychology.

By 1987, more than 10,000 guests participated in Kripalu programs and retreats.[37] Eisenstadt's keen observation that the charismatic personality attracts followers who are willing to "give up all resources, wealth, time, energy, existing social bonds and commitments—for the implementation of [the leader's] vision" clearly applies to the Kripalu community.[38] In the case of Desai, the strong desire to contact and experience the transference of charisma, *shakti*, or *prana* from guru to disciple

Figure 3.2. Kripalu and students watch Amrit Desai perform meditation-in-motion (Photo courtesy of Amrit Desai)

propelled the emerging Kripalu community into an overwhelmingly successful American institutional reality. In addition to the residents, a large lay community participated in the Kripalu lifestyle so they too could experience or contact Desai's charisma directly through his presence.

Kripalu Yoga and Meditation-in-Motion

Desai, as "an American yogi," both followed and deviated from his Indian-born guru in several ways.[39] Most notably, Kripalu was a *sannyasi* (renunciate), whereas Desai is not; he is a householder. He does not live the life of a solitary yogi (what Kripalu refers to as *nivritti* or *prana marga sadhaka*) in seclusion and silence, but rather lives within and among the community of disciples and devotees to whom he is spiritual guide, or "Gurudev." Desai's role can be defined as a *pravritti marga sadhaka* (lay ascetic) in the sense that he has patterned his life on teaching and practicing *asana*, *pranayama*, devotion, and meditation to the extent that he can manage his worldly affairs. He developed what he calls the "path of selfless service," or *seva*, rather than his guru's path of renunciation. His systematic method of teaching and practice called "Kripalu Yoga" emphasizes love, service, and surrender as a practical way to bring the so-called mystical experiences of yoga into daily life. As Desai puts it, "spirituality was no longer something I experienced only in solitary mediation but is included in every activity of life." Thus, in his own words, Desai's teachings on yoga reflect the "unique balance of living by the highest spiritual principles while fulfilling my responsibilities as a householder and an active teacher."[40] This is precisely the blend of "mysticism and worldliness" that appeals to his American devotees.[41]

As a lay practitioner, Desai developed what he describes as a radical approach to hatha yoga, using his own transformative meditation experiences after *shaktipat* as the starting point. More specifically, Desai cultivates techniques to balance *citta* (mind) and *prana* (energy) by synchronizing the flow of *asana* with various traditional *pranayama* exercises. By his own account, he intentionally draws parallels with Patañjali's *ashtanga* yoga (eightfold path), particularly limbs three to seven: *asana* (posture), *pranayama* (breathing), *pratyahara* (withdrawal of the senses), *dharana* (single-mindedness), and *dhyana* (absorption). However, his signature approach and primary contribution as a modern guru in America lies in his charismatic teachings on *prana* (energy) called "meditation-in-motion."

Broadly stated, meditation-in-motion describes a gradual five-stage approach to yoga that begins by harmonizing body and breath through stretching and strengthening. According to Richard Faulds, stage one nurtures, rejuvenates, and relaxes the practitioner, and provides introductory level technical training in postures. According to Desai, the practitioner is given primary instructions specifically for the opening and awakening of *prana*. In stage two, the practitioner learns to hold, extend, and intensify various postures. Here the intended purpose is to help the practitioner: (1) release tension; (2) strengthen and purify body and mind; (3) increase self-awareness; (4) cultivate preliminary meditative states; (5) become more flexible; and (6) stimulate *prana*.[42]

When viewed in conjunction, Desai claims these stages correspond to traditional hatha yoga. However, he provides an added instruction, that is, to pay particular attention to "subtle sensations and urges in the body during postures and *pranayama*."[43] Why? It is conducive for cultivating an awareness of *prana*. This special feature in Desai's approach establishes a harmony between mind and body that he maintains is essential in the higher stages of meditation referred to as raja yoga. Here Desai follows the rhetoric of modern yoga Vivekananda and others initiated. Raja yoga in this model is perceived not only as the fundamental goal of hatha yoga practice, but it is also perceived and reconstituted as an inner science. Thus, even though Desai portrays the postures and teachings of yoga as "ancient," he reiterates a modern interpretation whose history has recently been brought to light.[44] Nevertheless, the innovative element in Desai's approach is his central focus on *prana*.

Stage three and stage four correspond to Patañjali's eightfold path. Stage three corresponds specifically to *pratyahara* (the withdrawal of the senses) whereas stage four corresponds to *dharana* (the first stage of meditation) as outlined in the *Yogasutras*. Based on his own experience, Desai claims the practitioner must experience *nirodha* (stillness) of their thoughts (*citta-vrittis*) at every stage on the yogic path, not simply in the higher stages of *samadhi*. While scholars and practitioners can debate the viability of this point, it nonetheless emphasizes Desai's deeply personal and experiential approach to yoga practice. For Desai, hatha yoga and the raja yoga of the *Yogasutras* are not in conflict— they are interdependent. *Citta* (mind), *prana* (energy or breath), and body function spontaneously and harmoniously, meaning, in his words, that *asana* or posture cannot be separated from "the true purpose of yoga."[45] In the Kripalu™ approach, postures cultivate stillness of mind and the cessation of *citta-vrittis* (thoughts). Although we see a similar approach in other modern schools of yoga that are posture-identified (for example, the Krishnamacarya lineage), Desai markets this as a new or expanded perception of yoga leading to the embodied experience of "meditation-in-motion."[46]

In the fifth and final stage of Kripalu Yoga, the practitioner is introduced to specific techniques that foster deep relaxation and cultivate automatic movement or the spontaneous flow of *prana* during posture practice. Faulds and Desai describe this stage as a "form of moving meditation that reveals the essential mystical truth: Spirit [understood here as *prana*] dwells within you as the intelligent energy underlying body and mind."[47] In Desai's own words, this stage represents "the real experience of holistic yoga."[48] He claims, along the lines of other modern exponents of yoga including Swami Vivekananda (1863–1902) and Sri Aurobindo (1872–1950), that in the higher stages of consciousness, *prana* functions at an evolutionary level. While this line of thinking requires analysis beyond the scope of this chapter, what is most innovative in Desai's approach is that the movements (or *kriyas*) of the body, guided by *prana* or the inner cosmic evolutionary intelligence, emerge involuntarily. Mind acts as a "witness" to the automatic experiences of the body under the guidance and control of *prana*.

What becomes apparent is how deeply Desai's own meditation experiences align with the final stage of his Kripalu approach. One could argue justifiably that Desai's primary experiences of *shakti*, referred to earlier as *pranotthana*, are in large measure enshrined as the explicit goal of Kripalu Yoga. These experiences are then portrayed as the essential and ultimate goal of all spiritual practice. Using this method or approach, Desai remains at the forefront of the modern Anglophone yoga revolution in America for almost four decades. With a growing international reputation he also exports his teachings of Kripalu Yoga through personal demonstrations, talks, and teacher-training programs to more than forty countries and acquires thousands of worldwide adherents. Thus Desai's most noted innovation is that he was the first Indian-born "American yogi" to introduce systematic teachings and techniques on *prana* in the United States. By emphasizing *pranayama* such as *anuloma viloma* (alternate nostril breathing) and *ujjayi* (breathing with glottis partially closed), Desai cultivated a progressive five-stage posture flow as his so-called signature approach to facilitate a state of deep relaxation called *yoga-nidra* (yogic sleep), particularly in the final relaxation phase of posture practice (for example, *shavasana*, or the corpse pose). For Desai, this method is essential to gaining access to the higher stages of meditation, such as *dhyana*. Desai also maintains that the synchronization of breath and movement is critical to physical healing—it promotes states of bliss, clarity, and, most importantly, the spontaneous movement of *prana*. One also could argue that Desai's methods, like any set of rigorous spiritual exercises, induce embodied experiences as well as receptivity to his charismatic message.[49]

In many schools of modern yoga, including Iyengar, Ashtanga, and Vinyasa, postures are performed deliberately and voluntarily. Thus, Desai's teachings on *prana* constitute a unique contribution and a radical and innovative approach to yoga practice in America. In a recent interview, Desai shared how he learned the postures of yoga from a poster hanging on the wall at his father's gymnasium in India. That is, Desai practiced the various sequences as a young boy deliberately and with willful or conscious control. However, after *shaktipat* initiation when Desai's *prana* was partially awakened by Kripalu, postures, *mudras*, and other purificatory movements, or *kriyas*, manifested and flowed spontaneously during meditation. This experience is not only the source of his teachings on yoga; it is also the source of his charisma.

Desai's Kripalu Yoga is a modified version of Swami Kripalvananda's *pravritti marga* (teachings on hatha yoga for lay practitioners), infused with the rhetoric of Western contemporary New Age discourses such as holistic health and growth psychology. One may also argue that Desai's innovations and creative adaptations are rooted firmly in his lived experience of yoga in America. Desai developed an innovative and systematic approach to hatha yoga using his guru as the "circular construction of authority"—to borrow a phrase from Mark Singleton and Richard Smith,[50] but he tempers Kripalu's rigorous monastic approach to kundalini yoga for his American disciples with insights on *prana* from his own meditation experiences and his life as a lay practitioner in America. When we examine Desai's approach more closely, we see that he developed a cross-cultural style of posture practice that broadly resonates with other modern Anglophone schools that are practiced in community.

Quite often Desai demonstrated spontaneous postures at Kripalu. One may argue that these demonstrations are responsible in part for launching Desai's charismatic role as Gurudev (divine guru) and for the success of the American-born Kripalu approach to modern yoga on the transnational stage. Students were personally touched by Desai's charisma during these sessions. Cope refers to one of these demonstrations as "ecstatic dance." He writes:

As Amrit entered deeper into the dance, the entire room seemed to be pulled down by a deep undertow of absorption. We were lost with him in the dance of energy. . . . I noticed a change in my perception. Colors had become brighter, bolder. The blue and gold tiles behind the altar were fairly pulsing with flashing hues. Light itself had become a palpable golden presence. At moments the whole room dissolved into waves of light, particles of energy. And all the while, I felt the whole

room breathing together and somehow moving together, pulsing and expanding and contracting. At one point, I had an
experience of energy rushing up and down my spine, as I'd
had when he'd touch me, a tingling at the crown of my head,
my whole body suffused with an intense heat.[51]

Desai's "dance" and "state of absorption" pulled students into what
Eisenstadt and Weber define as "contact charisma." Desai's energy and
charisma were not only tangible, but also seemingly contagious. That
is to say, students repeatedly report (even today) their own dramatic
personal experiences of spiritual energy in his presence. The source of
this charisma is *shakti* or *prana*—the vital energy that propels the hatha
yoga Kripalu style.

Desai's specialty then lies in his ability to adapt and adopt what he
calls the "ancient esoteric techniques of *prana*" that he learned from his
guru and repackage them not only for a modern homegrown audience
but also for export. Desai says, "I have tested it and taught it to thousands of students." They report "greater physical health and strength,
more vigor and vitality, greater mental clarity and creativity, and feelings of love and compassion."[52] Furthermore, he claims his form of yoga
also opened students "to a new dimension of intuitive perception not
visible through the five physical senses or conceivable through reason
or logic of conditioned mind."[53] This, he maintains, is a direct result of
prana—a dimension of yoga that has been overlooked in traditional and
even modern Anglophone approaches to hatha yoga in America until he
adapted them from his guru and introduced them in the 1970s through
the Kripalu Center.

Fall from Grace: Phase Two

Phase two refers to Desai's fall from grace or the withdrawal of charismatic legitimacy. It began with allegations of sexual impropriety and
ended in 1994 with Desai's resignation as spiritual director of the Kripalu
Center for Yoga and Holistic Health. Although details of the scandal
are relevant, in this section we are more concerned with the implications of Desai's actions for himself and for the American-born Kripalu
community. Earlier I showed that in Weber's model, the charismatic
requires a reciprocal relationship of social recognition to maintain his or
her elevated status as leader within the community. Under this model,
Desai and the Kripalu Center engaged in a mutually reinforcing (though
unspoken) contract. Like any charismatic, Desai's authority and spiri-

tual legitimacy required validation in order to thrive in a community or institutional setting. In phase two, that validation is withdrawn and, consequently, his role as Gurudev is denied.

So, too, the members of Kripalu constituted a "charismatic community"—a term Guenther Roth introduced.[54] That is, they sought their own personal experience of transcendence and found it through Desai. As previously mentioned, the members exhibited a strong desire to participate in the charismatic act, for example, to receive *shaktipat* or become absorbed in Desai's "ecstatic dance," as Cope calls it. Thus the transference of charisma or *shakti* motivated individuals to follow Desai, often at great personal cost (for example, wealth, time, energy, preexisting social bonds, and so on). Furthermore, charismatic appeal, as we noted earlier, is ultimately tied to the quest for meaning and salvation. In Desai's case, the quest for meaning is reinforced by eliciting "powerful feelings and strong emotions" in members, particularly during the practice and demonstration of yoga.[55] Eisenstadt defines this as the charismatic's ability to "restructure the emotional components of the personality." Out of this restructuring charismatic communities such as Kripalu arise.[56]

Eisenstadt's argument that profound personal engagement with the charismatic can shatter preexisting psychosocial bonds is persuasive.[57] Eisenstadt claims that as a result, new or controlled norms of behavior must be predefined and prescribed by the charismatic leader in order to "give meaning" as well as to "reassure" the devotee or disciple of his or her new "status" and role within the collective.[58] As we have seen, after *shaktipat* initiation, Desai prescribed monastic or ascetic norms of behavior, including new Sanskrit names; a diet based on vegetarianism, macrobiotics, or both, including weekly fasts; wearing white clothes; rigorous spiritual exercises including postures, chanting, and meditation; the practice of *brahmacarya* (celibacy); work based on *seva* (selfless service); and vows of simplicity and obedience—all in the name of *sadhana*.[59] These newly prescribed ritual activities and norms of behavior conferred meaning. They also affected identity-formation and elevated the initiate's special status as a spiritual virtuoso within the Kripalu collective by acting as voluntary rites of passage.

More important, as Lindholm argues, the charismatic contract informed by these new prescriptive norms defines a moral bond that connects a leader with his or her followers.[60] The moral bond that linked Desai and members of the Kripalu community was established during phase one of institution building, using the strategies listed above. Desai's disciples voluntarily, willingly, and substantively altered their lifestyles to follow him. Residents believed that, in exchange for a life of *seva* (selfless or volunteer service), they would be supported in an alternative yoga lifestyle by Desai's charismatic presence and by his spiritual guidance, as well as be provided with the daily necessities of life including stipend, health care, vacation time, food, housing, and so on.

However, in phase two the moral bond between guru and disciple was radically challenged amidst allegations of Desai's sexual infidelity. That is, the alleged transgressions severed the moral bond of trust and *dharma* (duty) that was cherished by members of the charismatic community and caused Desai's eventual fall from grace. How? Kripalu members withdrew their validation of Desai's charismatic authority. This catapulted the community into a virtual crisis.

It's an old and familiar story. Desai was accused of extramarital affairs with five female residents of the Kripalu Fellowship. Desai prescribed new norms of behavior for members of the charismatic community after initiation that included foregoing normative sexual relations (that is, celibacy for nonmarried residents and moderation for married residents), and living a life of simplicity and selfless volunteer service. These were two essential criteria of the spiritual life that Desai as guru ultimately did not adhere to himself, especially since Desai received a salary as head of the organization that was much higher than the typical resident's stipend. However, to be fair, the residents were well aware of this legal financial structure and entered the Kripalu lifestyle by choice.

The scandal tore at the heart of the Kripalu community. In 1994, the directors of the Kripalu Fellowship confronted Desai on various charges of sexual impropriety. Desai openly and publically admitted the truth of his culpability to the community. As his daughter Kamini relayed in a personal correspondence, "He was aware that his actions were not in keeping with the teachings or the regulations at Kripalu." He also "shared his own fear of admitting his mistakes and of losing the love and respect of his students."[61] Nonetheless, the board of directors forced Desai to resign immediately as Spiritual Director, thereby relinquishing his role as Gurudev. His open admission of guilt triggered a storm of viciousness and anger, and the "tide of mass opinion turned against him."[62]

James Ambro captures one of the central issues when he writes:

> The spiritual authority that had been given to Yogi Desai for the past twenty-five years was based on the shared belief that Yogi Desai did not engage in this kind of behavior, and that if he did, he would have been honest and forthright about it. If his actions betrayed those beliefs, and trust, then what had the spiritual community been based on all these years other than a grand delusion. . . . In less than an hour, Yogi

Desai had gone from being a respected teacher and figure of reverence, to yet another symbol of spiritual hypocrisy and derision, and for the first time in its history, the Kripalu community was without a leader, or a firm direction.[63]

Andrew Cohen adds:

I remember my own disappointment, for I had seen Yogi Desai as the last of the few modern pioneer masters of yoga in the West who, up until that point anyway, had remained free from scandal. What is going on here? I found myself asking over and over again. These great men were true masters after all, men who not only had experienced glorious heights of bliss and ecstasy that most only dream about, but in this case, who also had the power to transmit that experience to others. . . . So what gives?[64]

The only explanation is the cherished moral bond between guru and disciple was broken by the allegations and admission of guilt, and thus the recognition of Desai's charismatic authority over the community was withheld. Members of the community refer to this as "the darkest period in Kripalu's history."[65]

Resilience and Restructured Organizations: Phase Three

Phase three began in 1999 after a period of readjustment. Kripalu redefined its legal status, changing from a nonprofit religious organization to a new nonprofit secular center for yoga education (formalized in 2004). Under the direction of a professional management team consisting of a board of directors, the new leadership of Kripalu, including several long-standing former residents, established Kripalu as a transnational secular yoga retreat and experiential program. Senior disciples took on teaching roles Desai previously held. According to Kripalu's press kit made available by Richard Faulds, chairman of the board (at the time of writing), Kripalu advertises itself as one of the "largest and most established retreat centers for yoga and holistic living in North America." As proof of this, its total 2008 revenues were approximately $27.3 million (IRS form). The new Kripalu is no longer predicated on the Hindu-inspired guru-disciple ashram model because, according to Faulds, it "proved problematic in so many spiritual communities across America."[66] In its place, Kripalu implemented a model of spiritual ecumenism.

Even though Kripalu has dropped almost all reference to Desai, the center promotes Kripalu Yoga under the name of "meditation-in-motion." Though developed by Desai, Kripalu owns the intellectual property rights to Kripalu Yoga as well as all of Desai's writings. Gone is the traditional connection to guru and lineage—replaced by more than 700 experiential programs in yoga, health, and holistic healing, including *ayurveda* (Indian traditional medicine), meditation, food and nutrition, as well as classes in *qigong*. According to its own self-promotion, "many of the world's most accomplished teachers in yoga, self-discovery and holistic health"[67] lead the programs. Consequently, Kripalu is no longer the only style of yoga found on its impressive roster. It features any style or approach that will draw guests—its main goal. In addition, Kripalu features personal retreats that work on weight loss, fitness, stress reduction, and healing. Thus we see that professional training and the medicalization of yoga play a large part in the ongoing educational thrust of the center. Through its newly formed Center for Professional Training, it offers certificates in yoga, massage, *ayurveda*, and bodywork.

Each year the Kripalu Center serves more than 28,000 guests. In 2005, the Kripalu School of Ayurveda was launched, offering one of the few professional certification programs in the United States. According to the website, thirty-five health services are available to choose from, including bodywork, facials, neuromuscular therapy, Thai massage, individual nutritional consultation, saunas, whirlpools, and of course, yoga—giving it the flavor of a spa along the lines of Canyon Ranch. The Kripalu School of Ayurveda opened in 2005, with forty-two graduates in its first class. According to the center's figures, in 2007 more than 27,600 students enrolled in various programs and 340 students were certified as Kripalu Yoga teachers. In 2009 Kripalu opened yet another new building called the Annex. Designed by Peter Rose, it is a six-story ecobuilding with eighty additional guest rooms including private baths.[68] Photos of the rooms, designed with natural, locally made furniture, are available on the Kripalu website. In 2010 Kripalu's Institute for Extraordinary Living, in partnership with Harvard University, began groundbreaking research on the effects of yoga. Thus we see that Kripalu has completely secularized the context and environment for the teaching and dissemination of yoga.

One also could argue that the various programs and international teachers the Kripalu community recognized replaced the role of guru at Kripalu. Thus residents and inside members of Kripalu still constitute a "homegrown" charismatic community seeking transcendence through the role of guru—a role Desai no longer holds, but rather is represented by an international roster of recognized teachers. Thus, at the core,

Figure 3.3. Amrit Desai, current photo (Photo courtesy of Amrit Desai)

the process of redefinition after the internal crisis represents a radical reinvention of the guru-disciple relationship and Hindu-inspired *ashram* model.

After a period of retirement, Desai has resumed teaching at the Amrit Institute in Salt Springs, Florida. Desai has been recognized internationally as a yogi, particularly for the innovations he brought to his teaching style of American yoga. As stated earlier, Desai developed a unique blend of so-called "traditional' yoga" alongside contemporary advances in holistic health and self-growth psychology. Thus, Desai's brand of or approach to yoga is still relevant. Even though he is not permitted to use the trademark "Kripalu Yoga," he fully recognizes that Americans are still looking for ways to improve their health and develop effective techniques for spiritual and personal growth.

After his resignation from Kripalu in 1994, Desai faced a moment of truth. As he stated in a recent interview, he was "stripped of everything" and "there was no going back." He had "lost face in a very public way." How he lived going forward would be "the true indicator of his ability to live his teachings or not." Desai seems to have learned from this. He refers to this time as "a blessing" because it "deepened" and "accelerated his own personal reflection and growth." His teachings at the Amrit Institute reflect a renewed commitment to his knowledge and experience of yoga and his dedication to his guru and the Kripalu lineage. As his daughter Kamini writes, "My father's greatest teaching is not in the words he has spoken or the experiences he has conveyed, but in the example he has given of what it means to surrender to life and the mistakes we make as the medium to liberation."[69]

Conclusion

This chapter examines Desai's life according to a threefold schema that includes the founding of the Kripalu Center, his fall from grace, and ultimately, his resilience and resurgence as "Gurudev" at the Amrit Institute in Salt Springs, Florida. Weber's ideal charismatic type provided a useful heuristic tool to frame the analysis and help us understand the interdependent relationship between guru and charismatic community. Desai developed his own style of yoga in the 1960s and 1970s based on the legacy of his guru Swami Kripalvananda, which continues to reach thousands of students worldwide. As such, his accomplishments as well as his failures, including his contributions to modern Anglophone yoga in America, are noteworthy.

Desai's style of teaching has been adopted and assimilated into American life by a large and diverse community of yoga practitioners and teachers. Kripalu Yoga as it is currently being taught at the Kripalu Center for Yoga and Holistic Health has removed the guru-disciple paradigm they claim proved problematic in so many spiritual communities across America. Kripalu replaced the role of guru with a mode of nonsectarian experiential and ecumenical education that has also proved successful. In contrast, we see the ideal of the guru is alive and well at the Amrit Institute under Desai's current leadership. Both models are currently thriving in America.

Notes

1. Lola Williamson defines the term "Hindu-inspired" in her recent book *Transcendent in America: Hindu-Inspired Meditation Movements as New Religion* (New York: New York University Press, 2010).

2. I interviewed Amrit Desai on May 16–18, 2010, at his home on the property of the Amrit Institute in Salt Springs, Florida.

3. Charles Camic, Philip Gorski, and David Trubek, "Introduction," in Max Weber's *Economy and Society: A Critical Companion*, ed. Charles Camic, Philip Gorski, and David Trubek, 1–28 (Stanford, CA: Stanford University Press, 2005), 8.

4. Philip Smith, "Culture and Charisma: Outline of a Theory," *Acta Sociologica* 43 (2000): 101–111; and, Guenther Roth, "Socio-Historical Model and Development Theory: Charismatic Community, Charisma of Reason and the Counter-culture," *American Sociological Review* 40 (1975): 148–157.

5. Max Weber, *Economy and Society: An Outline of Interpretive*, Guenther Roth and Claus Wittich, ed. (Berkeley: University of California Press, [1922] 1978), 358.

6. Ibid., 328.

7. Ibid., xx.

8. Douglas F. Barnes, "Charisma and Religious Leadership: An Historical Analysis," *Journal for the Scientific Study of Religion* 17 (1978): 1; and S. N. Eisenstadt, "Introduction: Charisma and Institution Building: Max Weber and Modern Sociology," in *Max Weber, On Charisma and Institution Building*, ed. S. N. Eisenstadt (Chicago: Chicago University Press, 1968), xxx.

9. Weber, *Economy and Society*, 49.

10. See also, Eisenstadt, "Introduction"; Barnes, "Charisma and Religious Leadership," 1; Ann Willner and Dorothy Willner, "The Rise and Role of Charismatic Leaders," *Annals of the American Academy of Political and Social Science* 358 (1965): 79; and Gauri Vishwanathan, "The Ordinary Business of Occultism," *Critical Inquiry* 27 (2000): 8.

11. Barnes, "Charisma and Religious Leadership," 2.

12. See Benjamin Smith, "'With Heat Even Iron Will Bend': Discipline and Authority in Ashtanga Yoga," in *Yoga and the Modern World: Contemporary Perspectives*, ed. Mark Singleton and Jean Byrne, 140–161 (London: Routledge, 2000).

13. Ibid., 109.

14. Desai has been awarded numerous titles including Jagadacharya (conferred in 1986 by the World Religions Parliament), Vishwa Yoga Ratna (conferred in 1987 by the Vishwa Unnyayan Samad), and Yogacharya (conferred in 1988 by his guru Swami Kripalvananda).

15. Desai graduated in 1964 with a bachelor's degree in fine arts and design.

16. At this stage in his early career, Desai himself trained more than fifty teachers and gave classes at the YMCA, YWCA, Rotary Club, and other community centers and colleges in Philadelphia.

17. For more details on Swami Kripalvananda, see Ellen Goldberg, "Swami Kṛpalvānanada: The Man behind Kripalu Yoga," *Religions of South Asia* 4 (2010): 67–88.

18. When Desai was fourteen years old, Kripalu took him under his tutelage.

19. Amrit Desai, *Kripalu Yoga: Meditation-in-Motion* (Lenox, MA: Kripalu, 1981), 35.

20. Ibid., 35.

21. Ibid., 35.

22. Ibid., 35.

23. Ibid., 35.

24. Ibid., 36.

25. Ibid., 36.

26. In the pamphlet "The Stages of Kundalini Yoga," Kripalu confirms that he gave Desai "light *shatkipat*" in 1969 to help him progress. Desai returned to India in 1971 to receive full *shaktipat* initiation from Kripalu. In a letter to Desai, Kripalu writes, "After you return from here having had *shaktipat diksha* from me, you will be able to bring many great changes in the atmosphere of America. Whatever progress you have made so far in teaching the message of yoga was only ordinary. Now you will be able to give these higher teachings as a true representative of God. Your message will become more powerful, popular, and will be of great service to mankind" (Swami Kripalvananda, *Stages of Kundalini Yoga.* [Pransali, India: Muni Mandal Ashram Trust, 1975], 50). See also, Chris Wallis, "The Decent of Power: Possession, Mysticism and Initiation in the Śaiva Theology of Abhinavagupta," *Journal of Indian Philosophy* 36 (2008): 247–295.

27. Douglas Brooks et al., *Meditation Revolution: A History and Theology of the Siddha Yoga Lineage* (New Delhi: Muktabodha Indological Research Institute, 1997), xxxviii.

28. Paul E. Muller-Ortega et al., *Meditation Revolution: A History and Theology of the Siddha Yoga Lineage* (New Delhi: Muktabodha Indological Research Institute, 1997), 407.

29. June McDaniel, "Spiritual Biography / Autobiography: Response" (Montreal: American Academy of Religion, 2009). This text is considered authoritative to Kaula *tantrikas* (practitioners of Tantra) in India. It is set in the form of a dialogue between Shiva and Shakti and deliberates on various topics including the guru-disciple relationship, the importance of initiation, yoga, mantra, and the secrets of self-realization.

30. See also the section of the Shiva Purana known as Vayavaiyasamhita 15: 7–10.

31. Andrew Cohen, "Yoga, Ego and Purification," *EnlighenNext Magazine*, http://www.enlightennext.org/magazine/j17/desai.asp, 1 (accessed June 22, 2011).

32. Weber, *Economy and Society*, 1136.

33. It is important to note that Kripalu initiated and ordained three disciples (swamis), Rajarshi Muni, Vinit Muni, and Ashutosh Muni.

34. See Steven R. Wilson, "Becoming a Yogi: Resocialization and Deconditioning," *Sociological Analysis* 45 (1984): 301–314.

35. In 1974 Desai led a contingent of devotees from the United States and Canada to attend the installation ceremonies of *jyotir lingam* of Lord Lakulish at the Brahameshvara Temple at Kayavarohan, India. In 1977 Swami Kripalu announced his decision to visit America. He lived in silence on the property of the Kripalu Ashram until several months before his death in 1981. For more information on the life of Kripalu, see Ellen Goldberg, "Kṛpālvānanda: The Man

behind Kripalu Yoga," in *Gurus of Modern Yoga*, ed. Mark Singleton and Ellen Goldberg, chap. 8 (New York: Oxford University Press, forthcoming).

36. Weber, *Economy and Society*, 1143.

37. http://kripalu.org/blog/thrive/ (accessed June 22, 2010).

38. Eisenstadt, "Introduction," xxii; see also, Weber, *Economy and Society*, 241–245.

39. Cope refers to Desai as an "American Yogi," an accurate designation. Desai became and was recognized as a "yogi" in America. In fact, his status in India is debated given his householder or lay lifestyle. Stephen Cope, *Yoga and the Quest for the True Self* (New York: Bantam Books, 1999), 69.

40. Desai, *Kripalu Yoga*, 45.

41. Vishwanathan, "Ordinary Business," 6.

42. See Richard Faulds, *Kripalu Yoga: A Guide to Practice On and Off the Mat* (New York: Bantam, 2005), 4–6; see, also, Desai, *Kripalu Yoga*, 83.

43. Desai, *Kripalu Yoga*, 80.

44. See also Mark Singleton, "The Classical Reveries of Modern Yoga: Patañjali and Constructive Orientalism," in *Yoga and the Modern World: Contemporary Perspectives*, ed. Mark Singleton and Jean Byrne, 77–100 (London: Routledge, 2009); Peter van der Veer, "Spirituality in Modern Society," *Social Research* 76 (2009): 1097–1120; Elizabeth De Michelis, *A History of Modern Yoga: Patañjali and Western Esotericism* (London: Continuum, 2005); Meera Nanda, *Prophets Facing Backwards: Postmodern Critiques of Science and Hindu Nationalism in India* (New Brunswick, NJ: Rutgers University Press, 2003); and, Vishwanathan, "Ordinary Business," 6.

45. Desai, *Kripalu Yoga*, 1–4.

46. In brief, Desai outlines five essential elements in his "meditation-in-motion" approach: (1) deep relaxation during postures; (2) continuous rhythmic breathing during postures; (3) slow and meditative movements synchronized with inhalation and exhalation; (4) attention focused internally inducing meditation or *dharana*; and (5) mind witnessing the movement of *prana* in the mind-body. By practicing in this way, Desai claims the "paradox of motion (hatha yoga postures) and the meditation (raja yoga) happen spontaneously" (*Kripalu Yoga*, 79).

47. Faulds, *Kripalu Yoga*, 6.

48. Desai, *Kripalu Yoga*, 82.

49. See David Lewis-Williams and David Pearce, *Inside the Neolithic Mind: Consciousness, Cosmos and the Realm of the Gods* (New York: Thames and Hudson, 2005) for an excellent discussion of the various experiences generated by spiritual exercises.

50. See Ellen Goldberg, "Swami Kṛpalvānanada," 68.

51. Cope, *Quest*, 50.

52. Desai, *Kripalu Yoga*, 100.

53. Ibid., 100.

54. Roth, "Socio-Historical Model," 149.

55. Eisenstadt, "Introduction," xxxix.

56. Ibid., xxix, ccviii.

57. Ibid., xxxi, xxviii; see also Charles Lindholm, *Charisma* (Cambridge, MA: Basil Blackwell, 1990).

58. Eisenstadt, "Introduction," xxviii.

59. Richard Faulds writes, "If you had walked through the doors of Kripalu Center as a guest in the ashram's heyday, your first impression would have been one of entering a Hindu religious community. Three hundred ashram residents lived on-site, almost all of whom were known by Sanskrit names. White clothing was worn to symbolize a commitment to purification, an endeavor made real by a strict vegetarian diet and a weekly fast day. Mornings started before dawn with yoga, *pranayama*, and meditation. Long hours of selfless service to the community were punctuated by an extended lunch break designed to encourage vigorous exercise. After dinner, the community gathered to chant, dance, and listen to spiritual discourses by the guru in residence, Yogi Desai" (*Kripalu Yoga*, 181).

60. Lindholm, *Charisma*; see also, Edward Shils, "Charisma, Order, and Status," *American Sociological Review* 30 (1975): 199–213; and Weber, *Economy and Society*, 241–245.

61. Kamini Desai, personal correspondence with author, Sept. 24, 2010.

62. Ibid.

63. James Abro, *An American Yoga: The Kripalu Story Ebook* (N.p.: 32 Beach Productions, n.d.), 154. http://beachproductions.com/kripalu.html (accessed January 22, 2013).

64. Cohen, "Yoga, Ego," 2.

65. Desai's daughter Kamini explains that as the residents became more mature, they wanted to participate in the decisions and the direction the community would take. Desai, as founder and director, though willing to make some changes, was not willing to make drastic changes in the basic vision of the organization as a service-oriented community. It was in this environment of frustration with the old structure that knowledge of Yogi Desai's former relations came to light. This information was the spark that caused an already slow-burning fire to burst into a firestorm. Personal correspondence with author, Sept. 24, 2010.

66. Faulds, *Kripalu Yoga*, 2.

67. Kripalu Press Kit, Kripalu Center for Yoga and Holistic Health.

68. Costs for the building are reported to be $18 million.

69. Kamini Desai, personal correspondence with author, Sept. 24, 2010.

4

Swamis, Scholars, and Gurus

Siddha Yoga's American Legacy

Lola Williamson

I want to see the world full of saints.

—Muktananda

Just prior to departing on his second world tour in 1974, Swami Muktananda (1908–1982) addressed several thousand disciples who had gathered at Mumbai's Santa Cruz Airport. "I am going abroad to initiate a revolution, a meditation revolution," he told the audience.[1] Muktananda attracted tens of thousands of followers worldwide with his charismatic personality and his ability to awaken spiritual energy, or *kundalini*, in others. He was called a *"shaktipat* (descent of grace) guru" because *kundalini* awakening occurred so readily in his presence. Muktananda taught that once the *kundalini* was awakened, meditation would occur spontaneously.

His revolution continues today as new gurus and spiritual teachers he and his successor, Gurumayi, influenced spread the teachings of Siddha Yoga, the tradition Muktananda established. The word *siddha* refers to an enlightened master and highlights the importance of the guru in this tradition. Muktananda named two successors: Malti, whom he named Chidvilasananda (later known as Gurumayi) when she became a *sannyasi* (renunciate), and her brother Subhash, whom he named Nityananda—the name of his own guru—upon becoming a *sannyasi*. However, Swami Nityananda broke his vow of celibacy and was ousted from the Siddha Yoga organization in 1985. He continued to function as a guru, though, and founded his own organization, Shanti Mandir. Nityananda is, therefore, not officially part of the Siddha Yoga lineage as it is proffered by Siddha Yoga Dham Associates (or SYDA, the legal arm of Siddha Yoga).

This chapter helps to delineate the growing tide of American Hinduism by illustrating how two Indian gurus, Muktananda and Gurumayi, have spawned many types of Hindu practice. Covering the dozens of gurus and teachers Siddha Yoga influenced would be impossible, so I have chosen three foci: two individual gurus, Master Charles and Sandra Barnard, and a complex of teachers who were first introduced to the public through Anusara Yoga founder John Friend. This chapter provides an overview of Muktananda's "meditation revolution" in its complex variety.

Because practitioners of American Hinduism, as well as those who study it, are still in the process of developing its nomenclature, a few notes on terminology may be helpful. In Sanskrit, the word "guru" translates as "teacher," and therefore the two words could be used interchangeably. However, the word has a useful place because it allows us to differentiate between those teachers who set themselves apart, or are set apart by their students, in a way that gives them a more extraordinary or sacred quality than others. Often, they serve as a focus of *bhakti*, or devotion, for those who follow them. Therefore, I use the word "guru" when referring to Master Charles, even though he has taken on the Western honorific "Master" as his title. "Guru" is also used for Sandra Barnard, even though most of her students refer to her as their "spiritual teacher." In contrast, I employ the word "teacher" when referring to John Friend and the spiritual leaders associated with him. Teachers in this network maintain that *jñana*, or knowledge, will free their students from the bondage of limited awareness if Hindu texts are deeply imbibed and then applied in a practical way. When referring to each guru or teacher specifically, I use the names their students use: Master Charles for Charles Cannon, Sandra for Sandra Barnard, first and last name for John Friend, and first names for the teachers in the Anusara network.

The chapter is based primarily on ethnographic research carried out over three years, beginning in the summer of 2009. I conducted interviews with each of the gurus and engaged in informal conversations and, in some cases, formal interviews with their students. I also attended classes and retreats in order to experience firsthand the various forms of the Siddha Yoga legacy.[2]

Master Charles: The High-Tech Guru

According to Master Charles's spiritual autobiography, he was born in Syracuse, New York, where he began to have mystical experiences at a very young age. As early as age nine, for example, he was suddenly plunged into an altered state of awareness in which all form disappeared and he knew himself to be pure awareness.[3] Raised in the Catholic tradition, throughout his life he reports that he had visions of Mary during which he would hear her voice, sounding "motherly, loving, and nurturing."[4] When he was in his mid-twenties, he saw a picture of Muktananda and had a profound mystical experience that lasted for three hours. A week later, he reports that he had another vision of Mary, the "Divine Mother," who directed him to go to Muktananda.

In 1970, at age twenty-five, Charles left a career in the performing arts to live as a monk named Swami Vivekananda under Muktananda's guidance. While serving as Muktananda's personal secretary, his mystical experiences continued to unfold. The only time he reported

Figure 4.1. Master Charles leading satsang (Photo courtesy of Synchronicity Foundation)

experiencing doubt in his path was after accidentally discovering Muktananda engaged in sexual intimacy with one of his female assistants. That night he was tormented by thoughts that his guru was "a liar and a fraud." His confusion did not last long, however. When he walked with Muktananda the next morning, he noted, "His truthful reverberation entrained a meditative balance in me, and I expanded in awareness to a new perspective on the reality of the moment."[5] In an interview, Master Charles explained how he reconciled Muktananda's behavior:

> Within the ashram we all knew about this, but we were educated that this had nothing to do with sex. It was about *kundalini* evolution. I know of so many women who said it was the most empowering, magnificent experience of their life.[6] Tantra is a vast system; it's the oldest model on the planet; it even preceded Veda. The fuel of *kundalini* is seminal fluid, which both men and women have. The principle of celibacy is used in initial stages of development—awakening and post-awakening—to provide that fuel in greater abundance. When the *kundalini* reaches its substantiation point, then downward flowing energy reverses and becomes an upward flowing energy. There can be no ejaculation. Many of the Tantric gurus used this throughout 10,000 years of history. Really, it is a very advanced form of *shaktipat*.[7]

Master Charles described in his autobiography how his mystical experiences culminated in enlightenment:

> Wherever I look, I see the shimmering indigo blue play of unitive consciousness dancing and delighting as all and every-thing. . . . This Sourceful inebriation saturates the whole of my multidimensional being with a lucid rapture that pleasures every cell of my physical body, and encompasses all forms, simultaneously radiating in all directions to infinity.[8]

My own skepticism prompted me to ask Master Charles if this experience of intense ecstasy is really a permanent state. He replied, "It is a constant state. This is a most important philosophical point: when the state of unified consciousness becomes constant—that's what's called enlightenment."[9]

Shortly after Muktananda's death, when Gurumayi and Nityananda were the official gurus of Siddha Yoga, Swami Vivekananda left the organization, took on the name Brother Charles, and settled in a home in the Blue Ridge Mountains of Virginia. He was among the first Siddha Yoga swamis to begin to teach on his own. The *Siddha Path* magazine, published by SYDA, contained a strongly worded message at the time stating that Swami Vivekananda, who goes by the name of Brother Charles, has no affiliation with Siddha Yoga. This was among the first of many SYDA efforts to control Muktananda's meditation revolution outside of official SYDA channels.

People slowly began to gather around Brother Charles in his home near Charlottesville, Virginia. At one point, a small group asked him if they could refer to him as Master Charles rather than Brother Charles. He agreed that this was appropriate as, he stated, his role had clearly become that of a master. Just as he had previously chosen the name Brother Charles to signify equality of consciousness, he now accepted the name Master Charles to signify his role in relationship to those who had chosen him as their guide on their spiritual journey.[10]

In many ways, Master Charles is a traditional guru who guides his disciples on the "enlightening" path. (Master Charles teaches that there is no end to spiritual evolution; generally, he does not use the term "enlightened.") Yet, at the same time, he describes the guru-disciple relationship in a unique way that points to a Westernization and secularization of the phenomenon. In Siddha Yoga parlance, both under Muktananda and later under Gurumayi, spiritual energy, or *shakti*, was awakened by the guru through touching or looking at the disciple. The term *shaktipat*, which means descent of grace, was used to describe this transmission of energy. While Master Charles also speaks of *shaktipat*, more often he refers to "entrainment." The guru is understood to vibrate at a high spiritual frequency, and disciples simply need to be in the presence of this in order to naturally and spontaneously begin to vibrate in the same frequency.

Master Charles employs scientific narrative in several ways. For example, using a term like "entrainment" rather than the religious concept of "grace" is in keeping with Master Charles's mission to Westernize yogic concepts. He explained in an interview that he had explored the work of Nobel Prize–winner Ilya Prigogine, who, among his many accomplishments, theorized that the brain is a nonlinear open system. While mechanical systems tend toward entropy and collapse, open systems tend toward increased order and efficiency. Master Charles correlated this idea with the view that clarity of the mind increases through yogic practices and that using a mantra plays a key role in this. He surmised that both the sound and the meaning of the mantra help to create a state of balance between the hemispheres of the brain. After visiting meditation caves in the Himalayas, he determined that environment was also important to experiencing deep meditation, and that caves, with their round shape and reverberation of 7.4 hertz, similar to the alpha brainwave pattern, constitute an ideal environment. His goal then became to create a way for people to experience "synchronized entrainment" in their apartments or homes, which may be less supportive of meditative states. This resulted in his system of "high-tech meditation" in which sound vibrations are fed into the brain through stereophonic earphones. Thus, the technique of "Synchronicity Contemporary High-Tech Meditation" consists of sitting quietly for an hour each morning while listening through earphones to soothing music underlain with subliminal sound frequencies and affirmations. The music serves two purposes: it simulates a "cavelike" environment, and it creates a positive state of mind. Traditional meditation techniques, such as focus on one's breath or on a traditional mantra, can be used simultaneously.[11]

Serious students supplement high-tech meditation with retreats with Master Charles at the Synchronicity Sanctuary in Virginia. In the meditation room, disciples sit in chairs equipped with earphones that allow them to experience holistic brain synchronization. When Master Charles enters the room, everyone stands until he has taken his seat on a large chair set on a platform slightly above the others. A retreat consists of periods of meditation and chanting, which Master Charles intersperses with talks in which he dispenses wisdom from sources from around the world. He may tell a traditional Indian folk story he heard from Muktananda, then a tale from a Zen master, followed by a quote from a modern physicist. Sometimes he instructs his disciples to dance to heavily rhythmic music while a strobe light mounted to the ceiling twirls around in a manner reminiscent of a 1980s disco club. He stresses maintaining good health, which is achieved through physical exercise and proper nutrition. Meals are prepared so that a systematic balance of protein, fat, and carbohydrates is provided. A variety of physical therapies are available at the Sanctuary, from Shiatsu to "vibrational stimulation," a therapy originally designed for astronauts.

Master Charles gives *shaktipat*, or "high-tech empowerment," during retreats. He created twelve rooms in modules, all of which are hooked up to a control room. Each of these rooms contains a bed with a mattress that vibrates at specific frequencies. Students receiving the empowerment are surrounded by a metallic grid made of copper and other metals that transmit sonic entrainment. Thus, the vibrations enter the whole body rather than just the brain as occurs when using headphones for meditation. Special lighting and fragrances help to create a supportive environment for experiencing balance. Master Charles guides the initiates with his voice and music from a control room. After twelve minutes, he goes to each room and focuses his energy into the initiates to "entrain" them to awakening, touching them on the head or heart region as a way of increasing his laser focus. The result, according to Master Charles, is *kundalini* unfolding.[12]

Master Charles's home is located at the top of a hill within walking distance of the sanctuary. There he creates artwork, including jewelry. He is also a musician and plays the instruments on the recorded music they listen to. The fourteen people who live full-time at Synchronicity Sanctuary hike up the hill one evening each week in order to have *satsang* (holy company) with Master Charles. A retreat might attract fifty to sixty people. This small size allows Master Charles to maintain a personal relationship with his disciples.

Along the hilly pathways that wind through the property are simple shrines to personifications of *shakti*, or the Divine Mother. Recently, according to followers of this path, the Divine Mother in apparition has begun to appear at the Shrine of the Heart, which Master Charles prepared for her after she had told him, "The time has come." The organization's website contains quotes from visitors to the shrine who have experienced great peace, smelled roses or gardenias, received personal messages, or actually seen the apparition.[13] On May 11, 2011, Master Charles joined a group of students at the shrine. During his talk, he described his experience:

> The downloading from subtle, universal consciousness into dense manifest consciousness is slowly proceeding. The gaze of Her eyes is downward and inward as if in ecstatic trance, absorbed in Herself. She is absolutely still. The light . . . the radiant light increases its intensity and is almost blinding to these physical eyes, and wave upon wave of bliss and peace floods the whole of my being and radiates outward in all directions filling all and everything with light and love and peace and bliss—a blanket of grace.[14]

Both Master Charles and a female guru of Indian heritage, Sai Maa Lakshmi Devi, who heads an ashram in Crestone, Colorado, led the retreat I attended at Synchronicity Sanctuary. He has also collaborated with Eckhart Tolle (author of the popular book, *The Power of Now*), Nityananda (Gurumayi's brother), Shankarananda (former Siddha Yoga swami who now teaches in Australia), and Chetanananda (disciple of Rudi, discussed in chapter 2). According to Master Charles, collaborating is beneficial because the combination of two gurus increases the amplitude of the power that is available to disciples. I asked him if this ever created confusion in disciples, and he replied that the benefits outweigh the challenges:

We feel that it's important to break down the barriers of separation—to share equally and honor the unity of diversity, the different expressions of the same truth. It's really important, especially with Sai Maa and myself, having a man and a woman expressing the same truth in unique ways. If someone feels drawn to go to another guru, I'm totally supportive. I trust in the consciousness that orchestrates the experience.

This sentiment is contrary to that of many earlier Indian gurus, who emphasized commitment to only one guru for a lifetime.

Sandra Barnard: The Guru Next Door

Pam Green and Sandra Barnard have been friends for thirty-five years. They met while attending Penn State and later, both became disciples of Muktananda. While they remain friends today, the relationship changed over the last few years when Pam began to view Sandra as her spiritual

Figure 4.2. Sandra Barnard leading satsang (Photo courtesy of Full Spectrum Center)

teacher. According to Pam, her experience with Sandra is more profound than the one she had with Muktananda. Earlier, she did not have the discipline to meditate regularly, but now, with Sandra's guidance and the support of a community, she is very committed to her *sadhana* (spiritual practice).

Pam was not alone in discovering that the person she had known as a friend was now a guru. Sandra Barnard had opened a healing school in 1994 in which students participated in seven weekend workshops per year for four years. The school trained students to work with subtle energy using psychological and body techniques along with relational therapeutic exercises, based on the work of psychoanalyst Wilhelm Reich (1897–1957). Before graduation, Sandra would take the class on a trip to a country of their choice, including Turkey, India, Bali, and Peru. While they continued to work on psychological and personality issues during these trips, they also experienced opportunities for spiritual growth. Meditating at the tomb of Rumi in Turkey or circling the hill of Arunachala in India, a spiritual dimension began to manifest in the group.

As their guide and teacher, Sandra was always held in esteem. And now she is viewed by many graduates from this healing school as more elevated—even literally, as she sits in a special chair on a raised platform, clothed in white, with a Persian rug in front that physically demarks a sacred space and serves as a subtle reminder that a difference exists between the one who sits behind the rug and those who gather in a semicircle in front of it. For her students, the change, which they refer to as the "transition," was gradual. Some of her students did not feel comfortable with the change and left, but about seventy-five students have made the transition, much to their surprise. Several told me they would never have accepted a guru or Hindu practices if they had not had the extended period of time working with Sandra at a different level. Even for Sandra the change was a bit of a surprise:

> A guiding voice led me into this role. I didn't wake up one day and say, now I'm going to be a guru. It came from a deep calling. There's a part of me that witnesses it all. Sometimes I think, "Well, this is a fine situation you've gotten yourself into, Sandra. Here you are, sitting here and shining light out the best you know how, and others are receiving it, and together we're caught in this great play."[15]

Sandra felt herself to be different from others as she was growing up. At age four, she saw what she believed to be "the face of God" filling the sky and looking down on her with kindness. She had many experiences throughout her childhood and teen years in which she clearly saw and heard people who had passed away. As a young adult, she had, in her words, "bigger experiences than I could understand." While many people learn about the possibility of spiritual experiences and then look for a way to achieve these, Sandra had the experiences first and later sought understanding about what they might mean.

While attending college, she began to practice meditation, although she had no teacher and no knowledge of yogic traditions. She simply lit a candle and sat with her eyes closed for an hour or two. Almost immediately she began to have a series of what she now interprets as *kundalini* experiences. In one of these, she had a vision of someone she later recognized as Nityananda (Muktananda's guru). The person approached her, but as he did, he took on different forms, such as Shiva Nataraj (Shiva in the form of a dancer). The meditation continued throughout the night. All of this occurred before she had any exposure to gurus or Eastern practices. Her final vision was of a dancing and whirling being coming down a middle aisle next to where she was sitting. When the person stopped by her side and looked at her, she felt so much energy that she swooned.

Several months after this experience, Sandra heard about a guru named Muktananda and decided to visit his *ashram* in South Fallsburg, New York. As soon as she arrived, she began to feel the same kind of energy she had months previously during her all-night meditation. She soon moved into the Philadelphia Siddha Yoga *ashram* where she lived for some years, performing different forms of service for programs. At the end of her stay, she had a series of profound experiences:

> It was like a second opening similar to the wild ride of *kundalini* I experienced when I first entered Siddha Yoga. It transformed how I understood the nature of reality. The teachings of nondual *advaita* became very alive for me, and I had the sense of being one with everything. Some people started coming to me and I would work with them energetically. I think that was more disturbing than anything. I felt I was unbaked and I didn't want to bring distortion to them. At that time, something seemed not right in my being a part of Siddha Yoga. It wasn't due to anything external; I just felt a strong urge that it was time to move on.

After leaving the *ashram* in 1987, Sandra moved to Chicago, but continued to attended Siddha Yoga programs occasionally. She later moved to Ithaca, New York, where in 1990 she studied for a period of time with Levent Bolukbasi, a healer from Turkey. Based on the model of his IM School of Healing Arts, in 1994, she created her own school called Full Spectrum Healing Arts School, which she directed for fourteen years. As students graduated from the four-year program, many did not want to leave, so she developed graduate and teacher training programs for them. In 2008 she dissolved the school's corporation and replaced it with a board-run nonprofit center and changed the name to Full Spectrum Center for Spiritual Awakening. She felt it was time for her students to enter a new dimension of learning:

> I think a lot of people who came to the healing program were responding to the energy and miracles of it and to the deep care that was given to them as human beings. They wouldn't have articulated that they were looking for God or were spiritual seekers. As much as I talked about wholeness, I saw it wasn't getting translated to anything more than enhanced egos. They were confusing the experience of love, seeing it as caused by a person outside them rather than a source within them. Or they would have these extremely *shakti*-filled experiences and then it would quickly dissipate through unconscious behavior. They didn't have a way to contain it. I saw that they needed a *sadhana*. That's when I started to introduce Eastern practices.

The transformation from a healing school to a center for spiritual awakening occurred slowly. New practices of meditation, hatha yoga, and chanting were incorporated beginning in 2006. Meditation had always been a part of the school's training, so deepening the practice and extending the time spent in meditation was not a difficult transition. They had also done bioenergy work, so the transition to hatha yoga made sense. "Sounding techniques" morphed into chants using Hindu-based mantras. They had always worked with the mind, but now classical yogic teachings about the nature of the mind were introduced. Yet work at the psychological level continued. According to Sandra, "For people who just do traditional meditation and chanting, there can be a big disconnect because there's no integration with their lower self. This integration is what was missing in Siddha Yoga."

The biggest change came with the introduction of the guru concept. *Pujas* (altars) were created with pictures of Nityananda, Muktananda, and Sandra. This changed, however, when SYDA objected to the use of pictures of the "Siddha Yoga lineage." Now only pictures of Sandra remain. However, of the students I interviewed, all had pictures of the other gurus on their home altars. While most of Sandra's students

refer to her as their "spiritual teacher," some students declare she is a
"*shaktipat* guru." The term "disciple" is not widely used. Both of these
concepts—guru and disciple—are evolving. Sandra explained:

> Some come with their understanding of the guru-disciple rela-
> tionship that they got from Siddha Yoga or Swami Nityananda
> or Ammachi. They have this picture in their mind of what
> the guru is. So we work on what these images are and what's
> limiting and what's expansive about them. I present them with
> the problem: Who is the guru? And who are you, and what is
> love? There are two things: love and confronting imperfection.
> As I serve in this role, I don't want to fuel any distortions of
> their projections onto me. And yet there's so much opportunity
> for expansion and for deep love to form. The notion of the
> [guru's] chair itself carries authority. My being willing to sit
> there carries a certain potency. I feel myself changed when I
> sit in the chair. There's a unique energy that comes into the
> room that very much reminds me of Siddha Yoga—especially
> in longer retreats that last for a number of days. The *shakti* is
> strong and potent. And I know they're having dreams about
> me and having teachings from me at other levels.

Some students of the center are experiencing *kundalini* awakening,
which reinforces the idea of Sandra as a *shaktipat* guru. One person who
is new to the program and so did not go through the healing school,
related:

> My *kundalini* has been awakened, and it is energetically very
> powerful. Energy just shoots up. It's because of Sandra and
> because of people seeking fervently all coming together. Sandra
> is good at facilitating experiences to open us up. For me, the
> experiences come through chanting, or listening to her talks
> or to people sharing their experiences. My heart opens up
> and huge waves of love come over me. The *kundalini* cleans
> out things from the past. Some have fits of rage for a few
> minutes and then it'll just pass. For me, it's intense deep sad-
> ness for the suffering of everyone. I feel it in my core, and I
> just wail. But I don't feel that it's me crying. When it passes,
> I feel intense energy going through me.[16]

The goal of the healing school had been "to engender within its
participants powerful mystical/visionary states of consciousness."[17] The

goal of the Full Spectrum Center for Spiritual Awakening is a sustained state of enlightenment that goes beyond brief flashes of mystical or ecstatic experience. This requires ongoing *sadhana* as well as intellectual understanding of what is occurring. Sandra describes enlightenment as the experience of unity, of the true Self, yet this experience does not take a person beyond the imperfect mind and body. In her words:

> In the ultimate sense, all is perfection. God's perfection includes human imperfection. This is true even in those who are spiritually enlightened. If you are embodied, then there will be imperfection, because to be human is to have flaws. This doesn't mean that the state of perfection is not experienced by an enlightened person—but rather that it is an inner attainment. Someone seated in the Divine Self sees perfection even in the imperfect world, even when acting in every other way as a flawed, limited human being—as one who catches colds, expresses anger, enjoys the delights of this world, has this or that bad habit, and so on. That someone manifests imperfectly, given human nature, does not mean that divine perfection is not also there to be enjoyed or realized.

I asked some of Sandra's students what their spiritual goal was. One person replied, "To be so fluid that I could just move with whatever happens in my life." Another said, "Experiencing myself in the deepest ways. When I feel the energy within me, possibilities are limitless." And another replied, "To be completely identified with my true self and with the universal flow of consciousness."[18]

The first thing that struck me about the group of about seventy-five people at the weekend workshop I attended was their sense of cohesiveness as they worked together to carry out the many tasks that made the weekend flow smoothly, from preparing and serving food to singing a poem by Rumi in delightful harmonies that had been practiced during weekly choir rehearsals. Many came from Pittsburgh or from the small town of Meadville, Pennsylvania, where the center is located. Those who came from a distance had at one time studied with Sandra in the healing school. The students who live in Meadville meditate and chant together every morning. The fact that it is not a residential ashram, however, is significant because Sandra emphasizes that one must integrate spiritual and worldly life so that, eventually, there is no differentiation between the two.

Sandra engages her students in exercises to reinforce the idea that the transcendent is to be found in the world. An example is "wholeness healing." Students line up on opposite sides of the room, and each person is paired with another. Both lines of people are instructed to bring their awareness to the divinity of the other person and of his- or herself. One line is seated on the floor; the other is standing. Those who are standing are told to slowly approach the partner sitting, and then to kneel next to him or her. The gazes of the partners are continuously interlocked. The person approaching is offering love, and the person seated is receiving it, yet both are aware that they are equal in divinity. This is a form of *darshan*, which literally mean "to see," and is an ancient practice of Hinduism. However, it is usually directed toward a deity in the form of a picture or statue, or toward a guru. This unique "Americanized" *darshan* practice brings focus to the equal divinity of everyone.

When Sandra spoke during the workshop, she was not teaching students in general, but was offering advice to the very specific group who sat in front of her and who had come to know each other so well over the years. As with Master Charles, the smaller size allows direct communication with her students, similar to traditional *ashrams* in India in which the guru knew each of his students, allowing for individualized guidance. As with Master Charles, Sandra drew from various sources as she delivered her talks. Thus, a humorous story about Sheik Nasrudin (a well-known Sufi character in India), a Native American tale, and a *Peanuts* comic strip all help to bring a particular message home. Sandra also shares experiences from her own life, and her openness and candor seem to endear her to her students.

John Friend and Friends

Research for this section was conducted in 2010 and 2011. Before publication, in February 2012, a scandal surfaced about John Friend that involved several allegations, including questionable financial practices, sexual relations with several married female employees (through a Wiccan coven), and use of marijuana, as well as placing employees in legal jeopardy by having them unknowingly accept mailed packages of marijuana at the office headquarters. The consequences of Friend's behavior are still surfacing. Currently a new structure without Friend's leadership is being developed, and the organization may survive the crisis. A new group formed by some disaffected Anusara Yoga instructors who follow the Tantric teachings of Douglas Brooks (discussed below) has also formed. These recent developments do not affect the history presented here. However, we should note that the Anusara network discussed below has been, perhaps irreparably, dismantled. Therefore, the following section should be viewed as a snapshot in time, during which both Anusara Yoga and

Figure 4:3. Anursara retreat discussion panel, from left, Douglas Brooks, John Friend, Sally Kempton, and Eric Shaw (Photo courtesy of Anusara, Inc.)

networking between John Friend and other teachers were at a peak. John Friend no longer teaches Anusara Yoga and has founded a new system called The Roots. The others discussed in this section continue to teach along the lines presented here, and Anusara Yoga under new leadership continues to conduct classes in the fashion outlined below.[19]

⟿

John Friend, founder of Anusara Yoga, is well known in the world of hatha yoga, or "Modern Postural Yoga," a term scholar Elizabeth De Michelis coined. Anusara has, at the time of this writing, more than 1,000 trained teachers and is established in more than 70 countries. Students attending an Anusara Yoga class typically begin by chanting the "Anusara mantras" together. However, these students probably did not recognize the words as the "introductory mantras" of Siddha Yoga that have been chanted daily in its ashrams for forty years. A translation of the verse reads: "Om. Salutations to the Guru, which is Shiva! His form is being, consciousness, and bliss. He is transcendent, calm, free from all support, and luminous."[20] With this short ritual, students of Anusara are taken into the heart of Siddha Yoga teaching. The Guru is understood to be the embodiment of Shiva and of the Self. The Guru/Shiva/Self is believed to consist of: *sat*, the ground being of all; *chit*, the consciousness that illuminates everything; and *ananda*, bliss that permeates and supports everything. John Friend's mother first taught him these mantras, and he was exposed to them again during the time he spent in Gurumayi's ashrams throughout much of the 1990s, when he was also exposed to the texts of Shaiva Tantra, which provide the philosophical underpinning for Anusara Yoga.

John Friend met Gurumayi while he was a teacher of Iyengar Yoga. He received *shaktipat* from her and shortly after began teaching yoga courses in her ashrams. Participating in the Teachers and Scholars Department, he befriended Paul Muller-Ortega and Douglas Brooks, both professors of religion at University of Rochester (New York); William Mahony, professor of religion at Davidson College (North Carolina); Sally Kempton (then Swami Durgananda) and Carlos Pomeda (then Swami Gitananda), both teaching monks of Siddha Yoga. They all taught courses in Gurumayi's ashrams and continue to teach today outside of the Siddha Yoga context. Their contributions to the development of an American Hinduism had already begun while they worked under the auspices of SYDA.

Douglas Brooks, William Mahony, Paul Muller-Ortega, and Sally Kempton were key authors and editors of the 700-page volume *Meditation Revolution: A History and Theology of the Siddha Yoga Lineage* (Agama Press, 1997). Sally Kempton also wrote an accessible book on meditation, *The Heart of Meditation*, now republished as *Meditation for the Love of It* (Sounds True, 2011). William Mahony directed the Muktabodha Indological Research Institute, which has published translations and commentaries of Hindu texts, established an online digital library of Sanskrit texts, recorded performances of Vedic rituals, and offered fellowships for training and research in Indological studies. While each of these scholars and swamis teaches independently today, they have all benefitted from Anusara's popularity and John Friend's endorsement. In fact, those who are undergoing the teacher training program for Anusara Yoga are encouraged to study with one or all of these teachers. In this way, Siddha Yoga–inspired practices and philosophies are finding their way into the American landscape.

At the end of the summer of 2004, Friend had just finished training teachers of Anusara at Shree Muktananda Ashram when he was told that this would be his last course at the ashram. He was surprised to hear this, especially since SYDA had recently constructed a 7,000-square-foot studio specifically for Anusara classes. John Friend has referred to it as the most beautiful studio in the United States. After many years of hosting thousands of visitors each summer, suddenly Shree Muktananda

Ashram was closed to visitors. Only those engaged in long-term *seva* (service to the guru) remained. The public, including the teachers who had offered their services for many years, is not privy to the reason for the sudden change. Gurumayi stopped giving public talks, books and DVDs published by SYDA were taken off the market, and the Teachers and Scholars Department was dissolved.

By this time, Swami Durgananda and Swami Gitananda had already relinquished their association with Siddha Yoga and had become established teachers of meditation. Not long after the closing of the ashram, Paul Muller-Ortega and Douglas Brooks began to develop their own systems for teaching meditation and Tantric philosophy outside of the college setting. Paul Muller-Ortega eventually left his position at the University of Rochester in order to devote himself full-time to teaching meditation and Tantric philosophy, which he calls Neelakantha or Blue Throat Yoga. In a course I attended he said:

> I left the university because I couldn't do there what I'm doing now—talking to sincere intelligent people who are yearning for the truth. I want to talk sincerely without academic jargon. People all over are awakening and going to hatha yoga studios with their questions about life and death, and these yoga teachers aren't trained for this. I want to help fill this gap and make a positive contribution toward the science of consciousness.[21]

Douglas Brooks maintains his university position, but travels on weekends across the United States to offer workshops in his system of practices called Rajanaka Yoga, which is based on Shrividya Tantra, a South Indian style of Shakta (goddess-centered) Tantra. Recently, he initiated an Internet-based series of courses called Shriviyalaya. In a brochure, Douglas writes that the intention of the curriculum is to advance understanding of "the history, practice, and interpretation of yoga as it originated in India, as it has developed in the west, and as it is relevant to our lives." While both Douglas and Paul taught in Siddha Yoga ashrams and once considered themselves "Siddha Yoga scholars," each now harkens back to other traditions as well. Douglas refers to his former and now-deceased professor who lived in Tamil Nadu, Dr. Gopala Aiyer Sundaramoorthy, or Appa (Father), as his guru. Even though he rarely mentions Gurumayi, he would not have made the connections he did in the Teachers and Scholars Department if it had not been for his time with Siddha Yoga.

Paul Muller-Ortega, on the other hand, loves to relate stories about his time with Gurumayi and yet she must share the stage with

Maharishi, whom Paul first encountered through the Transcendental Mediation program he learned at Yale University when he was sixteen. Today Paul's curriculum combines the practices and philosophies he has learned through these two gurus, as well as through his academic study of Tantra. More recently, William Mahony, still teaching at Davidson College, has begun to offer workshops at Esalen and at yoga studios. In 2011 he published a book with Anusara Press, *Exquisite Love: Heart-Centered Reflections on the Narada Bhakti Sutra*.

Another younger scholar of Sanskrit and Tantra, Christopher Wallis, also known as Hareesh, has joined these teachers in offering workshops in yoga philosophy and Tantric teachings inspired in part by his Siddha Yoga experience. Hareesh grew up around Siddha Yoga as his mother was a devotee of Muktananda and later of Gurumayi. He rejected the path when he was twelve, only to return when he had his own experience of *shaktipat* at age sixteen. He studied under Douglas Brooks and Paul Muller-Ortega at Rochester University, and then earned several master's degrees in Sanskrit and Indian religions. He is currently researching at the University of California, Berkeley, while simultaneously teaching at yoga studios throughout the United States and abroad. He has published a book, *Tantra Illuminated*, with Anusara Press (2012). Like the older teachers, Hareesh finds an audience through the network of Postural Yoga studios, primarily Anusara studios.

Teachers of Anusara Yoga are expected to be familiar with Tantric philosophy. They might take courses at Anusara "Grand Gatherings" where several of the above teachers provide mini-workshops after spending the morning in class with John Friend. Some find that they like a particular teacher's style and sign up for an extended course of study in which they delve deeply into specific Tantric texts. Sometimes a student considers one of the teachers to be his or her chosen guru or spiritual teacher. Others feel they attain the most benefit by studying with all of them. Anusara instructor Scott Lewicki is one of these. He considers the guru to be "any person, thing, or experience that removes the darkness of ignorance in order to make room for an experience of spaciousness and light." He continued, "Each teacher opened my eyes to a new way of thinking or practicing or connecting to my own heart. A lot of the joy in my life comes from my association with these teachers."[22] While he has studied with all of the teachers, he has spent extended time with Paul Muller-Ortega and Douglas Brooks and reflected on their teaching styles:

> I feel very blessed to have both of them. I have learned so very much from both of them. Paul is very systematic. He

always goes back to texts, gives you a quote, and provides the context. Douglas does this too and also uses deconstruction. He looks at essential truths or themes and then finds ways the texts promote these tenets. Douglas helps you to learn how to study any text. They have different approaches and different personalities. This is great for all of the teachers and students in Anusara.[23]

Since Douglas Brooks focuses on the South Indian Shakta tradition that he learned in Tamil Nadu while Paul Muller-Ortega focuses on the Shaiva tradition of Kashmir, particularly as it was articulated by masters of the tenth and eleventh centuries such as Abhinavagupta, John Friend recently attempted to close the gap between the two viewpoints. He wrote to his Anusara community:

In order to distinguish our school of Tantra among classical Tantra and neo-Tantra schools, we are now designating our philosophy as Shiva-Shakti Tantra. It is the integration of all the Tantric schools that see everything as a vibrating dance of Divine polarities full of freedom and the highest creative delight. We honor and glorify Supreme Consciousness (Shiva) and Its unlimited Creative Power (Shakti), spirit and matter, male and female; one is not higher than the other and one cannot exist without the other.[24]

According to Hareesh, the gap was an artificial one. The original tradition always presented Shiva and Shakti as two aspects of one divine reality. While he agrees with John Friend's description above, he argues that it needs to be expanded. He asserts that many Anusara students lack clarity on just what the Tantric philosophy is because each of the teachers John Friend introduced has such a different presentation of it due to their individual preferences and the incorporation of other influences (such as Transcendental Meditation in the case of Paul Muller-Ortega and Theosophy and New Thought in the case of John Friend). John Friend readily admits that American metaphysical traditions such as New Thought, which emphasize the power of positive thinking, influenced him more than Indian traditions. In an interview, Friend described his attraction to Tantra because of its focus on goodness: "After studying everything, Tantra is not only the most elegant and sophisticated system, but it's the one that aligns with my heart because it sees that the very essence of life is joy or love and that there's a goodness to life."[25] Hareesh claims that although this understanding can be found in some of the original

Tantric sources, it is also open to misinterpretation in a way that would not be aligned with classical Tantra:

> What Tantra actually seeks to do is go beyond positive and negative, beyond our conceptions of good and bad. That's the Tantric vision. It's not picking and choosing: "I like this bit of reality and I don't like that bit of reality." This is something the mind will always do. Classical Tantra seeks to embrace the whole of reality beyond the preferences of the mind, taking our joy from the very act of being conscious rather than from what we're conscious of. While I know John understands this, it is not yet a widespread understanding in the Anusara community from what I've seen.[26]

Hareesh teaches his students who are studying the thousand-year-old Shaivite Tantric text *The Heart of Self-Recognition* to experience the whole of consciousness by using a technique called *tattva-bhavana*, or contemplation of reality, in which one notices everything that is arising in the present moment, whether in the outer world of the senses or the inner world of thoughts and feelings. When one pays careful attention to the entire field of consciousness without differentiating between the so-called outer and inner, one becomes aware that everything is one field of energy manifesting as different vibrations.

Hareesh feels that the concepts of Tantric Shaivism have become deeply rooted in his being. He honors his past experiences with Siddha Yoga, but now states that when he sees a conflict between Siddha Yoga and the Tantric view, he feels a deeper alignment with the latter:

> There's not a conceptual conflict between those two because, of course, Siddha Yoga adopted so much of the Tantric Shaivism of Kashmir. The conflict is with the culture and the institution of Siddha Yoga, which doesn't look very much like the culture and institution we would expect to arise out of a path that was thoroughly embracing Tantric Shaivism. The teachings of Tantric Shaivism tend to be quite a bit more radical in their critique of things that we hold as socially and culturally valid in terms of hierarchy, power, and gender relations. Siddha Yoga shies away from this kind of critique. What has manifested in Siddha Yoga is fairly conservative and dogmatic. The teachings of Kashmir Shaivism given in Siddha Yoga are beautiful and great and yet there's a way in which students

of Siddha Yoga are not given full license to experiment with the teachings and make mistakes and bring them to life in a way unique to each person. Any kind of deviation from the standard interpretations in Siddha Yoga is often branded as wrong understanding. This happens when we have a highly structured organization that believes in copyrighting and concepts like intellectual property. I want to see a revival of the teachings and practices of Tantric Shaivism independent of organizations.[27]

Hareesh also argues that Siddha Yoga has represented the role of the guru quite differently from the ancient tradition. Siddha Yoga teaches that *shaktipat* is a transmission from the guru to the disciple. According to Tantric Shaivism, which originated the concept, *shaktipat* is a spontaneous event, a transmission of grace from the divine itself. It may happen in the presence of the guru, but the guru is not causing it.[28] The guru's role is to initiate the disciple. Hareesh asserts:

In Siddha Yoga, there is a conflation of the words *shaktipat* and *diksha* (initiation). In the original tradition, these are two different terms. *Shaktipat* can occur during *diksha*, but it is something separate. The former is a spiritual awakening, whereas *diksha* is a powerful ceremony meant to consecrate the disciple to a lifelong practice commitment in a graduated curriculum determined by the guru, something that has been lacking in Siddha Yoga.[29]

Hareesh sees his role as helping to change the direction of the American yoga phenomenon so that it moves closer to what it was originally intended to be: a means for cultivating subtle internal states that illuminate our deeper nature. Exercise is a good thing, but if it is not taught in a way that refines awareness, then it should be called exercise and not yoga, he argues. Ultimately, he would like to create a center with the same academic standards of a good university, but in the context of a residential *ashram*-like practice environment. Students would study under scholar-practitioners every type of yoga and religion that comes out of the Indian culture, including both Buddhism and Tantric Shaivism.

Unlike the other teachers discussed here, Sally Kempton has not studied Sanskrit. "I'm not a scholar," she says of herself. She may not have multiple degrees, yet a "scholar" is often defined as simply a learned person, and this she is. In an article she wrote for *Yoga Journal*, she referenced several scriptures from the Tantra and Vedanta traditions, poets, scientists, psychologists, musicians, and even a mathematician.[30] Sally first met Muktananda in the early 1970s and traveled and studied with him until he died in 1982. She edited many of his books and was eventually initiated into the Saraswati order of swamis. She continued to teach and write under Gurumayi until 2002 when she decided to leave *ashram* life to become a teacher outside the context of Siddha Yoga. A former journalist, she brings acumen and wit to her writing for *Yoga Journal* and to teaching her students in monthly telecourses and retreats, as well as in yoga studios, Esalen Institute, and other centers for developing spiritual awareness.

The study of the texts of Kashmir Shaivism was never purely intellectual for Sally. She has always looked for the practical angle in them, searching for ways they can help her to live in the world with an enlightened awareness. This is what she now teaches others:

> For me, the texts are a frame for spiritual teaching, as well as a way to help the truth land deeply for people. My concern when I teach is always how I can help people apply these beautiful, esoteric teachings to their actual life in the world, to the way they perceive themselves and the world and the way they act in it.[31]

She encourages people not to become rigid in their practices, but to be open to the leading of *shakti*, the inner energy. However, the practices she teaches are deeply grounded in the texts, not only of Kashmir Shaivism, but of Vedanta and the yoga tradition, and she emphasizes daily meditation as a core practice. She speaks to all levels of students, from those who want to explore meditation in depth to those who may have only a few minutes in a busy schedule to briefly center themselves. In addition to Indian philosophical texts, she draws on depth psychology and on mystics and poets from around the world, wraps them up in an accessible package, and delivers them to students around the United States. Sally also teaches longer trainings that combine text study with meditation practices, awareness exercises, group work, and her own ongoing personal guidance.

While each of the teachers discussed in this section has a different teaching style and sometimes philosophy, they are held together by their common past with Siddha Yoga and their vision for establishing a greater understanding of Tantric concepts and practices in America. They all believe that we can and should be living in a more enlightened way. Enlightenment is not held out as some future goal, however, but as something that is available in each moment. In the words of John Friend, "I see enlightenment as a heart connection, an open delight and love for life. When these moments grow and become regular, and we become established in love and wisdom, then that's enlightenment."[32] Sally Kempton said:

> My experience is that enlightenment is a very real, and constantly unfolding way of being in the world. There's that paradox in enlightenment, in that in our core we are already enlightened, and yet it requires a lot of focused effort to continually touch and act from the enlightened consciousness that's at our heart. We wake up to it, but then we go through a deep psycho-spiritual, emotional, physical process so we can learn to live it, and that means cleaning up our act in every sense of the word.[33]

Douglas Brooks quipped, "Well, I'm happy to argue with those who use the word enlightenment as if it meant a final, or finished or realized state. Like if they go, 'Oh he was a realized being.' Well my thought is I hope he just keeps realizing. I think that anything that comes to finality strikes me as problematic."[34] Paul Muller-Ortega said, "Enlightenment is not a rare state. It's implicit in consciousness itself. The point is to bring that consciousness to our life."[35] Hareesh commented:

> Enlightenment, or awakening, is a central concept in Shaivism. Muktananda taught that the awakened *kundalini* would organically guide you to enlightenment. But you have to be able to listen, and you can't listen if your body isn't clear and your mind isn't quiet due to lack of exercise or healthy food or meditation. Cultivating yogic practices is primarily about creating a vehicle in which you can perceive the promptings of the inner *shakti*.[36]

Conclusion

Even though each of the teachers discussed in this chapter is unique in his or her approach, several themes emerge that indicate patterns to be aware of when considering American Hinduism as a whole. One is a de-emphasis on a future state of enlightenment compared to earlier gurus. Maharishi Mahesh Yogi, for example, described seven states of consciousness that occur on the path, promising his followers that they would attain particular stages within set timeframes if they practiced Transcendental Meditation regularly. Thus, *sadhana* is conceived as the means to an end. This view continues with American Hinduism, and yet the bifurcation between an unenlightened and enlightened state is not as solidly drawn. Enlightenment is sought in small ways each day, and the reification of a future state is diminished. To some extent, the means and the end are the same. Of the teachers and gurus discussed in this chapter, Master Charles holds a view most similar to that of second-wave gurus as he creates a sharper distinction between the unenlightened disciple and the enlightened guru.[37] However, even he conceives of evolution as continual and uses the term "enlightening" rather than "enlightened." With this view, everyone is simply at a different place on a level playing field.[38]

A leitmotif of second-wave gurus is the view that a disciple must follow one guru and one path in order to attain the final goal of enlightenment. This understanding continues to some extent as students within the Siddha Yoga legacy often choose a particular spiritual teacher. However, many homegrown gurus from the Siddha Yoga tradition are open to collaboration. Similarly, students of American gurus may move from one teacher or guru to another, depending on what they feel they need at a particular point in their lives. This is encouraged by American gurus in sharp contrast to second-wave gurus. Furthermore, criticism of the guru or the guru's organization was not tolerated in the second wave. In contrast, many American gurus work through critical issues together with their students in a more egalitarian way.

A third theme that recurs in the Siddha Yoga legacy is the promotion of Tantra, often the form known as Kashmir Shaivism, which simply refers to a body of works Tantric masters from Kashmir wrote. Tantra proffers a nondual philosophy, but one that is different from the monism found in Advaita Vedanta. In Advaita the one reality is Brahman, and the spiritual seeker needs only to realize this in order to wake up from the delusion of multiplicity, or *maya*. In Tantra, waking up consists of realizing that all of reality, whether inner thoughts or outer phenomena or the consciousness that encompasses them, is of one fabric. This fabric is personal, dynamic, and alive with self-awareness, another characteristic that distinguishes Tantra from Advaita Vedanta. Tantra's acceptance of all realms of existence, including the emotional, the psychological, and the physical, is expressed through practices of these groups, such as Hareesh's *tattva-bhavana*, Sally's "practical" yoga, Sandra's focus on personality, Master Charles's use of physical therapies, and of course, the Postural Yoga practices that are a part of every group. In considering the legacy of Siddha Yoga, Muktananda's Tantric sexual activity cannot be ignored as it has been by the Siddha Yoga organization. As long as the memory of Muktananda is revered, the controversial elements of his life must be confronted. Master Charles is one who has openly examined this issue.

A final consideration concerns the propagation of the meditation revolution. Many second-wave gurus held that their ideas and the practices they taught must be tightly contained within a system, and the container was a legal organization. Indeed, the organization sometimes took on a life of its own so that allegiance of students was not to the guru, who was continually changing, but to an organization that tended to ossify. An organization also limits the proliferation of teachers and the freedom of those who, as Muktananda desired, were becoming "saints." This is a curious facet of the guru phenomenon in America that has no precedent in traditional Indian Hinduism. In the system Adi Shankaracharya established in the early ninth century, people become monks, or *sannyasis*, under the auspices of one of ten orders. Once a person becomes a *sannyasi*, he or she is free to teach and initiate others. A guru may or may not be part of this system; many gurus are married. In either case, whether a teacher of yoga and meditation is a monk or a householder, he or she teaches and initiates many people, and some of these go on to become teachers or gurus in their own right.

A new pattern emerged in America. Gurus established legal corporations to handle organizational details and protected their teaching by creating trademarks and intellectual property rights. The very fact that these legal precautions are taken indicates a mistrust in the unrestricted unfolding of spiritual energy and intelligence. Muktananda stated he would create a world full of saints, yet the actions SYDA takes to prohibit the proliferation of teachings indicate disbelief that these saints are actually being produced. In spite of SYDA's efforts, the Siddha Yoga legacy is vibrant. Swami Shankarananda, an American guru and former Siddha Yoga swami, created the website Nityananda, the Living Tradition, in which gurus and teachers who trace their spiritual influence to the official Siddha Yoga lineage are discussed. There are more than sixty entries listed in an A-to-Z index. The fact that only one of the teachers included in this chapter is discussed on this site is an indication that there are most likely many more.

The *parampara* (guru lineage) of Siddha Yoga is clearly defined as beginning with Nityananda, flowing through Muktananda, and ending with Gurumayi. This simple lineage is, however, contradicted by facts. For example, several disciples of Nityananda besides Muktananda are listed in a book the trustees of Nityananda's Samadhi Shrine in India produced.[39] Furthermore, the younger Nityananda, Gurumayi's brother, is functioning as a guru as well as Gurumayi. SYDA has systematically erased these facts from Siddha Yoga's history. Furthermore, the idea that the earlier Nityananda is the "first" of the lineage, that he was born in a state of realization and thus had no guru, removes him from a historical and cultural context, mythologizing him as the one source. Little is known about his background, but pictures are available of him sitting on the lap of a Tantric guru; he may have had other teachers as well. Many groups trace their influences back to Nityananda himself, skipping Muktananda. Chetananda, for example, discussed in chapter 2, traces his lineage from Rudi back to Nityananda.

Moving forward, we see no end to the proliferation. I have recounted here a few American examples; other strands are becoming established in India, Australia, and elsewhere. The global nature of the legacy becomes evident by considering the example of the American Swami Shankarananda, founder of Shiva Yoga Ashram in Melbourne, Australia, who was awarded the title of *maha-mandaleshwara* in India in 2010. This is an honor bestowed on swamis by their peers; only eighty *maha-mandaleshwaras* exist today, and only one is an American by birth.

Thus, rather than a linear progression, we find a multilayered expansion of *shakti* (power, capacity, potency). An apt metaphor to close with would be the rhizomatic theory Gilles Deleuze and Felix Guattari proposed in *A Thousand Plateaus*. The metaphor could be applied to the expansion of Siddha Yoga–inspired groups. It might also apply to the networks and collaborations found in American Hinduism. Finally, it could be compared to the view of enlightening in each moment rather than the conception of a linear path from ignorance to enlightenment. In the following excerpt, the linear tree analogy is contrasted with the rhizome, a horizontal root that shoots out stems and new roots. When rhizomes are separated, each piece produces a new plant.

> A rhizome has no beginning or end; it is always in the middle, between things, interbeing, intermezzo. The tree is filiation; but the rhizome is alliance. The tree imposes the verb "to be," but the fabric of the rhizome is the conjunction, "and . . . and . . . and. . . ." This conjunction carries enough force to shake and uproot the verb "to be." Where are you going? Where are you coming from? What are you heading for? These are totally useless questions. Making a clean slate, starting or beginning again from ground zero, seeking a beginning or a foundation—all simply a false conception of voyage and movement. . . .[40]

Notes

1. "Dhyana Chakra Pravartana," *Dhyana Chakra*, Feb. 26, 1974, 8. Quoted in *Meditation Revolution*, ed. Douglas Brooks et al., 71–113 (South Fallsburg, NY: Agama Press, 1997), 82.

2. Retreats were Synchronicity Sanctuary, Nellysford, VA, June 25–28, 2009 (Master Charles); Royal Way Ranch, Lucerne Valley, CA, June 30–July 5, 2010 (Paul Muller-Ortega); Anusara Grand Gathering, Estes Park, CO, Sept. 19–22, 2010 (John Friend, Sally Kempton, and Douglas Brooks); Full Spectrum Center, Meadville, PA, June 2–3, 2011 (Sandra Barnard).

3. Master Charles Cannon, *The Bliss of Freedom: A Contemporary Mystic's Enlightening Journey* (Malibu, CA: Acacia Publishing, 1997), 11.

4. Ibid., 10.

5. Ibid., 160.

6. However, Joan Bridges, one of the woman Muktananda had Tantric sexual relations with, declared that she felt she had been abused. See http://www.leavingsiddhayoga.net/frames2.htm (accessed June 13, 2011).

7. Interview with the author, Sept. 5, 2010.

8. Cannon, *Bliss*, 237–238.

9. Interview with the author, Sept. 5, 2010.

10. Cannon, *Bliss*, 241.

11. Interview with the author, Sept. 5, 2010.

12. Ibid.

13. http://www.blessedmotherapparition.com/index.html (accessed June 13, 2011).

14. http://www.blessedmotherapparition.com/Blessed_Mother_Messages_Current.html (accessed June 13, 2011).

15. This quote and the following narrative with quotes by Sandra Barnard draw from an interview with the author, Apr. 9, 2011.

16. Interview with the author, Apr. 26, 2011.

17. G. William Barnard, http://www.aarmysticism.org/documents/Barnard03.pdf, 2 (accessed June 1, 2011).

18. Interviews with author conducted during May–April 2011.

19. I explore the scandal and current developments in Anusara Yoga Virginia Commonwealth University's website, World Religions & Spirituality: http://www.has.vcu.edu/wrs/profiles/Anusara.htm, post date: Jan. 3, 2013.

20. *The Nectar of Chanting* (South Fallsburg, NY: SYDA Foundation, 1975), 2.

21. Blue Throat Yoga retreat, Lucerne Valley, CA, June 30–July 5, 2010.

22. Interview with the author, Aug. 8, 2010.

23. Ibid.

24. http://www.anusara.com/index.php?option=com_content&view=article&id=58&Itemid=103 (accessed June 2, 2011).

25. Interview with the author, Dec. 9, 2010.

26. Interview with the author, Aug. 14, 2010.

27. Ibid.

28. See Christopher Wallis, "The Descent of Power: Possession, Mysticism, and Initiation in the Shaiva Theology of Abhinavagupta," *Journal of Indian Philosophy* 36 (2008): 247–295.

29. Interview with the author, Aug. 14, 2010.

30. "It's All in Your Mind," *Yoga Journal*, Oct. 2009, 63–68.

31. Interview with the author, Aug. 14, 2010.

32. Interview with the author, Dec. 9, 2010.

33. Interview with the author, Aug. 14, 2010.

34. http://srividyalayaamrta.blogspot.com/ (accessed June 9, 2011).

35. Blue Throat Yoga retreat, June 30–July 5, 2010.

36. Interview with the author, Aug. 14, 2010.

37. See introduction for an explication of second-wave gurus.

38. For an examination of American transformations of the Asian enlightenment discourses, see Ann Gleig, *Enlightenment after the Enlightenment: American Transformations of Asian Contemplative Traditions* (Ph.D. diss., 2011, ProQuest).

39. "Gurudev Nityananda," ca. 1990, http://www.leavingsiddhayoga.net/history.htm (accessed June 14, 2011).

40. Gilles Deleuze and Felix Guattari, *A Thousand Plateaus*, trans. Brian Massumi (Minneapolis: University of Minnesota Press, 1987), 25.

5

A Life in Progress

The Biographies of Sivaya Subramuniyaswami

Richard Mann

This chapter studies the biographies of Sivaya Subramuniyaswami (1927–2001), or Gurudeva as his followers more commonly referred to him. Subramuniyaswami was the American-born founder of the Saiva Siddhanta Church, the Himalayan Academy, and the Kauai Aadheenam.[1] He claimed to be a guru within the South Indian Hindu tradition of Saiva Siddhanta and through his guru lineage the true *satguru* of 2.5 million Tamil Sri Lankans. Saiva Siddhanta originated in the north of India, but developed into the most important ritual and doctrinal system of Shaivism in Tamil, South India. Tamil Saiva Siddhanta combines the devotional traditions of the Nayanars (Tamil Saiva saint-poets) with an extensive temple system based in the *Agamas* (Saiva texts oriented towards religious practice).[2] From the 1980s until his death, Subramuniyaswami became a prominent voice not only for some Saiva Siddhantins, but also for the Hindu diaspora around the world. By the 1990s, Western commentators and scholars presented Subramuniyaswami as representing an orthodox and authentic voice within Hinduism.[3]

The following maintains that Subramuniyaswami's biographies are constructed documents designed to respond to particular circumstances he and his group find themselves in over the course of time. Biography becomes an important tool Subramuniyaswami and his followers use to define his status, role, and legitimacy within the traditions of Saiva Siddhanta and Hinduism in general. As the biographies are designed to establish the reputation of this guru, they do as much to illuminate

Figure 5.1. Sivaya Subramuniyaswami (Photo courtesy of Himalayan Academy on May 13, 2012)

aspects of his life as they do to obfuscate other aspects of it. An examination of the biographies and the historical circumstances of their production demonstrate a steady shift in the image of Subramuniyaswami from the 1950s to his death in 2001. He began as part of the esoteric movements found in 1950s California, many of which were influenced by various forms of Theosophy, and developed from there into an Aquarian Age guru by the late 1960s and early 1970s as part of the counterculture movement. His biographies emerge in the 1970s and 1980s and play a significant role in recharacterizing Subramuniyaswami as an orthodox Hindu guru by the 1990s. As such, Subramuniyaswami's biographies and the contexts of their production mirror broader shifts in Hinduism as it was found in America through the 1950s to the end of the millennium. A study of Subramuniyaswami's biographies and their depiction of his shift from teaching esoteric ideas primarily to Westerners to a conservative image as a Hindu guru who primarily addresses diaspora Hindus illustrates the integration of Hindu thought and practice into American life as well as the shifting perception of the guru in the United States in the second half of the twentieth century.

Adopting the work of Russell McCutcheon on myth, I approach sacred biography-hagiography or biography as an example of an ordinary process of narrative construction.[4] From such a perspective, the point of these narratives is not their felicity to some "truth" or lack thereof. I am not, then, interested in locating the original or correct narrative, but rather in locating the forces that lead to the process, or processes, of narrating the events of a particular life in particular forms. Hence, I have two general goals in studying the biographies of this particular guru: first, I hope to understand the historical circumstances that led to their production, and, second, I hope to understand how these narratives function—the role they play for the group or individual that uses them.

This chapter begins with a summary of Subramuniyaswami's life as gleaned from the biographies found in official publications of his organizations. It proceeds by reconstructing the guru's teaching career by arguing for four distinct periods of historical development. The first period discussed is in the 1950s and 1960s when Master Subramuniya, as he was then known, presented a mixture of esoteric and theosophist, Hindu, and Christian practices and teachings to his followers. In the 1970s, he entered into a second period of development. He relocated his core disciples to Kauai and established an Adhinam there. This period represents a transitional phase for Subramuniyaswami. Many of his publications still drew on esoteric and Aquarian Age teachings, but he was also increasingly in contact with the larger Tamil and Hindu diaspora around the world. The third period of the guru's development began in the late 1970s and early 1980s with extensive tours in Tamil and Hindu communities in Malaysia, Singapore, Tamil Nadu, Sri Lanka, and Mauritius. During this phase Subramuniyaswami took on the full persona of a Tamil guru. He began targeting Hindu diaspora groups and gained a following among such groups. With this success, Tamil Saiva Siddhantin organizations, the tradition Subramuniyaswami claimed as his own, began to scrutinize him. Other Adhinams and Sri Lankan Tamil groups questioned Subramuniyaswami's knowledge of Saiva Siddhanta and the legitimacy of a non-Tamil guru within Tamil Saiva Siddhanta. These questions culminated in a series of published debates between the Kauai Aadheenam and other groups between 1981 and 1984 that are discussed in this section. The fourth period (1985–2001) considers the aftermath of the debates. Subramuniyaswami's authority was shaken through the debates and his biographies emerged during this period as one means of reaffirming his authority within the tradition. His biographies present him as a strict, traditional, and orthodox voice within the tradition, and they address some of the issues raised in the debates.

Sivaya Subramuniyaswami's Biographies

Narratives of Subramuniyaswami's life began to appear, at least in print, during the early 1970s. Several versions of the biography exist, and I use nine accounts in this chapter.[5] According to the biographies, Subramuniyaswami was born in Oakland, California, in 1927 as Robert Hansen. The biographies make no mention of his family in terms of their class, occupations, or religious affiliations. Most of the accounts have little to say about his early life, but two early biographies from 1970 and 1972 are exceptions. In these, Subramuniyaswami recalls his first mystical experience as a baby. He claims to have become conscious of a tall man dressed in a yellow robe looking down at him. He reports shifting his consciousness to that of the man looking down at the baby, and then back to the baby looking up at the man. He states that he realized the man "was the body of my soul," and "that as I continued maturing spiritually, the soul body would finally fully inhabit the physical body." He records that the fulfillment of the vision happened "in a tremendous spiritual experience" in 1956.[6]

His parents died not long after a second mystical experience in which he recalled seeing "awareness coming out of the area of the mind that always worries and entering a total consciousness of here and now." Who raised him after their deaths is not clear. At around age ten or eleven, he decided he wanted to be a dancer and began his training. This training led him to meet what he calls his "first catalyst on the path of enlightenment," a dance teacher who had lived as the guest of the Maharaja of Mysore for five years in the 1920s where she studied dance, yoga, "and the mystical teachings and practices of India." He studied with this unnamed woman every summer for four years at her chalet at Fallen Leaf Lake, California. He reports that through her he "was brought up in Hinduism first through culture, music, art, drama, dance and all the protocols of Indian life." According to the biographies, she also taught him the fundamentals needed for meditation and the worship of Shiva Nataraja (Shiva in his form as a dancer).[7]

During his teenage years, he attended lectures at the Vedanta Society in San Francisco and began to pursue Vedanta philosophy. He reports being particularly inspired by the work and life of Swami Vivekananda. At about this time he met his second catalyst, also an unnamed female dance instructor. She trained him in dance starting when he was fourteen or fifteen, but she was also "well acquainted with various forms of mysticism, occultism and meditation." She taught him astral travel as well as aspects of Kundalini Yoga. He studied with her for two years and claimed to have had his first "inner light experience" under her instruction.[8] During this period he also began studying with the San Francisco Ballet and became their lead dancer.

His third catalyst is another unnamed woman with whom he studied for four years. He reports learning how to read people's auras, intentions, their subconscious motivations, and their aptitude for mystical study. In short, this third teacher appeared to instruct him in various aspects of what were likely esoteric traditions.[9] She also predicted that he would find his guru in Sri Lanka, and, as a result, he left the ballet company and traveled to South Asia by boat.[10]

He arrived in Sri Lanka in 1947 and met his fourth catalyst. Reportedly, this individual attained enlightenment in a cave in Thailand. The Thai connection is rather obscure, but other aspects of Subramuniyaswami's time with this fourth catalyst suggest he was Buddhist, although this is never explicitly stated in the biographies. Subramuniyaswami spent eighteen months with this figure, who set him to work in developmental projects in rural villages rather than allow him to spend his time meditating. He credits the fourth catalyst with giving him knowledge of how to get things done in the material world.[11]

Subramuniyaswami met his fifth catalyst, Mustan, a Muslim mystic, in the caves of Jalani. Following their meeting, Subramuniyaswami located a special cave, which had apparently been occupied by the Muslim saint Abdul Cadar Duster Jalani 300 years ago. Here Subramuniyaswami meditated and fasted until he attained enlightenment, an experience of *Parashiva*, the highest form of Shiva.[12]

After this enlightenment experience, Subramuniyaswami relocated to the YMCA in Colombo, Sri Lanka, where Kandiah Chettiar befriended him.[13] Chettiar introduced him to Yogaswami (1872–1964), who became Subramuniyaswami's guru. Before he could meet his guru, however, his sixth catalyst (Chettiar) prepared him by taking him "deep into Hinduism." Subramuniya claims Chettiar taught him "orthodox Hinduism," which seems to be a combination of instruction in Vedanta and temple worship. First, he learned "mysticism" and then ritual. The mysticism is, in part, described in the following manner: "I began meeting the Hindu Gods, the Deities, inside the inner areas of the superconscious mind, and learning how to relate to them." Through these experiences, Subramuniyaswami decided to become a Hindu and asked Chettiar to find him "a very pure priest" who had realized God.[14] Chettiar did not know of such a priest, but he did know of Yogaswami.

In the later biographies the two central elements of Subramuni-yaswami's life are his enlightenment experience and his initiation by Yogaswami. The two most detailed accounts of the initiation differ, how-ever, on certain details. The two accounts are the 1970/2002 and 1982 *Hinduism Today* biographies. The following blends the two accounts and important differences are endnoted. In the 1982 account, the guru-to-be traveled to Yogaswami's home in Columbuturai with Kandiah Chettiar and an unnamed Jaffna lawyer. They stopped off at the Kandaswamy Temple in Nallur where Subramuniyaswami had a vision of Yogaswami during the *puja*. He reported seeing an elderly Tamil man "appear in the sanctum, dressed in white, with silvery white hair and beard, radi-ant and smiling, looking like a sage from heaven."[15] After leaving the temple the three arrived at Columbuturai and approached Yogaswami's hut. Subramuniyaswami then narrates the following scene in the third person:

> As they walked closer, his voice rang out, "Have you seen me before?" "Yes," the American called right back, "I saw you just now at Nallur." They could see his face as he smiled at the American and spoke again, "I am in you." "I am in you," came the reply. "You are in me." "You are in me."[16]

Yogaswami then asked Subramuniyaswami a series of questions related to his training and understanding of Hinduism. Subramuniyas-wami tells us: "The questions were of the impossible type, subtle and profoundly simple, but the American answered right back every time, speaking out from intuition." Yogaswami was satisfied with Subramu-niyaswami responses, and decided to rename him: "You are white. Sub-ramuniya is white. You are Subramuniya," after which Subramuniya comments: "Having accepted his disciple into the Saivite religion by giving him his Hindu name, he then bestowed a mission—to return to America and bring Saiva Dharma fully into the mainstream of western culture." After this initiation, the two Tamils with the newly named Subramuniya were amazed. According to Subramuniyaswami, they had never seen Yogaswami "so open and at home with anyone, ever." Then, we are told, the three departed and were walking away when suddenly Yogaswami was upon them and gave Subramuniya a powerful slap on the back and stated, "This will be heard in America!"[17]

In the 1970/2002 version the slap on the back is described as an initiation. We are told: "Some of the Hindu devotees were startled, too, because that is one of the most powerful ordination initiations ever given."[18] He goes on to explain the four ways a guru will initiate an aspirant: through speech, through look, through thought, and, the most powerful, through touch when combined with the "actual inner power" of the guru and his lineage. According to Subramuniyaswami:

> Through this contact, with intent, he [the guru] begins to feed and transmit all of his inner knowing and inner power to the disciple. In this way, Yogaswami gave to me all his knowledge of how to be a guru. It later began to unfold within me from him, then from his guru and then from his guru's guru.[19]

As we shall see, lineage is important to Subramuniyaswami as a tool of his authenticity, and the previous quotation highlights his nature as a "guru" endowed with the spiritual power of a Sri Lankan Tamil guru lineage. In later accounts, he will claim that based on this initiation he is the "*satguru* of the Tamil Śaivite Hindu people of Sri Lanka, who now reside in many countries of the world."[20]

Following this last encounter, Subramuniya returned to America, but apparently maintained contact with Yogaswami through Chettiar. He states he was instructed not to teach until he was thirty, so he waits until 1957 to begin his teaching career. Yogaswami died in 1964 and Subramuniya reports having received letters from Sri Lanka asking him to return to be the guru there, "indicating that I was his successor." He did not immediately return, stating that he felt his mission was in the West. He did return in 1969 following his "inner direction" that the time was now right.[21] The 1970/2002 biography ends at around this point.

Other accounts of Subramuniyaswami pick up just after the initiation from Yogaswami. We are told in most that he established the Shri Subramuniya Ashram in Alaveddy just after his initiation and returned to America.[22] Once back in America in 1950, he began receiving "bursts of knowledge" that took the form of aphorisms.[23] These aphorisms and Subramuniyaswami's commentaries on them form the basis of his "first formal teaching ministry, in 1957."[24] At this point, Subramuniyaswami established the Saiva Siddhanta Church and opened a public temple and school in San Francisco. Here, he reports, students received weekly classes and a weekly Sunday sermon. His students wrote down these sermons and formed his first publications, *Inspired Talks*. In 1962, his center expanded by purchasing a property in Virginia City, Nevada, that he turned into a retreat center.[25]

Subramuniyaswami has little to say about his life until 1970 other than he published sections of his aphorisms and commentaries through the 1950s and 1960s, and that he established the Himalayan Academy, a publication and teaching center, in 1965. In 1970, Subramuniyaswami moved the Saiva Siddhanta Church to the Hawaiian island of Kauai and established an Adhinam, a Shaivite monastery-temple complex, there called the Kauai Aadheenam, and initiated the first of his lifelong monastics. During this same period, he opened the Wailua University of Contemplative Arts, also based in Hawaii.[26]

In the 1970s, he established two temples on the Kauai Aadheenam site. The first, Kadavul Temple, houses a Shiva Nataraja. The choice of the site and main *murti* (statue) were both "inspired by a vision of Lord Muruga," a vision Subramuniyaswami claims he had on March 12, 1973.[27] The temple was completed in 1979, and now functions as a private temple for the monastics attached to the Aadheenam.

The second temple, a Shivalingam temple named Iraivan, has been under construction on the island since 2001. It was inspired by a three-fold vision in 1975. In this vision Subramuniyaswami reports seeing Shiva walking near the Wailua River; the deity then looked into his face, and finally the two sat on a great stone with Subramuniyaswami to the left of Shiva.[28] After these visions, the guru was sure the location of this "great stone" was on the Aadheenam's property. He hired a bulldozer and began plowing his way through the brush. After about a half mile he stopped to rest near a tree and reports:

> Though there was no wind, suddenly the tree's leaves shimmered as if in the excitement of communication. I asked the tree, "What is your message?" In reply, my attention was directed to a spot just to the right of where I was sitting. When I pulled back the tall grass, there was a large rock, the self-created linga on which Lord Śiva had sat. The bulldozer's trail now led exactly to the sacred stone, surrounded by five smaller boulders. San Mārga, the straight or pure path to God, had been created.[29]

His later biographies present him as a great temple builder and as someone who revived temple worship among diaspora Hindus. After his death, his followers reported "he gave blessings to dozens of groups to build temples in North America, Australia, New Zealand, Europe, and elsewhere, gifting Deity images, usually of Lord Ganesha, to thirty-six temples to begin worship."[30] He guided numerous groups of temple trustees in the process of temple development, and he "thus authenticated and legitimized the establishment of the temple as essential to any Hindu community."[31]

The later biographies close with a list of his various accomplishments that feature recognition of Subramuniyaswami by other religious groups: in 1986 New Delhi's World Council of Religion named him one of five modern-day *Jagadacharyas* (world teachers). The Global Forum of Spiritual and Parliamentary Leaders for Human Survival named him a representative of Hinduism, and he attended their meetings in 1988, 1990, and 1992. He participated in the President's Assembly at the 1993 centenary Chicago Parliament of the World's Religions. In 1998, the Vishva Hindu Parishad sent an envoy to recognize Subramuniyaswami as the "Hindu Voice of the Century." Finally, in 2000 he received the United Nations U Thant Peace Award.[32]

Subramuniyaswami died, or attained *mahasamadhi*, on November 12, 2001. At the time of his death, twelve initiated swamis who had taken lifetime vows and nine celibate monks resided at his Aadheenam. Subramuniyaswami selected as his successor Bodhinatha Veylanswami, who had been a follower of the guru for thirty-seven years at the time of his death.[33]

Phase One of the Guru's Teaching Career: Master Subramuniya in the 1950s and 1960s

Now that we have a general understanding of the guru's various biographies, we can begin to reconstruct the historical phases of his teaching career by examining some of the material not discussed in the "official" biographical sources. The biographies have a significant gap between 1950 and 1957. Subramuniyaswami states that he was ordered not to teach until he was thirty to account for this silence. He was apparently not inactive during this time spending much of it exploring various untraditional religions. He traveled around the United States, experimenting with Christian Science, Theosophy, the Science of Mind, the Self-Realization Fellowship, Unity, Religious Science, and spiritualism. His shift to a teaching ministry as Master Subramuniya in 1957 blends elements of these new religious movements with Hindu yogic and Vedantic teachings in a language oriented to Westerners.[34]

Subramuniyaswami in the 1950s and 1960s might best be placed in an American metaphysical lineage that can be traced from nineteenth-century Theosophy to the New Age Movement in the late 1970s. During the 1950s, Subramuniya had contact with and practiced several new religious movements that largely blended theosophical and esoteric doctrines. These groups would become prominent in the eclectic spiritual counterculture movement in the 1960s and early 1970s. Among these loose networks of people and organizations were those who held a utopian vision of the future based in astrology. They understood themselves to be on the cusp of a "new age," the Age of Aquarius. The Aquarian Age would usher in a transformative era where humankind would witness an evolution of its social, spiritual, and psychological states.[35] Much of this utopian vision and the eclectic blending of psychological and Eastern thought typify Subramuniya's teachings beginning in the late 1950s and through the 1960s.[36]

The main philosophy Subramuniya used during this period is "Advaita Yoga." The goal of Advaita Yoga, according to the guru, is to attain a unitary vision of the self, the self as God.[37] While the realization of the *atman* (self) as the only ultimate reality fits an Advaita understanding of Hinduism, it cannot be described as part of Saiva Siddhanta. A more probable source for Subramuniya's perception of the self is Swami Vivekananda, a figure he mentions only in passing in his biographies, but whose Neo-Advaita perspective permeates much of Subramuniya's views on Hindu philosophy. A similar perception of monism is also central to Theosophical discourses, and schools related to it, and may have also influenced the guru's thoughts on this subject.

Subramuniya's early publications, *The Self-God* (1959), *Cognizant-ability* (1958), *Gems of Cognition* (1958), and *The Clear White Light* (1968) make no mention of Saiva Siddhanta, the term "Hinduism," or Shiva. They provide no biographical details on Subramuniya nor do they mention his guru or lineage. All of Subramuniya's early works stress meditation, an Advaita-based monism, and yoga, but make no mention of Subramuniya's Hindu religious or sectarian affiliations or his avocation of temple worship so prominently found in his later works.

Other reports of Master Subramuniya's teachings in the 1950s and 1960s also suggest a lack of attention to *bhakti* and temple worship. At his Virginia City retreat center, for instance, Master Subramuniya conducted retreats at which he taught a combination of breathing exercises, concentration, and *chakra* manipulation.[38] During this period, he stressed the achievement of a direct and complete unitive experience and, as a result, he "eschewed dualistic devotional exercises" and advocated "a kind of total dissociation from the body and the emotions."[39] In contrast to the biographies, the published evidence from the 1950s and 1960s suggests that Subramuniyaswami did not engage in or advocate temple worship to Shiva or other forms of *bhakti* common to Saiva Siddhanta.

While Subramuniyaswami blended elements of Aquarian teachings with Hinduism in one context during the 1950s and 1960s, he also combined aspects of Hinduism and Christianity in another context. Subramuniyaswami opened two centers in San Francisco in 1957: one nominally Hindu, the Subramuniya Yoga Order, and the other nominally Christian, the Christian Yoga Church.[40] A typical Sunday worship at the Christian Yoga Church included the singing of Christian hymns, readings from the New Testament and the *Bhagavad-Gita* or Upanishads, and a sermon related to Christian or Hindu mysticism. In this context, Master Subramuniyaswami was known as Father Subramuniya. All of the biographies are silent on this Christian aspect of Subramuniya's early career most likely because it would place his authority within the Hindu tradition into doubt.[41]

Phase Two of the Guru's Teaching Career: Steps Toward Gurudom, Master Subramuniya in the 1970s

The next major phase of Subramuniya's teaching career can be dated to 1970 with the establishment of the Kauai Aadheenam. Before discussing this development, I would like to concentrate on the guru's first biographies from 1970 and 1972. One way to gauge the shifts in Subramuniyaswami's characterization from the 1950s and 1960s to the 1970s is to compare the earlier material to the biographies that appear in the 1970s. The 1970s biographies share a strong esoteric theme with some of Subramuniya's early works, such as the appearance of the first three esoteric catalysts. Where the two 1970s biographies differ from the earlier publications is the introduction of specifically Hindu references, the inclusion of devotional practices as part of the guru's teachings, and the account of Subramuniya's initiation by Yogaswami.

Similar shifts can be detected in several of Subramuniya's other publications from the 1970s. In 1973, Subramuniya published Rajayoga, the renamed fifth edition of *Cognizantability*, first published in 1958. The two texts are essentially the same, except *Rajayoga* makes direct reference to Hinduism, Saiva Siddhanta, and the role of a Shaivite guru:

> Saiva Siddhanta Hinduism, man's spiritual, philosophical, and devotional laws and guidelines, leads him through practice to the Ultimate within himself. For many thousands of years each Saivite Guru has elucidated portions or all of these systematic teachings to his closest disciples, thus adding to the wealth of Hinduism.[42]

While the new title of the text and these references to Saiva Siddhanta and Hinduism do not change the content of the rest of the book from earlier editions, they do suggest a shift in the public presentation of Subramuniya. The guru and his teachings are now clearly labeled as Hindu, and he is affiliated with a specific sectarian movement within that tradition. Although Subramuniya's teachings still blend esoteric and Hindu beliefs, he now wishes to be recognized primarily as a Hindu guru.

Other publications from this period establish the guru's authority through accounts of his initiation. *The Wailua Story* (1972), for instance, provides a brief account of Subramuniya's lineage and his initiation under Yogaswami.[43] In *I'm All Right, Right Now* (1973) Subramuniya repeatedly refers to "My Guru Yogaswamī."[44] Again, the content of the teachings in both texts remains consistent with Subramuniya's previous teachings. What has changed is a re-visioning of Subramuniya. These shifts in representation establish Subramuniya's personal authority as a guru within Saiva Siddhanta and Hinduism through his initiation, but he also maintains his appeal with Western "seekers" who might be attracted to his more esoteric ideas.

Historical circumstances may account for these shifts in the presentation of Subramuniya. In 1969 Subramuniya traveled to Sri Lanka, his first trip back since 1949, and then he took two more trips in 1970 and 1972. In 1970, he moved the Saiva Siddhanta Church to Kauai and establishes the Kauai Aadheenam there with his first lifelong *sannyasins*. The introduction of printed biographies and related shifts in Subramuniya's publications in the early 1970s coincide with a period of transition and travel for the guru and his followers.

The death of Yogaswami in 1964 and the 1969, 1970, and 1972 trips began a process where the guru found himself in more contact with Hindu Tamils. There was a general agreement that Yogaswami initiated Subramuniyaswami as his heir. The devotees of Yogaswami would have expected Subramuniyaswami to act in the ways of a Tamil Saiva guru, but, as we have seen from his earliest publications, he has not practiced or taught Saiva Siddhanta or a distinctly Tamil tradition since leaving Sri Lanka in 1949. Part of the goal of the trips to South Asia between 1969 and 1972 may have been to establish Subramuniya's authority with Yogaswami's followers and to seek to legitimate his new Adhinam both in the eyes of his newly initiated Western *sannyasins* and with Tamil Sri Lankans. These factors may have helped to inspire the shifts in his self-representation found in his biographies and other publications in the early 1970s.

The shift toward incorporating more references to devotion to Shiva in the two early biographies may be based in the central role devotion plays in Saiva Siddhanta and at Tamil Adhinams. The Dharmapura Adhinam, in Dharmapuram, Tamil Nadu, provides an example of the ritual and devotional aspects of an Adhinam. The Dharmapura Adhinam is a Saiva Siddhanta religious institution Gurujñanasambandhar, a Saiva ascetic, founded in the sixteenth century Saiva. While the Dharmapura Adhinam is primarily a brotherhood of religious ascetics, it also administers twenty temples, and the daily worship of Cokkanatha, a Shiva linga, is central to the institution's identity. Gurujñanasambandhar's biography is focused on his acquisition of Cokkanatha and learning how to worship it. The secret knowledge initiates at the Adhinam receive is a knowledge of this worship.[45] Institutionalized devotion to Shiva is central to most Adhinam identities, and we begin to see the Kauai Aadheenam model such behavior in the 1970s.

Arguably the most important historical event during the early 1970s is Subramuniyaswami's decision to establish a Saiva Siddhanta Adhinam. While the guru tends to legitimate his personal authority to establish this center through his initiation by Yogaswami, we should note that Yogaswami did not run an Adhinam. Certainly, Yogaswami belonged to a lineage of Tamil Sri Lankan gurus, but an argument can be made that he comes from the *siddha* aspect of that tradition. He may not have been viewed as an orthodox representative of Tamil Saiva Siddhanta as it is known at most Adhinams. Subramuniya would not have learned of the traditions of an Adhinam from Yogaswami and his understanding of Saiva Siddhanta gained through his guru may have been atypical—issues that will reappear during the debates of the 1980s discussed below.

In the early 1970s, Subramuniyaswami appears caught between two worlds, or personas: one as guru to a group of Western born neo-Hindu/neo–New Age disciples, a group that has been taught little about the Siddhantin tradition; the other as Yogaswami's successor to his Tamil Sri Lankan following and the head guru of an Adhinam based in the Saiva Siddhanta tradition. To be viewed as the legitimate head of a Saiva Siddhanta Adhinam, Subramuniyaswami must not only allow for devotional worship, but he must actively facilitate such worship. The shift from ignoring devotion found in his earliest publications to a presentation of him engaging in temple worship in the biographies of the 1970s appears to facilitate Subramuniya's new role as an Adhinam guru. Nonetheless, the core of his teachings through the 1970s remains a blend of esoteric and Hindu ideas directed primarily at Western followers. His decision to base his Adhinam in Hawaii largely excluded Tamil Sri Lankans from visiting it and gives one the impression that the guru stayed focused on his Western converts.

Phase Three of the Guru's Teaching Career: The Emergence of *Satguru* Sivaya Subramuniyaswami and Challenges to His Authority in the 1980s

The next major biography appears in 1982 and many of the later biographies owe much to it. We can detect some shifts in Subramuniyaswami's characterization by comparing the biographies from the 1970s to the 1982 account. The key shifts are a progressive diminishing of esoteric references and a concomitant increase in Hindu–Saiva Siddhanta references. The 1982 biography skips much of the material related to the esoteric catalysts from the earlier biographies. Instead it begins in Sri Lanka with Subramuniya's vision of Yogaswami in the Kandaswamy temple, and many later biographies also begin in Sri Lanka. Those that do mention the catalysts only discuss the first from whom Subramuniyaswami is said to learn of Shiva Nataraja and Indian culture.[46]

These shifts between the biographies indicate a movement away from Aquarian Age and esoteric teachings and the elimination of references to religions other than Hinduism. The image of Subramuniyaswami in the 1982 account is of someone well established in Hindu Tamil culture and traditions. In the early 1980s, the guru also shifts his name from Master Subramuniya to Satguru Sivaya Subramuniyaswami in print.[47] The transition to a more Sanskritized name is part of a broader shift toward an image of Subramuniya modeled on Hindu ideals of a guru.

The 1982 biography also presents Subramuniyaswami as having always promoted temple worship and *bhakti*. The text states: "Temple worship is fundamental to the Saivite religion, and a keynote in the history of the [Saiva Siddhanta] Church. . . . Gurudeva stressed bhakti, or devotion, to the congregation from the start. . . ."[48] This emphasis on devotion and temple clearly was not part of his earlier recorded teachings. A concerted effort during the early 1980s shifted Subramuniyaswami's image from that of a neo-Hindu/neo–New Age guru to an authentic Adhinam guru within Saiva Siddhanta.

Events not recorded in the 1982 biography may help to explain some of these shifts in Subramuniyaswami's image. For a considerable period after 1972 Subramuniyaswami does not travel to South Asia. While he attempts to connect more with the Tamil Sri Lankan community in the early 1970s, whether these efforts were sustained is unclear. A distinct shift in his travel habits occurs in 1979. He goes to India and Sri Lanka each year from 1979 to 1983 visiting various Hindu diaspora communities in Malaysia, Singapore, Mauritius, and South Africa in the process. During this period, Subramuniyaswami's audience expands and changes from his early days with Western practitioners. The presentation of the guru shifts to a diasporic Hindu audience, a group that tends to be conservative and grounds itself in tradition.

In February 1979 the first edition of *The New Saivite World* also appears. This publication would become *Hinduism Today*, and Subramuniyaswami's main vehicle for promoting himself and his group during the 1980s. While the publication contains some aspects of esoteric teachings, the majority presents Subramuniyaswami as a voice of traditional Hinduism. In late 1979, the Kadavul Temple at the Kauai Aadheenam was also completed. *The New Saivite World* reports that after Subramuniyaswami's vision in 1973 a Shiva Nataraja was installed at the site with plans to build a temple around it. The project languished until a new fund-raising campaign was undertaken in 1979 and the temple completed.[49]

During that same year Subramuniyaswami returned to Sri Lanka and attempted to revive his ashram at Alaveddy. *The New Saivite World* reports that the ashram had gone into a state of dormancy. New leadership was established in 1979 and by 1980 a new building in Alaveddy was purchased and programs initiated.[50] The shift detectable in the 1982 biography is also reflected in a concerted effort beginning in 1979 to restart a variety of distinctly Hindu projects and efforts to reach out to Sri Lankan and diaspora communities with whom Subramuniyaswami has had little direct contact since 1972.

A decisive re-visioning of Subramuniyaswami and his organization occurs in 1979 for reasons that remain unclear. While what follows is speculation, we might hypothesize that the changes had little to do with events on Kauai and more to do with events in Guyana in November 1978. The mass suicides at Jonestown, Guyana, had a significant impact on new religious movements. A number of these groups after Jonestown were labeled as "cults" and saw their memberships drop. The response from some groups was to "rebrand." An example that echoes the shifts seen in the Kauai Aadheenam is the Holy Order of MANS. In response to negative publicity in the wake of Jonestown, the leadership of the Holy Order of MANS decided to move away from their New Age and Theosophist teachings and to adopt a more traditionally Christian program.[51] The Saiva Siddhanta Church responds similarly: it moves away from New Age teachings and adopts a more traditional program among diaspora Hindus. We cannot be certain what motivated Subramuniyaswami to change in 1979, but we may reasonably assume that it arose from the negative climate for untraditional groups produced after Jonestown.

Demographic shifts in America may provide a second factor that contributed to Subramuniyaswami's shift toward outreach to the Hindu diaspora and a more conservative persona. Before the Immigration and Nationality Act of 1965 very few South Asians immigrated to the United States. Subramuniyaswami's early teachings were most likely oriented toward Western esoteric seekers and counterculture practitioners in the 1950s and 1960s because very few South Asians were in California during that time. The numbers of South Asian immigrants to the United

States began to increase dramatically from the 1980s to the 1990s.[52] These shifts in the U.S. demographic landscape probably had an impact on Subramuniyaswami. He was already reaching out to diaspora groups outside of the United States in the late 1970s and early 1980s. By the late 1980s and early 1990s we find him traveling more within North America and orienting his message in *Hinduism Today* and other publications more specifically to Hindu diaspora groups in America. His shift toward a more conservative and politicized version of Hinduism may be in response to the diaspora community in America.

This period of increased publicity within India and diaspora communities, however, led to conflict. Subramuniyaswami entered into a series of debates with two Siddhantin groups from 1981 to 1984, initiating the debates when he issued the monograph "There Can only Be One Final Conclusion" in 1981.[53] This essay caused a strong reaction among some Saiva Siddhantin organizations. It elicited two published responses both attacking Subramuniyaswami's arguments. The first was "Souls Are Beginningless: This Has Always Been a Fundamental Tenet of Saiva Siddhanta" issued by the Selangor/Wilayah Persekutuan Ceylon Saivites Association from Kuala Lumpur, Malaysia, a lay Tamil Shaivite group. "Souls Are Beginningless" was written by V. K. Palasuntharam and released at a seminar, which Subramuniyaswami attended, on the topic of monism and pluralism in Saiva Siddhanta hosted by Palasuntharam's organization in July 1983.[54] The Dharmapura Adhinam issued the second response, *There Can only Be One Final Conclusion in Saiva Siddhanta (according to Thirumular): Dharmapura Adhinam's Reply to the Hawaii Saivites*, T. N. Arunachalam, a lay member of the Adhinam, wrote the Dharmapura paper, which was released at an international seminar on Saiva Siddhanta at Dharmapuram in May 1984.[55]

The Kauai Aadheenam was not present at the Dharmapuram Seminar, but they arranged for their second debate publication, "Monism and Pluralism in Saiva Siddhanta," to be distributed at the seminar. It was largely a response to Palasuntharam's "Souls Are Beginningless." Finally, at the 1984 Dharmapuram Seminar, V. K. Palasuntharam published, "There Has always been only a Pluralistic Śaiva Siddhanta Philosophy: A Reply to Hawaii Saivism's Brochure on Monism and Pluralism."[56]

In the debates, Subramuniyaswami declares that two schools exist within Saiva Siddhanta: a philosophically monistic school and a philosophically pluralistic school. He describes the monist school as practicing monistic theism. In this system, Shiva is both the efficient cause and the material cause of the universe and souls. The ultimate destiny of souls is an "undifferentiated union" with "God Siva."[57] Such a conclusion is a unique understanding of Shiva and the ultimate goal of souls within

Tamil Saiva Siddhanta. Most Tamil Siddhantins are what Kauai calls "pluralist."[58] This pluralist position believes in three eternal and coexistent entities—Shiva, souls, and the material universe. Here, Shiva is the efficient, but not material, cause of the universe. The ultimate destiny of souls is a nondual union with God.[59] Most Siddhantins view liberation of the soul to occur in an individual who has become all powerful and all-knowing like Shiva. Such an omniscient and omnipotent soul is viewed as *a* Shiva, but remains ontologically distinct from *the* Shiva. The phrase "nondual union" appears to refer to this equal but separate state of the soul when released from the bonds of the universe. Subramuniyaswami's "undifferentiated union," on the other hand, suggests that the soul and universe are Shiva, and release is the realization that there is no separate soul, but only Shiva. Subramuniyaswami argues that the monistic view is the better of the two.[60]

Monistic theism represents a shift in Subramuniyaswami's teachings. Subramuniya can be described as advocating a Neo-Advaita perspective from the 1950s to the 1970s. Such a perspective tends to delegitimize the material world of ritual and worship. His earliest work might best be described as monist, but not theist. The theism is most likely a product of his desire to model his Adhinam after other Tamil Adhinams, including their ritual practices. The shift toward supporting temple worship in the 1982 biography demands a shift in philosophical perspective to allow for such devotion. Monistic theism appears to be an attempt to keep part of the group's past (monism), while incorporating elements of its future in promoting the worship of Shiva (theism).

Returning to the debate, while Subramuniyaswami presents a variety of arguments to support his position for monism, we are primarily interested in only one aspect of it: his claim to know the "truth" because he speaks from an "enlightened" perspective. Subramuniyaswami argues that he has an enlightened knowledge of Saiva Siddhanta, which he contrasts with scholarly knowledge. He states: "One view is for the intellectual, the other is for the rishi. The intellectual will see it only one way, he will then discard the other view as wrong. The rishi can see it both ways, yet he knows the monistic view is the higher realization."[61] Subramuniyaswami argues he is the spiritual superior to the other authors in the debate because he is enlightened and knows the "truth." In placing such emphasis on his enlightened status, a status the biographies help to establish, the guru stakes his reputation and authority in the debate.

Also part of Subramuniyaswami's argument in the debate is an attempt to redefine the prominence of certain texts found in the Saiva Siddhanta canon. This canon comprises the *Vedas*, the twenty-eight volumes of Shiva *Agamas*, the twelve volumes of the *Tirumurai* (songs of the *bhakti* saints), and the fourteen volumes of the *Meykantar Shastras* (philosophical texts).[62] While all of these texts hold some prominence in the tradition, the thirteenth-century *Shivajñanabodham* of Meykantar is particularly revered by most Tamil Siddhantins. For many, Saiva Siddhanta does not truly exist until this text appears.[63] The pluralist philosophy Subramuniyaswami refers to in the debate originates with the *Shivajñanabodham*. In his attempt to discredit the position of the pluralists, he argues that Meykantar's text is not as authoritative as others suggest, nor does it represent the true philosophical teachings of Saiva Siddhanta.[64]

Subramuniyaswami posits that Saiva Siddhanta originated with the Tamil saint Tirumular and his text the *Tirumantiram*, part of the *Tirumurai* and is dated to the first century BCE by Subramuniyaswami, although others place it in the sixth or ninth century CE.[65] Subramuniyaswami claims this text is the most mystical, comprehensive, and earliest text in the *Tirumurai*. He posits that Tirumular and the *Tirumantiram* are based in monistic theism.[66] For Subramuniyaswami, this monism of the *Tirumantiram* represents the earliest and most legitimate version of Siddhanta.

Palasuntharam's "Souls Are Beginningless" questions Subramuniyaswami's reading of Saiva Siddhanta and, as a result, he implicitly questions the guru's authority in that tradition. Palasuntharam argues that in order to understand Tirumular's text, one must be "well versed in Tamil Literature, Tamil Grammar, Vedas, Agamas and the Saiva Siddhanta Philosophy of Meikandar."[67] He also presents a lengthy critique of the translation of the *Tirumantiram* he used to highlight Subramuniyaswami's inability to read Tamil.[68] Palasuntharam argues that because Subramuniyaswami cannot read Tamil, he cannot present a valid interpretation of the Tamil texts of the Saiva Siddhanta tradition.

Arunachalam presents similar critiques that privilege linguistic and cultural access to Tamil texts. He cautions those with no grounding in the other *Tirumurai*s from attempting to study the *Tirumantiram* because of its obscure nature. Both Palasuntharam and Arunachalam argue that Meykantar is central to Saiva Siddhanta and that Tirumular's text is pluralist and misread by Subramuniyaswami.[69]

Implicit in these attacks is a suggestion that only educated Tamils can correctly interpret Saiva Siddhanta and speak for the tradition. Palasuntharam situates the Kauai Aadheenam on the outside of Tamil tradition by referring to them as "Hawaii Saivism."[70] In doing so he presents Subramuniyaswami and his Adhinam as philosophically, geographically, and culturally outside of Tamil Saiva Siddhanta. Subramuniyaswami is branded as a foreigner to the tradition who is trying to bring new and non-Tamil teachings into it.[71]

While Subramuniyaswami attempted to discredit the idea that he brought ideas to Saiva Siddhanta and is a cultural outsider, evidence suggests that these debates damaged the guru's reputation with his Tamil followers. That Palasuntharam's group organized a seminar on the topic of monism and pluralism and used the venue to attack Subramuniyaswami speaks to the response from some within the diaspora. Most of the articles in *Hinduism Today* in 1984 and 1985 defend Subramuniyaswami's standing as an initiated guru within Saiva Siddhanta and his views on monistic theism, although these articles do not directly mention the debates. The publication of the 1982 biography with its elimination of Subramuniyaswami's esoteric training may also be a response to the first wave of reaction to his initial essay distributed in 1981.

Phase Four of the Guru's Teaching Career: The Postdebate Sivaya Subramuniyaswami

Subramuniyaswami and his group were placed in a difficult position after the debate. Subramuniyaswami tried to project a non-Western image in the debate, but that he and most of his *sannyasins* are not Tamil informed much of the argument against him. The public nature of the debate demanded that Subramuniyaswami address these issues if his authority as a spiritual leader within Saiva Siddhanta was to be taken seriously.

The biographies that appear in some of Subramuniyaswami's major works in the late 1980s and 1990s may be seen as responses to these challenges to his authority. Representative of them is one found in the 1987 edition of *Hindu Catechism*. This biography provides a paragraph on Subramuniyaswami's early life. It mentions his training in dance, but focuses on his receiving "a rigorous training in meditation and the disciplines of classical yoga," and mentions that he was tutored "in the occult sciences," but makes no reference to his catalysts from earlier biographies. The core of this biography is the account of his enlightenment experience and his initiation. The remainder of this biography focuses on the guru's founding of various temples and branches of his outreach programs. The biography provides no comments on the debates of the early 1980s, but instead focuses on the growth of the guru's international mission in the 1980s resulting in "a spiritual revival . . . within Saivite Hinduism in several nations."[72] This postdebate biography accentuates numerous shifts found in the 1982 account, concentrating on his training in meditation and yoga and presenting him as a legitimate guru, both through personal realization and through the sanction of an authentic guru. Finally, the biography projects an image of him as actively engaged in establishing temples and reviving Shaivism in diaspora communities.

Another example of the shift in depictions of Subramuniyaswami and his thought in the 1990s can be found in *Satguru Speaks on Hindu Renaissance* (1993), a collection of Subramuniyaswami's lectures delivered mainly between 1978 and 1983. He claims in the introduction that a Hindu renaissance is underway, a movement where "Hindus are rediscovering the beauties, the refinements and the deep philosophical and mystical depths of a faith they were born into but knew little about."[73] Part of this need for the rediscovery of one's faith, argues the guru, is brought about by Hindus living in the diaspora.[74] For Subramuniyaswami, this renaissance is primarily about preserving Sanatana Dharma, coming to terms with one's "Hinduness and with the forces in the world that even today seek to diminish Hinduism."[75] This and other elements of the introduction have something of a Hindutva orientation, reflective of political shifts in Hinduism in the 1980s and 1990s that also tended to view Hinduism as threatened and called for a revival and defense of the faith.

These shifts to a focus on diaspora communities and a more conservative, politicized, view of Hinduism are common in the guru's later publications. Through various media he provided instruction to diasporic Hindus on how to maintain one's tradition while living outside of India. Typically, his advice was presented in conservative terms, encouraging what he understood to be "traditional" Hindu practices. An example can be found in relation to his views on gender roles. He is credited with:

> Establishing a counter "women's liberation movement," reminding Hindus that family well-being lies in the hands of women, who with their special *śakti* are uniquely able to raise the children well and make their husbands successful by not working in the world, but following the traditional role of wife and mother.[76]

This appeal to a traditional lifestyle and values is found throughout the later work of the guru. His followers describe him as nurturing "a staunchly Hindu, highly disciplined, global fellowship, . . ." and as being "known as one of the strictest gurus in the world."[77] His legacy as described in the biographies of the 1990s is as a traditional and strict Hindu guru. More could be stated on these points, but Subramuniyaswami's teachings and "traditional" image garners him support with certain aspects of the Hindu diaspora community.

Conclusion

This chapter demonstrates the fluid nature of biography construction in the case of Subramuniyaswami, which sees the guru and his group respond directly to the historical circumstances in which they find themselves. The gaps between the biographies and historical record of the guru suggest that religious biography in this case is more a tool of image construction rather than an attempt to portray the life of Subramuniyaswami "warts and all."[78] The issue I wish to pursue, however, is not the potential accuracy of the accounts. Much like religious myths we should expect religious biographies to develop in this manner. The real value of this study is in its demonstration that the biographies mirror broader shifts in Hinduism in America. The guru's initial training in the 1930s and 1940s at Vedanta Society centers and among probable theosophists and esoteric practitioners reflects the general status of Hinduism in America at that time. His blending of Hindu and Christian thought in the 1950s and 1960s as well as his progressive movement toward Aquarian Age thought is also typical of trends in nontraditional religions that borrowed from Hindu and Asian thought. Perhaps the most significant shift, however, is a demographic one. The emergence of a vibrant diaspora Hinduism in America and around the world along with the proliferation of temples and other Hindu organizations outside of South Asia also has an impact on the career of this guru and the trajectory of his biographies. With the suspicion surrounding new religious movements in the United States in the early 1980s, the guru was already moving away from his base of support in Western converts to his group. His outreach programs to Tamil Sri Lankans and diaspora groups around the world made him aware of the needs of diaspora Hindus, their political perspectives, and the role most Adhinam gurus took. With the rise of the Hindu diaspora in America over the last two decades of Subramuniyaswami's life, we find a considerable distancing from his former esoteric and Aquarian Age teachings of his Western followers to better fit the Hinduism of the diaspora.[79] The life and times of this American-born guru are, in many ways, the life and times of Hinduism in America in the second half of the twentieth century.

Notes

1. An Aadheenam or Adhinam (Tamil Atinam) is a South Indian religious institution. The term is applied to non-Brahmin Saiva centers that function as independent institutions with their own internal system of authority.

2. A useful summary of Saiva Siddhanta can be found in Gavin Flood, *An Introduction to Hinduism* (Cambridge, Eng.: Cambridge University Press, 1996), 162–164, 168–171.

3. Andrew Rawlinson, *The Book of Enlightened Masters: Western Teachers in Eastern Traditions* (Chicago: Open Court, 1997), 539–540.

4. Russell McCutcheon, "Myth," in *Guide to the Study of Religion*, reprint, ed. Willi Braun and Russell T. McCutcheon, 190–208 (London: Continuum, 2007).

5. The oldest is from 1970, but it appears in the 2002 memorial edition of *Hinduism Today* after the guru's death. I refer to it as the 1970/2002 biography, Sivaya Subramuniyaswami, "Autobiography: The Making of a Master," *Hinduism Today*, Apr.-May-June 2002, 16–25.

6. Subramuniyaswami, "Autobiography," 16; also see Master Subramuniya, *Master Course, Part One*, 6th ed. (Kapaa, HI: Wailua University of Contemplative Arts, 1972), 80–81.

7. Subramuniyaswami, "Autobiography," 16–18.

8. Ibid., 18; also see Subramuniya, *Master Course*, 91–92.

9. Subramuniya never names the traditions to which these catalysts belong. It is my assumption that his catalysts were primarily Western practitioners of theosophy, occultism, and other traditions that would develop into New Age movements by the 1970s.

10. Subramuniyaswami, "Autobiography," 19. The account of this catalyst is more detailed in the 1972 version; see Subramuniya, *Master Course*, 92–97.

11. Subramuniyaswami, "Autobiography," 20.

12. Ibid., 21–22.

13. "Amma V. Sivayogam, from Alaveddy, Sri Lanka, Visiting U.S. Church Families," *New Saivite World*, February 1982, http://www.hinduismtoday.com/modules/smartsection.php?itemid=236 (accessed Sept. 21, 2010).

14. Subramuniyaswami, "Autobiography," 22.

15. "Saiva Siddhanta Church Celebrating Silver Jubilee," *New Saivite World*, Aug. 1982, http://www.hinduismtoday.com/modules/smartsection.php?itemid=247 (accessed Sept. 21, 2010).

16. Ibid. In the 1970/2002 account this conversation is depicted differently.

17. "Saiva Siddhanta Church Celebrating." In the 1970/2002 version the events detailed in the 1982 account are described as occurring over three meetings.

18. Subramuniyaswami, "Autobiography," 24.

19. Ibid.

20. Sivaya Subramuniyaswami, *Saiva Dharma Shastras*, http://www.himalayanacademy.com/resources/books/sds/ (accessed Sept. 20, 2010).

21. Subramuniyaswami, "Autobiography," 24.

22. "Master Subramuniya Returns from World Pilgrimage," *New Saivite World*, May 1979, http://www.hinduismtoday.com/modules/smartsection.php?itemid=175 (accessed Sept. 21, 2010); "Original Sri Subramuniya Ashram Building in Alaveddy Acquired," *New Saivite World*, May 1980, http://www.hinduismtoday.com/modules/smartsection.php?itemid=198 (accessed Sept. 21,

2010); Sivaya Subramuniyaswami, *Hindu Catechism: A Catechism and Creed for Saiva Siddhanta* (San Francisco, CA: Himalayan Academy, 1987), viii.

23. Sivaya Subramuniyaswami, *Merging with Śiva: Hinduism's Contemporary Metaphysics* (Kapaa, HI: Himalayan Academy, 1999), xii.

24. Ibid.

25. Subramuniyaswami, *Hindu Catechism*, viii; "Saiva Siddhanta Church Celebrating."

26. Subramuniyaswami, *Merging*, xii; Subramuniyaswami, *Hindu Catechism*, viii; "Saiva Siddhanta Church Celebrating." I have no firm figures on the ethnic makeup of Subramuniya's following at this time. Photographs of the guru interacting with his followers in publications from the early 1970s suggest that all of his lay followers in Hawaii were Westerners. Later images of his renunciates suggest that they also were initially all Westerners, but some South Asian renunciates begin to appear in the mid- to late 1990s. All of the renunciates appear to be male.

27. "Saiva Siddhanta Church Celebrating."

28. Subramuniyaswami, *Saiva Dharma Shastras*.

29. Ibid.

30. Sivaya Subramuniyaswami, *Yoga's Forgotten Foundation: Twenty Timeless Keys to Your Divine Destiny* (Kapaa, HI: Himalayan Academy, 2004), 183.

31. Ibid., 183–184.

32. Ibid., 185–186.

33. Ibid., 188.

34. Phillip Charles Lucas, *The Odyssey of a New Religion: The Holy Order of MANS from New Age to Orthodoxy* (Bloomington: Indiana University Press, 1995), 21.

35. Richard Kyle, *The New Age Movement in American Culture* (Lanham, MD: University Press of America, 1995), 9.

36. One of Subramuniya's books for this era that speaks directly to his adoption of Aquarian Age thinking is Master Subramuniya, *The Clear White Light: A Western Mystic's Transcendental Experiences*, 3rd ed. (San Francisco, CA: Tad Robert Gilmore, 1971). The first edition of the book was in 1968.

37. For an example, see the entire text of Master Subramuniya, *Self-God*, 7th ed. (Kapaa, HA: Wailua University of Contemplative Arts, 1970).

38. Lucas, *Odyssey*, 21.

39. Ibid.

40. Rawlinson, *Enlightened Masters*, 541.

41. Lucas, *Odyssey*, 13. Some have suggested, however, that Subramuniya was not a Christian during this period, nor did he truly desire to mesh Hindu and Christian ideals and practices. Rather, his followers claim that he used Christianity to transplant Shaivism in the West; Christianity and terms like "Church" were simply means of making Shaivism accessible to a Western audience; see Lucas, *Odyssey*, 23.

42. Master Subramuniya, *Rajayoga*, 5th ed. (San Francisco, CA: Comstock House, 1973), 17.

43. Master Subramuniya, *The Wailua Story* (Kapaa, HA: Wailua University of Contemplative Arts, 1972), 26.

44. Master Subramuniya, *I'm All Right, Right Now* (San Francisco, CA: Comstock House, 1973), 2, 14.

45. K. I. Koppedrayer, "Miraculous Abhiseka: Miracle and Authority in a South Indian Non-Brahmin Lineage," in *Images, Miracles, and Authority in Asian Religious Traditions*, ed. Richard H. Davis, 97–119 (Boulder, CO: Westview Press, 1998).

46. "The Path of the Nayanars," *New Saivite World*, Apr. 1983, http://www.hinduismtoday.com/modules/smartsection.php?itemid=267 (accessed Sept. 21, 2010); Subramuniyaswami, *Merging*, xxx.

47. One of the first occurrences of the new name is in "1981 India Odyssey Departs from Honolulu," *New Saivite World*, Jan. 1981, http://www.hinduismtoday.com/modules/smartsection.php?itemid=219 (accessed Sept. 21, 2010).

48. "Saiva Siddhanta Church Celebrating."

49. "Kadavul Hindu Temple on Kauai Completed," *New Saivite World*, Feb. 1980, http://www.hinduismtoday.com/modules/smartsection.php?itemid=181 (accessed Sept. 21, 2010).

50. "Master Subramuniya Returns"; "Original Sri Subramuniya Ashram."

51. Lucas, *Odyssey*, 2.

52. For census numbers see Raymond Bradley Williams, "Introduction," in *The South Asian Religious Diaspora in Britain, Canada, and the United States*, ed. Harold Coward, John R. Hinnells, and Raymond Brady Williams, 213–217 (Albany, NY: SUNY Press, 2000), 214–215.

53. The 1981 essay was republished in 1984. All of the citations in this chapter to "There Can only Be One Final Conclusion" are to the 1984 reprint, Sivaya Subramuniyaswami, *Monism and Pluralism in Saiva Siddhanta*, 2 vols. (Hawaii: Kauai Aadheenam, 1984).

54. Subramuniyaswami, *Monism and Pluralism*, vol. 2, 1.

55. T. N. Arunachalam, *There Can only Be One Final Conclusion in Saiva Siddhanta (according to Thirumular): Dharmapura Adhinam's Reply to the Hawaii Saivites* (Dharmapuram, India: Dharmapura Adhinam, 1984), title page.

56. I have discussed other aspects of this debate elsewhere; see Richard Mann, "The Kauai Aadheenam: The Challenge of Identity and Authority in an American Hindu Sect," *Journal of Religion and Culture* 14 (2000/2001): 101–125.

57. Subramuniyaswami, *Monism and Pluralism*, vol. 1, 5.

58. Ibid.

59. Palasuntharam, "There Can Be only One Final Conclusion in Saiva Siddhanta," 22.

60. Subramuniyaswami, *Monism and Pluralism*, vol. 2, 1.

61. Ibid., 1:27.

62. Mariasusai Dhavamony, *Love of God According to Śaiva Siddhānta: A Study in the Mysticism and Theology of Śaivism* (Oxford, Eng.: Clarendon Press, 1971), 4.

63. Dhavamony, *Love of God*, 200; K. I. Koppedrayer, "The Sacred Presence of the Guru: The Velala Lineages of Tiruvavatuturai, Dharmapuram, and Tiruppanantal," (Ph.D. diss., McMaster University, 1990), 6.

64. Subramuniyaswami, *Monism and Pluralism*, vol. 1, 6.

65. Ibid; Maithili Thayanithy, "The Concept of Living Liberation in the Tirumantiram" (Ph.D. diss., University of Toronto, 2010), ii.

66. Subramuniyaswami, *Monism and Pluralism*, vol. 1, 6–7.

67. Palasuntharam, *Souls Are Beginningless*, 22.

68. Ibid., 32–37.

69. Palasuntharam, *Souls Are Beginningless*, 4; Arunachalam, *There Can only Be*, 3, 18.

70. Palasuntharam, *Souls Are Beginningless*, 1.

71. I will not cover the second round of debates here as they largely repeat issues addressed in the first round.

72. Subramuniyaswami, *Hindu Catechism*, vii, ix.

73. Sivaya Subramuniyaswami, *Satguru Speaks on Hindu Renaissance* (Kuala Lumpur, Malaysia: Jiwa Distributors, 1993), iii.

74. Ibid.

75. Ibid., iv.

76. Subramuniyaswami, *Yoga's Forgotten*, 192.

77. Ibid., 185, 187.

78. One of the most authoritative biographies of Subramuniyaswami is the 1970/2002 account that appeared after the guru's death. His *sannyasins* appear to have selected a biography of the guru that lays bare his initial training among esoteric American practitioners, an image from which the guru actively distanced himself in the later stages of his life. Some of these *sannyasins* would have been followers of the guru since the 1970s, if not earlier. Perhaps for them the 1970 biography represented the identity of Subramuniyaswami with which they most closely identified. We might view in the manipulation of the biographies over time an attempt at deception, but the 1970/2002 biography acts as something of a correction to this.

79. Subramuniyaswami did occasionally return to New Age and esoteric themes in the 1990s; see Sivaya Subramuniyaswami, *Lemurian Scrolls: Angelic Prophecies Revealing Human Origins* (Kapaa, HI: Himalayan Academy, 1998), for an example.

6

Guru Authority, Religious Innovation, and the Decline of New Vrindaban

E. Burke Rochford Jr. and Henry Doktorski

The doubt was there about Kirtanananda but I kept covering it over with the justification that he is a pure devotee [who] knows what Prabhupada [ISKCON's founder] wants. As long he was following the four regulative principles of no meat, intoxication, sex, or gambling I could forgive him. But even after he fell down from these principles I still forgave him. I think the turning point came when I saw him preaching different philosophies from what Prabhupada had given us. Then I said, "That's not right. It isn't what Prabhupada wanted."

—Words of a Prabhupada disciple and long-time
resident of New Vrindaban, 2007

Charismatic authority has been central to the development of new religious movements. New religions are typically established by charismatic leaders preaching new revelations that in various ways challenge the legitimacy of the existing social order, including the established churches.[1] But as recent research suggests, charisma is a dynamic and collaborative process between leaders and followers and is thus more a social construction than a matter of individual personality. Charisma so defined represents a quality attributed to someone by others who place considerable trust and faith in their leadership.[2] At the group level, charismatic authority translates into high levels of organizational commitment, religiosity, and voluntary service directed toward realizing the goals of the leader and his or her organization.[3]

The concept of charisma Max Weber formulated applies to leaders whose authority is "endowed with supernatural, superhuman, or at least specifically exceptional powers or qualities . . . regarded as of divine origin or as exemplary."[4] But as Weber makes clear, charismatic authority is inherently unstable and remains in its pure form only in the short term.[5] Because of this volatility, charisma is subject to ongoing pressures toward routinization and rational-legal forms of authority. Yet charismatic leaders may resist such threats by employing a variety of counteractive strategies meant to preserve their authority including making sudden and dramatic changes in doctrine in order both to attract new followers and to push out dissenters.[6] While these strategies may or may not prove successful, they run the risk of provoking controversy and even violent behavior.[7]

This chapter focuses on charismatic authority, religious innovation, and the decline of one of the more significant new religious communities that emerged during the 1960s era in the United States—New Vrindaban located in West Virginia. New Vrindaban was founded and led by Kirtanananda Swami (1937–2011), one of the early disciples of A. C. Bhaktivedanta Swami Prabhupada, the founding *acarya* of the International Society for Krishna Consciousness (ISKCON), more popularly known as the Hare Krishna movement.[8] Following Bhaktivedanta Swami Prabhupada's death in 1977, Kirtanananda became one of ISKCON's eleven successor gurus.[9] New Vrindaban represents a worthy case study because Kirtanananda's charisma was never institutionalized a fact that had far reaching implications after he was violently attacked and subsequently charged with criminal activities and moral transgressions. His authority and leadership wavering, Kirtanananda devised several religious innovations that fundamentally altered the religious culture of New Vrindaban. These innovations were intended to Americanize Krishna Consciousness in an effort to make it less alien culturally and religiously. As we will see, however, such radical changes in the community's core teachings contributed to New Vrindaban's decline as a religious community. Before turning to these issues, we first provide a biographical sketch of Kirtanananda Swami as well as a history of the community he established and led for twenty-five years.[10]

Kirtanananda Swami and the
Development of New Vrindaban

Kirtanananda Swami was born Keith Ham in September 1937 in Peekskill, New York. He grew up in a conservative religious household as his father was the minister of the First Baptist Church in Peekskill. Keith contracted polio as a teenager leaving him permanently impaired with a noticeable limp. In 1959 he graduated with a history degree from Maryville College in Tennessee, a liberal arts college affiliated with the Presbyterian Church USA. Thereafter, he matriculated to the University of North Carolina to pursue graduate work in American history. After two years, however, Keith abandoned his studies and suddenly moved to New York City, where he discovered hallucinogenic drugs and Eastern philosophy. He later enrolled at Columbia University where he completed all course work for his Ph.D. but never finished his dissertation, choosing instead to travel to India in 1965 to find a guru with his friend and lover, Howard Wheeler. Unsuccessful, he and Howard returned to New York in April 1966. Ironically, in July, they found the Indian guru they were seeking walking the streets on the Lower East Side. As Kirtanananda described in a 2007 interview, Howard, or Hayagriva as he came to be known, encountered Prabhupada in their neighborhood:[11]

> Hayagriva was the one who ran into Prabhupada. We were both living on Mott Street at the time. At Bowery [Street], Hayagriva saw a holy man approaching. We had just been to India so he recognized him as a holy man. Hayagriva stopped and said, "Are you a holy man?" Prabhupada said to him, "Are you from India?" Hayagriva said, "No, but I have just come back from India." Prabhupada said, "Well, I have just opened a storefront on Second Avenue and I am holding classes on *Bhagavad Gita* on Monday, Wednesday and Friday." So Hayagriva came back and said, "I have just run into a holy man on Bowery. He told me there were classes." So the next night, I think it was a Wednesday, I went. That was my first introduction to Prabhupada.[12]

Although "Swamiji"—as they called Prabhupada initially—was difficult to understand because of his thick Bengali accent, Keith found the music and the overall atmosphere at the storefront temple attractive.[13] As he admitted, however, "At first I did not recognize Prabhupada as the spiritual master. . . . The realization came slowly."[14] In time, he came to realize that Prabhupada ". . . was like an old piece of iron that is magnetized, it brings all the iron to it. Prabhupada had that magnetic power which was not material but spiritual. He had a spiritual potency and for those seeking spiritual life he acted as a magnet."

When Prabhupada offered his few followers the opportunity to move into the storefront temple as full-time devotees, Keith was the first to take up the invitation. Prabhupada taught him to cook in the Indian style and he began wearing *dhoti* (traditional robes), adorning his face and body with *tilak* (sacred clay), and shaved his head with only a tuft of hair left on the back (*sikha*). On September 23, 1966, Keith became Kirtanananda *dasa* after accepting initiation from Prabhupada.[15] Initiation obligated him to chant sixteen rounds of the Hare Krishna mantra daily on a string of 108 beads and to strictly follow the four regulative principles—no meat, intoxication, illicit sex, or gambling.[16] Because of Kirtanananda's expertise at cooking, Prabhupada affectionately called him "Kitchen-ananda" and made him his personal servant.

In December 1966, a disciple who had relocated to San Francisco urged Prabhupada to go there because the potential for preaching was great, given the presence of a large and growing number of hippie youths migrating to the Haight-Ashbury section of the city. In January 1967, Prabhupada left New York for San Francisco, and Kirtanananda and Hayagriva drove cross-country to be with their spiritual master. At Prabhupada's request, Kirtanananda then traveled to Montreal to open ISKCON's first center outside of the United States.

When Prabhupada returned to New York in May 1967, Kirtanananda left Montreal to be with his spiritual master. Soon after, Prabhupada had a stroke and was hospitalized. Kirtanananda nursed him in the hospital and then accompanied Prabhupada to India to further his recovery. While in India, Prabhupada initiated Kirtanananda into the renunciate order of *sannyasa* and he became ISKCON's first swami. In this role, Kirtanananda committed himself to lifelong celibacy and to full-time preaching. As Prabhupada wrote to one of his disciples, "Kirtanananda is now a fully Krishna conscious person as he has accepted *sannyas*[a] on the birthday of Lord Krishna with great success. He is the first *sannyas*[a] in my spiritual family and I hope he will return back home to begin preaching work with great vigor and success."[17]

Kirtanananda was ill and generally miserable in the extreme heat of the Indian summer and he asked Prabhupada if he could return to the United States. Prabhupada granted his request with the understanding that Kirtanananda would stop in London and attempt to open a preaching center. Feeling homesick, Kirtanananda disobeyed his spiritual master and stopped in London only to change planes on his way to New

York. Upon his return, and without Prabhupada's blessing, Kirtanananda attempted to Westernize the devotees' style of dress and appearance believing it would enhance their preaching efforts. Kirtanananda shaved his *sikha*, grew his beard and hair, abandoned his *dhoti* in favor of a black robe and cape, and attempted to convince the other New York devotees to do the same but none were inclined to follow Kirtanananda's example without Prabhupada's approval. Kirtanananda reflected on those days following his return from India:

> I think I had a black robe on when I came back [from India]. I was talking about how *dhotis* were not necessary. And when Prabhupada heard about it, he was quite irate. And he said [to the devotees in New York], "Don't listen to Kirtanananda." So from that point I was excluded. EBR: At one point Prabhupada called you a "crazy man." K: Yeah. EBR: How did the devotees in New York react? Bewildered? K: That's true. Prabhupada's permission to experiment in my preaching depended on my doing it in a *new* place. Not where *he* already had a temple with devotees. . . . If I had stopped in London and done it there that would have been alright [*sic*] because there was no temple in London at the time. . . . But Prabhupada was of the opinion that that was not necessary. That we are doing these things because we are following the disciplic succession [lineage of gurus that followers of Prabhupada believe go back in time to Krishna] and this is the way the *acaryas* have done. He made that clear. But he said, "If you want to try it, try it."[18]

Having provoked controversy in the New York temple and angered his spiritual master, Kirtanananda left ISKCON. Initially, he lived with his friend Hayagriva who had taken a college teaching position in Pennsylvania. He also spent some time with his brother's family in Madison, Wisconsin. His unkempt appearance and renewed use of marijuana suggested that Kirtanananda had returned to the hippie lifestyle he enjoyed prior to becoming Prabhupada's disciple.

In February 1968, Kirtanananda telephoned Hayagriva with news that he was going to West Virginia to meet with someone starting a religious community in the hill country near Wheeling. He had seen a letter in the *San Francisco Oracle* promoting the community. Hayagriva agreed to accompany Kirtanananda to West Virginia to meet with the owner Richard Rose, who owned 300 acres of land. They both wore Western-style clothes and introduced themselves to Rose as *former* Hare

Krishna members who had left the movement because the Krishnas were too "closed-minded." They informed Rose that they were looking to join a "non-dogmatic" spiritual community where people holding different beliefs could exchange ideas and practice their faith peacefully.[19]

After the meeting, Hayagriva returned to his teaching duties in Wilkes-Barre, Pennsylvania, but Kirtanananda decided to stay on with Rose and Rose's few followers. Kirtanananda quickly learned however that Rose had little patience for views that differed from his own. Unable to coexist with Rose, Kirtanananda moved to a remote and largely inaccessible part of the property living in a run-down house without electricity or running water. There he subsisted on oatmeal and blackberries, pokeweed shoots, and other edible plants he found in the surrounding meadows and forest.

After weeks in isolation, Kirtanananda grew restless realizing he had no means to start a spiritual community on his own. Although a few of Hayagriva's students expressed interest, there was little to be optimistic about without committed people and sufficient resources. With few realistic options available, Kirtanananda decided to try and mend his relationship with his spiritual master in hopes that Prabhupada would accept him back in the fold and support his efforts to start a community in West Virginia. As the then-president of the New York ISKCON temple put it, "It was only after Kirtanananda and Hayagriva became frustrated because they found it difficult to attract followers to come and live there . . . that they decided to offer the land to Srila Prabhupada to develop as a Krishna consciousness project."[20] Kirtanananda, by contrast, remembered his motives for reconnecting with Prabhupada very differently:

> EBR: What were you thinking you would do with that land? That Kirtanananda Swami was going to start his own community? K: I was there on behalf of Prabhupada; definitely there on behalf of Prabhupada. In fact, I wrote to Prabhupada because there was the break between us, bad feelings or whatever. And I told him I was very sorry and that I could never forget him and I wanted to become his good disciple. Because Prabhupada wanted to create a place of pilgrimage, I suggested we do that. And he wrote back and said, "Yes, we will start New Vrindaban." Prabhupada said, "You were not able to stay in old Vrindaban [India] very long so therefore Krishna has sent you back to start New Vrindaban."[21]

After numerous failed attempts to secure a lease on a portion of the property, owner Richard Rose finally relented after he encountered legal problems. Hayagriva secured a 99-year lease on 132 acres of land for $4,000 and the West Virginia property became known as New Vrindaban, the name given by Prabhupada in a letter to Hayagriva four months earlier.[22] In the years to follow, the community purchased several adjacent properties and by the mid-1980s grew to approximately 4,000 acres.

New Vrindaban's formative years were difficult. Under the motto, "Plain Living and High Thinking," Kirtanananda and a handful of other devotees carved fields and pasture from the overgrown land to grow crops and provide grazing for cows. The goal from the start was to establish a self-sufficient community based on spiritual principles. But Prabhupada had a grander vision for New Vrindaban hoping it would come to mirror its namesake in India.[23] He envisioned seven major temples as found in Vrindaban, India, built on the surrounding West Virginia hilltops. New Vrindaban would serve as a sacred *dham* and place of pilgrimage for ISKCON devotees and Indian-Hindus throughout North America. Kirtanananda made it his life's work to realize his spiritual master's plans for New Vrindaban as did the other Prabhupada disciples choosing to live in the community.

After laying the cornerstone for what was to be the community's first major temple, Kirtanananda decided instead to build a residence for Prabhupada. Prabhupada was delighted and stated, "[Kirtanananda] has actually understood our philosophy. All over the world my disciples are building temples for Radha and Krishna; but he is building a temple for me."[24] Begun in 1972, "Prabhupada's Palace of Gold" opened to the public on September 2, 1979, nearly two years after Prabhupada's death. The structure was built almost entirely by the devotee residents of New Vrindaban. The *New York Times* declared the palace "America's Taj Mahal" and the *Washington Post* called it "Almost Heaven." As Prabhupada's Palace was nearing completion, Kirtanananda announced plans to build the largest Radha-Krishna temple in the world at New Vrindaban.

Prabhupada's Palace proved a magnet for tourists with busloads coming daily from Pittsburgh and elsewhere. New Vrindaban publications indicate that in 1982 100,000 people visited the palace—a total that reportedly increased to some 500,000 between 1983 and 1985. With growing revenues from palace tourism and other sources, the community employed 187 nondevotees from the surrounding area as secretaries, gardeners, and construction workers making New Vrindaban one of the largest employers in Marshall County, West Virginia.

The success of Prabhupada's Palace as a tourist destination changed the overall mission of New Vrindaban. Agricultural production and self-sufficiency were largely set aside in favor of projects that would promote preaching and spiritual tourism. As Kirtanananda explained:

Figure 6.1. Prabhupada's Palace of God (Photo courtesy of Henry Dostorski)

> Prabhupada's Palace was built to glorify my spiritual master. Our desire was that Prabhupada would be so happy with the palace that he would stay with us at New Vrindaban. But when we saw hundreds of people coming a week you start thinking about how to capitalize on that asset. We were a regular stop on the bus tours. We built a restaurant and we began making other plans.[25]

Among those plans was building a "Land of Krishna" theme park; a spiritual Disneyland meant to attract large numbers of people who could be introduced to Krishna Consciousness.

Kirtanananda's dedication to building Prabhupada's Palace brought him respect and admiration, both from the residents of New Vrindaban as well as from many ISKCON devotees.[26] He was widely perceived as a "pure devotee" because of his austerity, scriptural understanding, and selfless dedication to Prabhupada as exemplified by the building of the palace and his unfailing determination to realize Prabhupada's vision for New Vrindaban. As a result, residents of New Vrindaban saw Kirtanananda as Prabhupada's rightful successor. As one stated on the occasion of Kirtanananda's birthday:

You once told us that there's no way to think of Srila Prabhupada without thinking of Krishna, and that we cannot think
of Krishna except by remembering what Prabhupada has told
us. Similarly, we only know Srila Prabhupada through you,
and as soon as we think of you we automatically remember
Prabhupada.[27]

Such widespread respect allowed Kirtanananda to make ever greater demands on both himself and his followers to "surrender more and
more to Krishna." As one longtime resident of the community commented, "Kirtanananda was very strict. He was also always visible. . . . He
was there in the trenches with the foot soldiers so it seemed that he
was exemplary."[28] As Kirtanananda acknowledged, his strictness and
dedication inspired others to sacrifice:

The secret of New Vrindaban is the sacrifices that people were
willing to make. EBR: But how did you get people to sacrifice?
K: Because I sacrificed myself. Because of this I could inspire
them to sacrifice. . . . I wasn't thinking of myself. I was thinking of the project. I gave my whole life to that project. And
because I was giving my whole life to the project, they gave
their lives to it. I was all day going back and forth dealing
with different facets of the project. Inspiring, asking people
what they needed and getting it for them. . . . I was always
up first [in the morning]; got the others up. We chanted
together. They saw me chanting with them. It wasn't that I
was off someplace else chanting my rounds. We ate together.
I ate the same food they did.[29]

One clear measure of New Vrindaban's success was the growing
number of devotees who chose to live there. In 1974 the community
had 108 adult residents and 10 children, a figure that grew to nearly 400 adults and more than 100 children in the mid-1980s.[30] Funds
in support of the community and its building projects also grew and
included revenues generated by Prabhupada's Palace and related tourist
businesses (restaurant, selling of Krishna-conscious literature); traveling
fund-raising parties (sankirtan); distributing candles, hats, records, and
stickers for donations or soliciting money for fictitious charities in public
places; and the financial contributions of the community's substantial
Indian-Hindu congregation. Collectively, these sources raised millions
of dollars yearly. For example, the New Vrindaban Community Income
Statement for 1984 reported a total annual income of just over $4 million

with *sankirtan* collections of $2,853,899 and palace income of $745,315. The statement did not however report the contributions made by New Vrindaban's Indian congregation.

Violence, Crime and Controversy

Charismatic authority is uniquely precarious because charismatic leaders face the ongoing task of sustaining their legitimacy in collaboration with followers. Actions on their part may establish, reinforce, or undermine their authority in the minds of followers. Because of this, maintaining charismatic authority demands continuous legitimation work, especially when questions arise about a leader's decision-making and behavior.[31] Under such circumstances, leaders may employ a variety of strategies meant to bolster their authority in the face of challenge.[32] Just such a chain of events unfolded at New Vrindaban in the mid-1980s that would raise serious questions about the legitimacy of Kirtanananda's leadership.

On October 27, 1985, Kirtanananda was violently assaulted by an enraged devotee while supervising community members who were laying bricks for the new temple parking lot. Michael Schockman (Triyogi dasa) snuck up behind Kirtanananda and forcefully hit him on the head and back with an iron bar. Schockman was angry because Kirtanananda had refused his request for *sannyasa* initiation. Kirtanananda was in a coma for ten days and hospitalized in critical condition for three weeks. When he returned to New Vrindaban, Kirtanananda had difficulty walking and talking and he was partially paralyzed due to the brain injuries resulting from the attack. He also suffered permanent hearing loss, problems with his vision, and lasting cognitive impairments, all of which severely limited his ability to lead the community. Because of his longstanding spiritual authority however, no one initially raised questions about his ability to lead the community. This only changed after it became unmistakable that Kirtanananda's injury had left him mentally unstable and spiritually weakened.[33]

Soon after Kirtanananda's return to New Vrindaban another act of violence occurred that would have far reaching consequences. On May 22, 1986, Stephen Bryant (Sulocana dasa) was murdered near the Los Angeles ISKCON temple. Bryant had been on a crusade against Kirtanananda after he initiated his wife and then gave his approval for her to divorce Bryant and remarry another New Vrindaban resident. Because of Schockman's recent attack on Kirtanananda and Bryant's threat to "destroy Kirtanananda," a surveillance team was formed to keep an eye on Bryant and to track his whereabouts. One member of this surveillance team followed Bryant to California and shot him from close range while he sat in his vehicle. Bryant's murder set off an extensive government investigation by the Federal Bureau of Investigation, the Internal Revenue Service, and police in Los Angeles and West Virginia. On January 5, 1987, police and federal authorities raided New Vrindaban and in May 1990 a federal grand jury indicted Kirtanananda on three counts of violating the RICO (Racketeer Influenced and Corrupt Organizations Act) statute for illegally using copyrighted and trademark logos during fund-raising, six counts of mail fraud, and two counts of conspiracy to commit murder.[34] ISKCON's leadership responded to Kirtanananda's legal problems by excommunicating him from ISKCON in March 1987 and one year later expelling New Vrindaban and its satellite temples and centers. No longer affiliated with ISKCON, Kirtanananda reorganized New Vrindaban under the name the "Eternal Order of the Holy Name, League of Devotees International" and began making radical changes to New Vrindaban's religious culture.

Authority, Innovation, and the Decline of New Vrindaban

In the midst of threatening criminal charges and growing concerns about his leadership, beginning in 1986, Kirtanananda introduced several radical and controversial changes to New Vrindaban's religious culture. He first incorporated Western literature and music and, in 1987 and 1988, further Westernized Krishna Consciousness by integrating practices from Christianity and other religious traditions with ISKCON's Vaisnava practices. Not unlike his aborted attempt in 1967, Kirtanananda sought to make Krishna Consciousness more attractive to the American public by uniting East and West:

> I made it [these changes] just to facilitate my wider vision for preaching. I thought that since America is basically a Christian country the more we could express our philosophy in terms that Christians could understand the better they would relate to Krishna Consciousness. I thought to reach Americans by strictly speaking in Vedic terms would be very difficult. But if you can relate what you are doing to something in Christianity then people will understand.[34]

Kirtanananda believed that the Indian cultural aspects of Krishna Consciousness, such as chanting in Sanskrit and Bengali, wearing *dhotis* and saris, and shaving the head except for the *sikha* were detrimental to preaching in the West and he attempted to "de-Indianize" New Vrindaban's religious culture. As he stated, "We are not interested in Indian culture as such. We're interested in what is productive for Krishna Consciousness—whatever is useful."[35] In the broadest sense, Kirtanananda's vision for New Vrindaban was to create an interfaith "City of God" that would unite people of all faiths.

Kirtanananda encouraged the use of English in chanting and in temple worship, meditative music performed with Western instruments, silent meditation, interfaith preaching that honored the value of all legitimate spiritual paths, sharing practices of other faiths such as Native American rock lodges, pipe ceremonies, and Sufi dancing, in addition to Christian rituals and religious practices. New Vrindaban devotees began wearing Franciscan-type robes and men grew short beards and short hair. A life-size *murti* of Jesus was placed next to the *murti* of

Figure 6.2. Kirtanananda during interfaith period (Photo courtesy of Henry Dostorski)

Prabhupada in the temple room. Both sat cross-legged in an elevated chair (*vyasasana*). In addition to these innovations, a choir known as the Krishna Chorale was organized that performed Christian hymns and Western classical-music masterpieces such as Handel's *Messiah*, with the lyrics rewritten to express the sentiments and philosophy of Gaudiya Vaisnavism.[36] A final change that had no precedent within the Gaudiya Vaisnava tradition was Kirtanananda's decision to initiate women as *sannyasis*. As he stated, "I was thinking that we are in America in the twentieth century where sex discrimination is a black eye. Our philosophy is the spirit soul is neither male nor female. And since *sannyasa* is on the spiritual level why not make it available, whether you have a male or a female [body]."[37]

In keeping with the turn toward interfaith, New Vrindaban hosted fifteen interfaith conferences that brought religious leaders and teachers from several religious traditions. Hundreds of religious seekers were attracted to each of these events, although few became Kirtanananda disciples or members of the New Vrindaban community. One New Vrindaban resident remembered the interfaith conferences in very favorable terms:

> Looking back, what I thought was groundbreaking at New Vrindaban was the interfaith conferences. They opened my eyes; they were so unique, so precious. . . . I feel blessed to have been a part of that; trying to show the world that although there are many faiths, there is one common truth behind each tradition. The festivals allowed people to experience their faith and others' faith, to share joy with each other. It was a monumental experience.[38]

Although many New Vrindaban residents embraced Kirtanananda's interfaith, others saw reason to challenge changes to the community's religious culture. The latter included both New Vrindaban residents as well as the community's Indian-Hindu congregation. Following the introduction of interfaith, many Prabhupada disciples abandoned the community as they remained firmly committed to Prabhupada and his Krishna conscious teachings.[39] Among those who chose to remain, some embraced interfaith at least for a time while others moved to the margins of the community and reduced their involvement. For the most part, devotees enthusiastically embracing interfaith were Kirtanananda's own disciples. But, over time, some of these disciples also became disillusioned with the interfaith experiment as can be seen in the following comments:

I thought the interfaith was a real mistake. Prabhupada would have never approved. No *mrdanga* [two-headed Indian drum]. No *dhotis* and no *kirtan* in the temple. That was ridiculous. I thought the whole thing was ridiculous. Prabhupada was adamant about keeping the Vaisnava culture so that we would be different. He wanted Vaisnava culture to be retained. So I was finished [at New Vrindaban] in [19]89. The interfaith, it was just completely wrong.[40]

Community census data demonstrate dramatically the consequences of Kirtanananda's legal problems and his innovations to New Vrindaban's religious culture. In July 1986, New Vrindaban had 377 adult residents; by July 1991, that number had dropped to 131. In five years New Vrindaban lost a total of 246 adult members, a reduction of 65 percent. Most of those leaving New Vrindaban rejoined ISKCON and moved to one of its temple communities.[41]

New Vrindaban's Indian supporters were equally confused and alienated by Kirtanananda's legal troubles and by his introduction of interfaith. Although Kirtanananda's criminal charges caused embarrassment, his turn to interfaith and his determined effort to de-Indianize New Vrindaban's religious culture provoked outrage among many within the Indian congregation. Statements by Kirtanananda such as, "We are not meant to be a sectarian Indian cult" caused concern among New Vrindaban's Indian supporters.[42] As one longtime New Vrindaban resident stated, the introduction of interfaith convinced many Indians to ". . . just stop coming because they felt that the mingling of Christianity and Vaisnavism was inappropriate because they came here [to New Vrindaban] with the motive of instilling Vedic theology into their children. And they felt the changes undermined that purpose."[43]

Especially disturbing to many Indian people was the realization that their financial contributions to build a Vedic style temple at New Vrindaban were being used instead to construct the "Cathedral of the Holy Name." The temple design had moved away from its traditional Indian architectural details to one that was modernistic, earth-based, and New Age in style. As a devotee who worked extensively with New Vrindaban's Indian congregation during this period explained:

This was very humiliating and very embarrassing. It was embarrassing because I was collecting funds to build this very beautiful Vedic temple designed by south Indian Brahman architects. It was going to be a gift to humanity. And then I had to go back to the same [Indian] people and show them this new design and give excuses to justify it. "We are sorry we have changed things on you. Now we are going to do it like this." And then it became even more embarrassing when I had to go back to the same people and ask for money to get Kirtanananda out of jail or get him out of his legal problems. . . . I think they felt like they had been cheated, which they [had been].[44]

Indian anger toward Kirtanananda only intensified when he publically stated, "I do not care about Indian people." In response, one Indian wrote to Kirtanananda, "I was extremely distressed by your ridiculous remarks about Indians. . . . If you have such racial inner feelings about Indians, you should realize that Indians do not need you for the spiritual knowledge but you need them for the *Lakshmi* [money] all the time."[45] A longtime resident of New Vrindaban likewise suggested that Kirtanananda appeared to hold racist attitudes toward Indian people: "It seems like he was what you might call racist. He had a demeaning attitude towards the Indians. I don't know the how or what that was behind it, but it was there. Whatever it was, it was belittling."[46]

The loss of substantial numbers of community residents collecting donations on *sankirtan*, in combination with the loss of Indian financial support, pushed New Vrindaban into a severe financial crisis. Beginning in 1990, New Vrindaban's householders were required to support their families independently. Desperate for income, the community supported itself initially by selling off heavy construction equipment and its printing presses when Palace Press was forced to close. Thereafter, the community raised money by selling parcels of land. Due to a lack of funds, the community's extensive dairy operation began downsizing and in 1999, the community closed its day school. Financial pressures intensified further in 2000 when New Vrindaban was named as a defendant in a child abuse case filed in Dallas, Texas, by former students who attended ISKCON schools, including the one at New Vrindaban.[47]

The end of Kirtanananda's controversial interfaith experiment came with the demise of his leadership. Although rumors and specific allegations had persisted at least since 1986 about Kirtanananda's sexual behavior, it was not until a 1993 incident that a substantial portion of the community turned against his leadership.[48] On his return to West Virginia from the World Parliament of Religions centennial celebration in Chicago, Kirtanananda was observed by the driver having sexual relations with a young Malaysian adult male in the back of a Winnebago mobile home. When questioned about the encounter by two senior members of the community, Kirtanananda vaguely confessed to some unspecified spiritual weakness. Yet in a subsequent meeting with his disciples, he denied the allegations claiming a conspiracy against him. Tensions between Kirtanananda's supporters and his critics escalated to the point that some left the community, fearing for their safety.[49]

As Kirtanananda continued to deny any wrongdoing, a number of Prabhupada disciples defiantly returned to an ISKCON-style of worship, first at Prabhupada's Palace and later in the temple when two morning programs were held to accommodate the split between those continuing to favor interfaith and those determined to return to Prabhupada's program of Krishna Consciousness. Devotees turning against Kirtanananda and interfaith abandoned their Franciscan robes in favor of traditional *dhotis* and saris. Finally, after a petition to end interfaith and return to Prabhupada's standards of worship and practice was signed by sixty-seven community residents in March 1994, Kirtanananda terminated his radical experiment the following July at the urging of his godbrother Bhaktitirtha Swami. By then it was clear that Kirtanananda's authority and leadership had been forever destroyed at New Vrindaban.

Following his release from prison on June 16, 2004, Kirtanananda moved to his New York temple, Sri Sri Radha Murlidara, where a small number of committed disciples awaited him. Virtually all his other North American disciples had previously abandoned Kirtanananda. Upon his release from parole in November 2007, Kirtanananda traveled to India where he found a substantial number of disciples and followers who remained committed to his spiritual leadership. On March 7, 2008, Kirtanananda and his longtime friend Radha Vrindaban Chandra Swami left New York for India. He stated before leaving that he had no intention of returning to the United States as, "There is no sense in staying where I am not wanted." In India, he took up residence in temples managed by his disciples in Rishikesh and Ulhasnagar.[50]

Conclusion

Unlike many other Hindu and Buddhist groups that appealed to Westerners in North America, ISKCON was unique in that it sought to create a religious culture in keeping with the religious teachings and practices promoted by the movement's founder Prabhupada. The religious culture that ISKCON aspired to was in various ways oppositional and even hostile to conventional American culture, a fact that made the movement appealing to some counterculture youths in the 1960s and 1970s.[51] ISKCON devotees sought to reproduce Indian cultural practices and styles in matters of dress, diet, gender roles, marital relations, child rearing, and the like. ISKCON, therefore, was as much a cultural movement as a religious or spiritual one as it required members to radically alter their beliefs and lifestyles as part of the membership or conversion process.

Because culture is dynamic, religious organizations face the ongoing task of introducing innovations in order to better serve the needs of their members and to adjust to shifting environmental circumstances.[52] However innovation has limits as it runs the risk of compromising a religious organization's core teachings and its related religious culture. Core teachings specify individual and collective religious activities, form the basis of member commitment, and shape distinctive religious identities. Core teachings also establish social boundaries with the dominant culture, and with other religious groups, and build emotional and social ties between believers. Core teachings thus directly and indirectly define a religious culture and its distinctive religious capital. Religious capital represents the degree of mastery and attachment members gain from participating in a specific religious culture.[53] Retaining core teachings safeguards members' religious capital which, in turn, upholds the vitality of the religious organization.[54] Conversely, significant changes to a religious group's core teachings reduce members' religious capital and thereby: (1) decreases their mastery of the religion; (2) erodes their emotional ties to the group's religious culture; and, (3) threatens the certainty of their faith.[55] It was just such a pattern that transpired among New Vrindaban residents beginning in the mid-1980s after Kirtanananda implemented radical changes to the community's religious culture.

Interfaith proved a failure because it ultimately robbed New Vrindaban devotees of years of accumulated religious capital. By turning away from the community's traditional teachings and religious practices, Kirtanananda undermined the Krishna worldview so central to New Vrindaban's identity and mission. As their existing religious capital lost relevance to everyday life, many community members found reason to challenge Kirtanananda's leadership as well as their place within the community. In combination with his moral failings, interfaith signaled to Kirtanananda's followers that he had broken his connection with Prabhupada and the Gaudiya Vaisnava tradition in favor of establishing his own independent authority. For in crafting what can only be described as a new religion, Kirtanananda broke from the tradition's lineage (*parampara*) and thereby forfeited the religious authority he had inherited from Prabhupada and previous teachers (*acaryas*), which his disciples believe can be traced back in time to Krishna. The failure of Kirtanananda's leadership left New Vrindaban struggling to survive and the community faced years of decline.[56]

Although Kirtanananda's attempt to Americanize the community's religious beliefs and practices proved a failure, other Hindu- and Buddhist-inspired organizations have experienced greater success as many of the case studies in this volume demonstrate.[57] In large part this is because the primary focus of these groups is to teach spiritual practices rather than promote religious cultures that are alternatives to dominant American institutions and cultural forms. While perhaps overly critical in tone, A. L. Basham refers to the guru leaders of Hindu-inspired groups such as Transcendental Meditation as "streamlined swamis" because they teach yoga meditation without emphasizing the culture from which these practices are derived.[58] Spiritual practices and beliefs are instead fitted onto existing American identities.[59] By contrast, ISKCON's communities, including New Vrindaban, have traditionally sought to reproduce aspects of Vaisnava culture as central to their mission and identity as new religious communities.[60]

Notes

1. Eileen Barker, "Perspective: What Are We Studying? A Sociological Case for Keeping the 'Nova,'" *Nova Religio* 8, no. 1 (2004): 96; Lorne L. Dawson, *Comprehending Cults: The Sociology of New Religious Movements* (New York: Oxford University Press, 2006), 152–153; J. Gordon Melton, "Perspective: Toward a Definition of 'New Religion,'" *Nova Religio* 8, no. 1 (2004): 76; E. Burke Rochford Jr., "Social Building Blocks of New Religious Movements: Organization and Leadership," in *Teaching New Religious Movements*, ed. David G. Bromley, 159–185 (New York: Oxford University Press, 2007), 165–168.

2. Lorne L. Dawson, "Crises of Charismatic Legitimacy and Violent Behavior in New Religious Movements," in *Cults, Religion and Violence*, ed. David Bromley and J. Gordon Melton, 80–101 (New York: Cambridge University Press, 2002), 82–84; Roy Wallis, "The Social Construction of Charisma," *Social Compass* 29, no. 1 (1982): 25–39.

3. Dawson, "Crises of Charismatic Legitimacy," 82.

4. Max Weber, *Economy and Society*, vol. 1, trans. Guenther Roth and Claus Wittich (Berkeley: University of California Press, 1978), 241.

5. Weber, *Economy and Society*, 246.

6. Dawson, "Crises of Charismatic Legitimacy," 92–94.

7. Dawson, "Crises of Charismatic Legitimacy," 85; E. Burke Rochford Jr. and Kendra Bailey, "Almost Heaven: Leadership, Decline and the Transformation of New Vrindaban," *Nova Religio* 9, no 3 (2006): 6–23.

8. ISKCON's historical roots are traced to sixteenth-century Bengal, India. The Krishna Consciousness ISKCON's founder preached is part of the Krishna *bhakti* movement of Caitanya Mahaprabhu (1486–1533). A distinctive feature of the Gaudiya Vaisnava tradition to which ISKCON belongs is that Caitanya is believed

to be an incarnation of Krishna. The movement was brought to the United States in 1965 by A. C. Bhaktivedanta Swami Prabhupada (1896–1977). ISKCON was incorporated as a religious organization in 1966 in New York City and is dedicated to spreading Krishna Consciousness with communities and preaching centers throughout the world. The aim of the Krishna devotee is to become self-realized by chanting Hare Krishna and living an austere lifestyle that requires avoiding meat, intoxicants, illicit sex, and gambling. While young Westerners were drawn to the movement in the 1960s and 1970s, today the largest portion of ISKCON's North American and Western European membership is comprised of immigrant Indian-Hindus and their families. For a discussion of the movement's growth and development in North America, see Francine Daner, *The American Children of Krsna: A Study of the Hare Krsna Movement* (New York: Holt, Rinehart and Winston, 1974); Satsvarupa dasa Goswami, *Srila Prabhupada-Lilamrta* (Los Angeles: Bhaktivedanta Book Trust, 1993); Stillson Judah, *Hare Krishna and the Counterculture* (New York: Wiley, 1974); E. Burke Rochford Jr., *Hare Krishna in America* (New Brunswick, NJ: Rutgers University Press, 1985); E. Burke Rochford Jr., *Hare Krishna Transformed* (New York: New York University Press, 2007); Larry Shinn, *The Dark Lord: Cult Images and the Hare Krishnas in America* (Philadelphia: Westminster Press, 1987); Federico Squarcini and Eugenio Fizzotti, *Hare Krishna* (Salt Lake City, UT: Signature Books, 2004). For descriptions of New Vrindaban's history, see Hayagriva dasa [Howard Wheeler], *The Hare Krishna Explosion: The Birth of Krishna Consciousness in America (1966–1969)* (New Vrindaban, WV: Palace Press, 1985); Henry Doktorski, *The Great Experiment: Sacred Music and the Christianization of the New Vrindaban Hare Krishna Temple Liturgies* (unpublished manuscript, 2003); Henry Doktorski, *Gold, Guns and God: Swami Bhaktipada and the West Virginia Hare Krishnas* (unpublished manuscript, 2010); Rochford and Bailey, "Almost Heaven," 6–23; E. Burke Rochford Jr., "Knocking on Heaven's Door: Violence, Charisma and the Transformation of New Vrindaban," in *Violence and New Religious Movements*, ed. James Lewis, 275–292 (New York: Oxford University Press, 2011).

9. In 1979 Kirtanananda took on the honorific name "Bhaktipada," which translates as "he at whose feet the *bhaktas* [devotees] sit." For the sake of consistency, we use the name "Kirtanananda" throughout the chapter.

10. Rochford has been studying the Hare Krishna movement for thirty-five years. Beginning in 1993, he began researching New Vrindaban, conducting fieldwork and interviewing current and former members of the community. Formal interviews were completed with two of the community's leaders, twelve residents, and ten devotees who previously lived at New Vrindaban. In addition, informal interviews were completed with numerous devotees who at some point had lived at New Vrindaban but at the time of the interview were residing in communities affiliated with ISKCON. Doktorski was a member of the New Vrindaban community from 1978 to 1994 where he served in various capacities such as artist during the design and construction of Prabhupada's Palace of Gold, school teacher, fund-raiser, codirector of Palace Publishing, and minister of music. He was a disciple of Kirtanananda Swami and has completed a manuscript on the history of New Vrindaban, *Gold, Guns and God: Swami Bhaktipada and the West Virginia Hare Krishnas.*

11. Rochford interviewed Kirtanananda Swami in New York City in February 2007. Quotes from Kirtanananda that appear throughout the chapter are from that interview unless otherwise noted.

12. Kirtanananda explained that meeting Prabhupada "was destiny, as a fortune teller in Calcutta told me that soon after you return to the U.S. you will meet your guru."

13. In 1968 "Swamiji's" followers began calling him "Prabhupada" in recognition of his guru status. "Prabhupada" means one who is always found at Krishna's lotus feet and is a title signifying reverence and respect (see Satsvarupa dasa Goswami, *Srila Prabhupada Lilamrta*).

14. Daner, *American Children*, 80–81.

15. A few weeks earlier, Kirtanananda's friend Howard Wheeler was among the first group of followers Prabhupada initiated and received the name "Hayagriva." Kirtanananda missed the first round of initiations because he was in the psychiatric ward at New York's Bellevue Hospital at the time.

16. The Hare Krishna mantra is as follows: Hare Krishna Hare Krishna, Krishna Krishna, Hare Hare, Hare Rama Hare Rama, Rama Rama, Hare Hare. On average, it takes between ninety minutes and two hours to chant sixteen rounds of the mantra.

17. Prabhupada letter to Woomapati [Umapati], Sept. 5, 1967, in *Letters of Srila Prabhupada*, vol. 1. (Culver City, CA: Vaisnava Institute, 1987), 205.

18. Prabhupada acknowledged that while he had doubts he was not totally against Kirtanananda trying out his innovative preaching ideas. As he wrote to his disciple Damodar in October 1967, "Kirtannda [*sic*] suggested to me when he was here that the Americans do not like the robes [*dhotis*] & flag [*sikha*]. I told him personally if you think that Americans in great numbers will follow you, simply for not having robes & flag, I therefore advi[s]ed him to drop for a few days in London & test this theory" (Prabhupada letter, Oct. 13, 1967, in *Letters of Srila Prabhupada*, 227); interview 2007.

19. David Gold, *After the Absolute: Real Life Adventures with a Backwoods Buddha* (Lincoln, NE: Writers Press, 2002).

20. Personal communication to Doktorski, Oct. 8 and 9, 2003.

21. Interview, 2007.

22. The property in West Virginia was one of several attempts Prabhupada made to establish a farm community he planned to name "New Vrindaban." He had encouraged a number of his disciples, including Hayagriva, to acquire land for a country ashram. Prabhupada first suggested to his disciple Hansadutta that he acquire land to start a rural community. As he wrote to the president of the New York temple, "Hansadut[t]a will help me in establishing a New Vrindaban in the West" (Prabhupada letter to Brahmananda, Feb. 26, 1968, in *Letters of Srila Prabhupada*, 337). In July 1968, Prabhupada was encouraged when another of his disciples reported that a man in Florida wanted to use ten acres of his land to start a spiritual ashram. Again, Prabhupada replied that the property could be developed as New Vrindaban. Because neither of these projects materialized the West Virginia property became New Vrindaban after Hayagriva secured a lease.

23. Vrindaban (or Vrndavana) is a town in India located on the Yamuna River in present day Uttar Pradesh. The town and the surrounding area are

considered the location of Krishna's childhood and adolescence and it attracts thousands of pilgrims each year. For a discussion of ISKCON's presence in Vrindaban, India, see Charles Brooks, *The Hare Krishnas in India* (Princeton, NJ: Princeton University Press, 1989).

24. Quoted in Kuladri dasa, "Srila Bhaktipada's Vision," *Brijabasi Spirit* 6, no. 6 (Sept. 1979): 8–9.

25. Interview, 2007.

26. Before Prabhupada's Palace was completed and began attracting favorable media attention and large numbers of tourists, some ISKCON leaders remained critical of Kirtanananda's plan to build a residence for Prabhupada in the wilds of West Virginia. They were especially critical because the palace diverted the attention of New Vrindaban residents away from distributing Prabhupada's books (see Rochford, "Knocking on Heaven's Door").

27. *The Most Blessed Event: Sri Vyasa–Puja* (New Vrindaban publication, Sept. 4, 1978).

28. Interview, 2007.

29. Kirtanananda's consistent involvement with his followers stands in contrast to most charismatic leaders who manage their exposure in an effort to avoid revealing their human frailties. Too much exposure can delegitimize a leader and place the stability of the group at risk. Aware of such potential, charismatic leaders tend to err on the side of isolation from their followers. As this implies, charismatic leaders face the delicate task of maintaining an uneasy balance between exposure and isolation (see Dawson, "Crises of Charismatic Legitimacy," 86); interview, 2007.

30. "Community Census," *Brijabasi Spirit*, Nov. 31, 1974.

31. Dawson, "Crises of Charismatic Legitimacy," 85.

32. Ibid., 92–94.

30. Rochford, "Knocking on Heaven's Door."

33. After a three-week trial in 1991, Kirtanananda was convicted on the RICO and mail fraud counts, but the jury failed to reach a verdict on the murder charges. In July 1993, his convictions were overturned by the Court of Appeals and a second trial took place in 1996. After newly revealed incriminating testimony linking Kirtanananda to the murder of Stephen Bryant, Kirtanananda agreed to plead guilty to one count of federal racketeering and was sentenced to twenty years in prison. Because of failing health, Kirtanananda's sentence was reduced to twelve years and he was released from federal prison in 2004, having served eight years (see Doktorski, *Gold, Guns, and God*, and Rochford, "Knocking on Heaven's Door").

34. Interview, 2007.

35. Kirtanananda Swami Bhaktipada, "Our Purpose Is to Enlighten People" (from a conversation with Dr. Don Rich, a United Church of Christ minister, at New Vrindaban on July 23, 1986), *Brijabasi Spirit*, Nov. 1986, 2.

36. See Doktorski, *Great Experiment*.

37. Interview, 2007.

38. Interview with Doktorski, Aug. 6, 2003.

39. Rochford, "Knocking on Heaven's Door."

40. Interview, 2007.

41. Rochford and Bailey, "Almost Heaven," 12.

42. Quoted in Doktorski, *Great Experiment*, 226.

43. Interview, 2007.

44. Interview, 2007.

45. Ibid., 268.

46. Interview, 2007.

47. Rochford, *Hare Krishna Transformed*, 95–96.

48. Ibid., 36–38.

49. Doktorski, *Gold, Guns and God*; Rochford, "Knocking on Heaven's Door."

50. Hrishkesh dasa [Henry Doktorski], "Kirtanananda Leaves U.S., Moves to India Permanently," *Brijabasi Spirit*, Mar. 7, 2008, www.brijabasispirit.com/2008/03/07/kirtanananda-swami-leaves-us-moves-to-india-permanently/ (accessed Aug. 25, 2010).

51. Daner, *American Children*; Rochford, *Hare Krishna in America*.

52. Roger Finke, "Innovative Returns to Tradition: Using Core Teachings as the Foundation for Innovative Accommodation," *Journal for the Scientific Study of Religion* 43, no. 1 (2004): 23.

53. Rodney Stark and Roger Finke, *Acts of Faith: Explaining the Human Side of Religion* (Berkeley: University of California Press, 2000), 120.

54. Finke, "Innovative," 21.

55. Ibid., 21–23.

56. Rochford and Bailey, "Almost Heaven."

57. Also see Wendy Cadge, *Heartwood: The First Generation of Theravada Buddhism in America* (Chicago: Chicago University Press, 2005) on the Cambridge Insight Meditation Center; Harold Kasimow, John Keenan, and Linda Keenan, eds., *Beside Still Waters: Jews, Christians, and the Way of the Buddha* (Boston: Wisdom Publications, 2003); and Lola Williamson, *Transcendent in America* (New York: New York University Press, 2010) on Hindu-inspired meditation movements.

58. A. L. Basham, "Interview with A. L. Basham," in *Hare Krishna, Hare Krishna: Five Distinguished Scholars on the Hare Krishna Movement in the West*, ed. Steven J. Gelberg, 162–195 (New York: Grove Press, 1983), 166–167.

59. See Cadge, *Heartwood*; Kasimow, Keenan, and Keenan eds., *Beside Still Waters*; and Williamson, *Transcendent in America*.

60. As ISKCON became a more congregationally-based movement beginning in the 1980s, however, the goal of creating a religious culture based on the movement's Vaisnava beliefs was largely abandoned. See Rochford, *Hare Krishna Transformed*.

7

Neo-Advaita in America

Three Representative Teachers

Phillip Charles Lucas

Ramana Maharshi (1879–1950) was a prominent Indian exemplar of Advaita Vedanta during the first half of the twentieth century.[1] Advaita Vedanta philosophy asserts that *Brahman* or One Absolute Reality is infinite, formless, nondual awareness, and that the supreme goal of human life is the realization that *atman* or the inner self is not separate from Absolute Reality—"Atman is Brahman."[2] The Maharshi (great sage) was widely acclaimed in India as a *jñani*, a master who had realized complete identity with *Brahman*. He was seen by many of his followers as the spiritual descendent of the ninth-century sage Shankara and the Primal Sage, Dakshinamurthi.[3] Among his few written works is a translation of Shankara's most famous teaching, *Crest Jewel of Discrimination*, from Sanskrit into Tamil.[4]

Although the Maharshi gained widespread fame during his lifetime and seekers from around the world visited him, he never created an organization or movement in his name. In fact, he told Paramahansa Yogananda (1893–1952), during the latter's visit to the Maharshi's ashram in South India, that his path was not amenable to a mass movement or churchlike organization, but was an interior process for ripe souls only.[5] He maintained that authentic spiritual instruction must be tailored to the unique mentality and karmic disposition of the individual; he therefore eschewed lectures in front of large groups.[6]

Given this background, it is somewhat puzzling to observe the many contemporary teachers and organizations throughout the world that trace their lineage to, or at least claim a strong influence from, Ramana Maharshi. In North America alone, at least seventy-seven teachers and organizations acknowledge or claim the influence of the Maharshi, or of prominent followers of his such as H. W. L. Poonja (also known as Papaji, 1913–1997).[7] Many of these teachers fall into the category of Neo-Advaita, a term not always complimentary from a traditional Advaita perspective. What most of these teachers have in common is independence from established or traditional religious institutions or hierarchies. They are free agents, as it were, although a few have taken steps to create their own organizations, institutes, or teaching networks. Many Neo-Advaitin teachers have published books, such as Eckhart Tolle (b. 1948) and his best-selling *The Power of Now*.[8] Most have websites where viewers can read excerpts from their published works or get streaming audio or video of their *satsangs*. Some Neo-Advaitin teachers, such as Francis Lucille (b. 1944), A. Ramana (1929-2010), and Gangaji (b. 1942), have offered private counseling, weekend seminars, longer retreats, and various levels of teacher training.[9]

The extent to which North American Neo-Advaitin teachers use the Maharshi "brand" varies. In some teaching centers—for example, that of Nome (b. 1955) in Santa Cruz, California—large pictures of the Maharshi hang on walls and shrines honor him. Many Neo-Advaitin websites feature a picture of the Maharshi or a link to Sri Ramanasramam's Indian website.[10] Others offer an explicit statement that a particular teacher is in the "lineage" of Ramana Maharshi. Still others make only the claim to be in the Advaita tradition and some mention of the Maharshi's books or teachings.

This chapter explains how the Maharshi, in spite of his disinterest in founding a mass spiritual movement, appears to have inspired a host of spiritual teachers and organizations dedicated to spreading their own interpretation and expression of his Advaitic teaching and practice in North America.

Framing the "Ramana Effect"

Ramana Maharshi was born Venkataraman Iyer into a Brahmin family near Madurai, in Tamil Nadu, India, and was educated in a British middle school and an American missionary high school. During a crisis at age sixteen brought on by an intense fear of death, followers believe he experienced *sahaja samadhi* (permanent Self-realization). Within six weeks he had left his school and family and moved to Tiruvannamalai, also in Tamil Nadu, located at the base of Arunachala, a large, red-granite hill

Figure 7.1. Ramana Maharshi (Photo courtesy of Sri Ramanasramam)

Hindus traditionally believe to be a local manifestation of Lord Shiva. Young Venkataraman took up the life of a *sadhu* (renunciate ascetic) and remained on the mountain the next fifty-four years, living in several caves and temples before moving to the site of the present ashram, which is called Sri Ramanashramam.[11]

The Maharshi's apparent disinterest in founding a missionary movement contrasts with Swami Vivekananda (1863–1902), a follower of the Bengali saint Ramakrishna. Following a series of lectures, fund-raising events, and his address at the 1893 World's Parliament of Religions in Chicago, Vivekananda organized small groups in the United States that studied and promoted Vedanta. Swamis of the Ramakrishna Order, who came to the United States after Vivekananda's return to India, helped found a network of Vedanta Societies, which today number about thirty-five.[12]

The Maharshi's attitude toward missionary outreach was also in contradistinction to that of Swami Chinmayananda (1916–1993), the Indian Advaita teacher who founded the Chinmaya Mission in India in 1953 and expanded it into the Chinmaya Mission West in 1976. Today the mission, under the leadership of Chinmayananda's successor, Swami Tejomayananda, has 250 centers in India and more than 50 missions around the world. Tejomayananda travels to these centers and missions teaching and overseeing outreach activities. The mission publishes classical Advaita scriptures and Sanskrit lessons, and it sponsors classes, seminars, retreats, and service projects. Chinmaya Mission self-consciously "makes available the ageless wisdom of Vedanta, the knowledge of the one Reality, and provides the tools to realize that wisdom in one's life."[13]

Although an ashram grew up around Ramana Maharshi in the last half of his life in Tiruvannamalai, most biographers indicate that he remained detached from the community's day-to-day administration, except for his practice of rising early to chop vegetables and help prepare food for the day's visitors. Organizational and managerial duties were left to others, who consulted him only when conflicts arose. Although he had no formal university training, after his enlightenment the Maharshi read widely in Vedanta scriptures in Tamil, Malayalam, Telugu, and Sanskrit, and even translated traditional Advaita texts from Sanskrit to Tamil and wrote introductions to them.[14] On several occasions he agreed to write short expositions of his spiritual teaching. The bulk of his teachings, however, appeared as transcriptions of his oral responses to various questioners who appeared at the ashram over some twenty-five years. The testimony of most devotees was that the Maharshi's most profound teaching occurred in silence and was transmitted through his presence.[15]

A useful way of understanding what I have termed the "Ramana effect" is to frame it within theories that examine how religious traditions move across diverse linguistic and cultural settings in the era of globalization. Thomas Csordas identifies two factors necessary for a tradition of rituals and beliefs to move successfully into a new cultural setting. The first is *portable practice*, rites or practices "that can be easily learned, require relatively little esoteric knowledge or paraphernalia, are not held as proprietary or necessarily linked to a specific cultural context, and can be performed without commitment to an elaborate ideological or institutional apparatus."[16] The second is *transposable message*, a term Csordas prefers over transmissibility or transferability in part because it "includes the connotations of being susceptible to being transformed or reordered without being denatured, as well as the valuable musical metaphor of being performable in a different key."[17] The most significant elements in this second factor are the transformability and universality of the teaching.

The Maharshi's influence is at least partly attributable to both the portability of his spiritual method and to the universality and transformability of his teaching. His basic method, called "self-inquiry," consists of an introversion of the mind grounded in the question, "Who am I?" Seekers attempt to follow this inquiry with single-pointed focus until they experience the deeper root of the "I-thought," which purports to dissolve the conventional ego-self in cosmic awareness of *Brahman*, the One Absolute Reality. As one Ramana devotee explained, "The fruit of self-inquiry is the realization that the Self is all, and that there is nothing else."[18] The method requires no paraphernalia and no esoteric practices, although practices of *pranayama* (breath control) and *japa* (the repetition of mantras) are permitted if found to be efficacious. Although the Maharshi was inscribed in a Vedantic culture/tradition, he did not require seekers to adopt it in order to practice self-inquiry. He also did not demand commitment to an institution or ideology, but only to the practice itself. As we will see, Neo-Advaitin teachers in North America use variations on this basic practice, and present it without its traditional Advaitic framing.

The Maharshi's teaching is universal in the sense that teachers have appeared in all the major world religions, including Islam, Christianity, Judaism, Buddhism, Sikhism, and Hinduism, teaching spiritual practices designed to bring followers into an intimate and immediate experience of unity with Divine Reality. Although these practices are often controversial and were more or less emphasized depending on historical, cultural, and sectarian factors, their presence provides seekers with a bridge from their own religious traditions to Advaita spirituality. The Maharshi made no demands that seekers leave behind their primary religious affiliations and often quoted Jewish and Christian scriptures to Westerners. By deemphasizing specifically Advaitic elements (that is, traditional language, philosophy, and theology) of their teachings and repackaging them within the psychologized thought-world of contemporary North Americans, Neo-Advaitin teachers are able to transform Maharshi's Advaitin teaching into a species of self-help accessible to a sizable number of adherents.

Csordas also examines the *means* by which religious traditions travel to other cultural settings in the era of globalization. The first of these, traditional *missionization*, does not really apply in the case of the Maharshi for reasons cited earlier: he did not create an organization designed to spread his teachings, and he did not send disciples into the world.[19]

The second means, *migration* of peoples, certainly has some salience in the Maharshi's case, especially given the rapid increase of South Asians in the population of North America since the liberalized changes in U.S. immigration policy beginning in 1965. South Asians constitute a segment of North American followers of Neo-Advaitin teachers, although exact numbers are difficult to ascertain. They also constitute a population of individual Ramana Maharshi devotees who practice self-inquiry in private and who are loosely affiliated with other devotees through *satsangs* and websites.

The third means, *mobility* of individuals in the era of globalization, also has played a part in the diffusion of Advaitic spirituality in the West.[20] During the late twentieth and early twenty-first centuries, many thousands of North Americans visited Sri Ramanasramam ashram in South India or listened to Advaitin teachers such as Papaji or Nisargadatta Maharaj (1897–1981) in other parts of India. Pilgrims to Tiruvannamalai today can attend retreats and *satsangs* during the winter season given by both traditional Advaitin and Neo-Advaitin teachers from around the world. Thus a global Neo-Advaitin subculture has emerged wherein teachers and students circulate freely among Europe, North America, India, Israel, Australia, New Zealand, Japan, and Korea. This global network has arguably fostered greater awareness of, and appreciation for, the Maharshi's tradition of Advaita Vedanta.

Csordas's final factor, *mediatization*, has perhaps been the most important element in the growing popularity of Advaitic-based modes of spiritual practice and teaching.[21] The Internet, for example, provides sophisticated representations of Neo-Advaitin teachers, teachings, and organizations. These representations include streaming audio and video of *satsangs*, transcripts of teaching discourses, articles and book chapters, and links to websites of other Neo-Advaitin teachers. In one instance, Neo-Advaitin teacher Eckhart Tolle answered questions from listeners around the world on a live webcast viewed by more than 11 million people.[22] Seekers can order DVDs, books, magazines, and teacher-training materials from teachers' websites, as well as find information on public *satsangs* or workshops.

The Neo-Advaitin phenomenon can also be viewed in historical perspective. As the research of historians Leigh Schmidt and Catherine Albanese has skillfully demonstrated, the United States has a long tradition of what Schmidt terms "religious liberalism."[23] This tradition of American spirituality—beginning with the Transcendentalists and continuing in Quakers, Unitarians, Vedantists, Western Buddhists and Sufis, Baha'is, Spiritualists, New Thought churches, New Agers, and Wade Clark Roof's "Generation of Seekers"—shares certain characteristics Harvard-educated metaphysician Horatio Dresser (1866-1954) first identified. These include: (1) aspiration to mystical experience or deepened religious feeling; (2) valorization of silence, solitude, and serene meditation; (3) sense of the immanence of the Divine Reality in persons and in nature; (4) cosmopolitan appreciation of religious variety as well as the deeper unity of the world's spiritual traditions; (5) engaged spirituality, meaning serious participation in progressive movements to reform society and to address specific injustices in the world; and (6) valorization of creative self-expression, self-empowerment, and an open-ended search for spiritual fulfillment.[24] I submit that the Neo-Advaitin movement fits very well within, and has indeed been shaped in some ways by, this long-standing tradition of American liberal spirituality.

Neo-Advaita in North America

To support these arguments, the following section examines representative examples of Neo-Advaitin teachers who have traced their spiritual lineage to Ramana Maharshi to demonstrate that, while no evidence suggests that he ever intended to do so, the Maharshi inspired a new wave of spiritual teachers and organizations in North America. These teachers and organizations are having a significant effect on the larger culture of liberal American spirituality, particularly with regard to Neo-Advaita's eclecticism, focus on interior transformation, privileging of experiential over conceptual dimensions of religion, mistrust of conventional religious organizations, ideal of the divinized human, and vision of human unity and solidarity across religious as well as national and ethnic boundaries.

Maharshi Devotees in North America

Before examining representative teachers, however, we should note a long-standing presence of loosely organized Ramana Maharshi devotees in North America. The Maharshi first came to the West's attention through publication of Paul Brunton's work, *A Search in Secret India*, in the 1930s. This widely read book detailed the English journalist's exploration of India in search of an authentic yogi.[25] After meetings with various yogis, fakirs, and wonderworkers, Brunton (1898–1981) visited the Maharshi's ashram in Tiruvannamalai. He reported a profound experience of transcendent awareness during his time at the ashram and wrote movingly of this experience. *A Search in Secret India* became a perennial bestseller in Western spiritual circles and prompted a small but influential number of Westerners to visit the Maharshi in India. One of these was the author W. Somerset Maugham, who referenced the Maharshi (using a pseudonym) in his novel *The Razor's Edge* (1944). Although some of these seekers wrote of their experiences, none returned to the

West with a plan to found an organization dedicated to spreading of the Maharshi's teachings.

Arthur Osborne (1906–1970), a British-born editor of *The Mountain Path*, an ashram publication, encouraged U.S. resident Bhagawat Singh, during Singh's visit to India in the early 1960s, to introduce the Maharshi's teachings to Western seekers. Singh organized a weekly meeting in 1965 at the American Buddhist Society in Manhattan, and later rented space that in December 1966 became Arunachala Ashrama. The ashram's mission was to transmit the teachings of the Maharshi through lectures, publications, and rituals. Interest in the ashram's activities grew slowly but steadily. Members were content to draw seekers by word of mouth without much missionary outreach. As Dennis Hartel, a resident during this period remembered, "The Maharshi never told us to go out and spread his teachings to the world, but rather to go inward and realize their truth. . . . For many devotees of the Maharshi in North America their spiritual aspirations are a private affair. They shun organizations."[26] The New York ashram moved to Queens in 1987 and now offers retreats, *puja*s (devotional worship to an image of the Maharshi), and meditation sessions at its residence in Jamaica Estates. The center distributes a quarterly newsletter, books, and video and audio CDs, many of which are published at Sri Ramanasramam in India. Although the number of residents is small, the ashram's sponsored events attract many attendees throughout the year.

A second ashram was founded in 1972 on acreage in the Annapolis Valley in Nova Scotia. The ashram built a temple, Sri Arunachala Ramana Mandiram, for daily chanting and meditation sessions, and offered extended retreats for Ramana devotees. Today it offers a summer camp for children and provides food and lodging for its guests without charge—similar to the services provided by the Tiruvannamalai ashram.[27]

Other Ramana devotees have organized periodic *satsang*s and *puja*s throughout North America over the past twenty years. At present, these *satsang*s are found in more than fourteen cities in the United States and Canada. The large wave of Indian immigration to North America in recent years—especially from South India—has spurred a greater interest in devotional practices at these events, and many are now held at the homes of Indian émigrés.[28] This subsection of the Maharshi's North American influence remains relatively small and has no organized administration or designated gurus or teachers. Periodically, these devotees sponsor small-scale tours around the United States by elderly Indian disciples who lived with the Maharshi during his lifetime.

Eckhart Tolle

Probably the most significant Neo-Advaitin teacher in North America is Eckhart Tolle, a native of Germany. Tolle attended the University of London, where he studied literature, languages, and philosophy. At age twenty-nine, he experienced a deep depression that culminated in a radical shift in his awareness:

> The fear, anxiety and heaviness of depression were becoming so intense, it was almost unbearable. . . . And the thought came into my head, "I can't live with myself any longer." That thought kept repeating itself again and again. And then suddenly there was a "standing back" from the thought and looking at that thought. . . . "If I cannot live with myself, who is that self that I cannot live with? Who am I? Am I one—or two?" . . . At that moment, a dis-identification happened. . . . "I" consciousness withdrew from its identification with the self, the mind-made fictitious entity . . . and its story. And the fictitious entity collapsed completely in that moment. . . . What remained was a single sense of presence . . . which is pure consciousness prior to identification with form. . . . There was no longer a "me" entity.[29]

This narrative of awakening parallels in some ways the reported awakening of Ramana Maharshi, which occurred when he was sixteen and was suddenly gripped by an intense fear of death. He decided to simulate his own physical death by assuming the posture of a corpse while reflecting on the meaning of the death experience. Suddenly his identity shifted from the ego-mind and physical body to the Absolute Self or *Brahman*.[30] Like the Maharshi, Tolle claimed that his transformation in awareness was permanent, although (as with the Maharshi) it required some ten years to "ripen." In an interview with John Parker, Tolle acknowledged the influence of the Maharshi on his present self-understanding:

> And there are other teachers . . . that I feel a strong connection to. One is Krishnamurti and the other is Ramana Maharshi. I feel a deep link. And I feel actually that the work I do is a coming together of the teaching "stream," if you want to call it that, of Krishnamurti and Ramana Maharshi. . . . It is the heart of Ramana Maharshi, and Krishnamurti's ability to

see the false, as such and point out how it works. . . . I feel completely at One with them. And it is a continuation of the teaching.[31]

Tolle worked in London with individuals and small groups as a counselor and spiritual teacher, then moved to Berkeley, California, and ultimately Vancouver, British Columbia, in the mid-1990s. While in Berkeley, he wrote *The Power of Now*, which outlined his core message:

> Enlightenment is simply your natural state of "felt" oneness with Being. . . . When you are present, when your attention is fully and intensely in the Now, Being can be felt, but it can never be understood mentally. To regain awareness of Being and to abide in the state of "feeling-realization" is enlightenment.[32]

Tolle asserts that this experience is accessible to each person in the present moment, and what prevents its realization is conditioned identification with the body, emotions, and mind. When one is able to observe the workings of the body, emotions, and mind without identification, one's "whole sense of identity shifts from being the thought or the emotion to being the 'observing presence.' "[33]

The Power of Now was published in North America in Vancouver and circulated mainly by word of mouth during the 1990s. In December 2002 Oprah Winfrey (b. 1954) featured it on her "Oprah's Favorite Things" show, claiming it had helped her get through her distress after the events of September 11, 2001. This publicity and the work's selection for Oprah's book club pushed the book to number one on the *New York Times* best-sellers list in Advice, How-To, and Miscellaneous books. The work is currently translated into thirty-two languages. Following an appearance on *Oprah and Friends*, Tolle accepted an invitation from Winfrey to coteach a class in spring 2008 on her XM satellite radio channel. Using the Internet link Skype over ten weeks, Tolle and Winfrey discussed his second book, *A New Earth*, and answered questions live from people around the world. The class grew from .5 million students to 11 million in three weeks. In May 2008, *A New Earth* and *The Power of Now* were numbers one and two on the *New York Times* best-sellers list in Advice, How-To, and Miscellaneous books.[34]

In congruence with the liberal American religious tradition mentioned earlier, Tolle's articulation of Advaita avoids traditional religious language, is nonsectarian, practical, and speaks to both churched and unchurched populations. He makes clear that "spirituality" is not the same as "religion," and that the spiritual experiences to which he points are found within many traditions, including Buddhism and Christianity. New Age writer Deepak Chopra characterized Tolle as "one who is not aligned with any particular religion or doctrine or guru, one who is able to do what all the great masters have done: show us, in simple and clear language, that the . . . truth . . . is within us."[35]

In *A New Earth* Tolle takes a more millennial or New Age tone, and claims that a planetary "transformation of consciousness is arising to a large extent outside of the structures of the existing institutionalized religions."[36] In his vision of the future, humanity is "coming to the end not only of mythologies but also of ideologies and belief systems."[37] "At the heart of the new consciousness," he observes, "lies the transcendence of thought, the newfound ability of . . . realizing a dimension with yourself that is infinitely more vast than thought."[38] Tolle claims that "millions are now ready to awaken because spiritual awakening is not an option anymore, but a necessity if humanity and the planet are to survive."[39]

Tolle's adaptation of traditional Advaita teaching concerning spiritual awakening to the cultural landscape of contemporary North America illustrates, to use Csordas's formulation, the *transposability* of the Maharshi's teaching. Tolle wraps his Advaita core message not only in apocalyptic or millennial language familiar to contemporary Christians and New Agers, but also in the therapeutic, self-help language of late modern Americans. His books address issues such as emotional suffering, addiction, dysfunctional relationships, ecological devastation, and consumerism. Whether this approach is an authentic reflection of Ramana Maharshi's Advaitic teaching—a matter of some dispute—it is bringing some of his basic insights to a *mass* audience in North America for the first time.

Gangaji

While Tolle has avoided many of the trappings of the guru persona, other Neo-Advaitins have taken on the traditional role of guru or enlightened master. A representative of this stance is Gangaji, a disciple of Papaji (H. W. L. Poonja), who was one of Ramana Maharshi's most influential followers in India. Born Antoinette Roberson, Gangaji grew up in 1950s Mississippi and taught school in Memphis. She relocated to San Francisco in the 1970s and began a search for spiritual enlightenment. Eventually she moved to Bolinas in coastal Marin County and married her second husband, Eli Jaxon-Bear. The couple began a Tibetan *dharma* center in their home under the direction of Tibetan teacher Kalu

Figure 7.2. Gangaji (Photo courtesy of Gangaji Foundation)

Rinpoche (1905–1989). She also participated in the 1981 protest at Diablo Canyon Nuclear Plant in San Luis Obispo County and spent time in jail where she participated in workshops, cocounseling, and Daoist exercises with fellow protesters. After a period of growing disenchantment with the San Francisco Bay Area's numerous spiritual groups, Gangaji and Jaxon-Bear moved to Mill Valley and opened an alternative health clinic in downtown San Francisco that offered acupuncture and neurolinguistic programming therapy. In 1990, Gangaji followed her husband to India, where she met Papaji and reported experiencing a deep awakening to her true spiritual nature.[40] Like several other Neo-Advaitin teachers, she was asked by Papaji to teach spiritual awakening.[41]

Gangaji began meeting with individuals for private sessions but soon decided that her teaching was better transmitted in *satsangs*:

> At first, I met with people individually who felt they needed it, but I was not satisfied with these meetings. Really what they wanted was better expressed in the group. Somehow

when they asked for an individual meeting it was as if they had an individual problem that was different from the individuals' problems in the group, and I found that not to be true. . . . I discovered that it does not have to be a personal relationship, that the problems that people speak of in *satsang* everyone can identify with. . . . It is the same problem; it is the problem of running away from the abyss or void or emptiness or nothingness. Of course the strategies, the attempts at solutions are infinite, and that's the individuality. But if you get at the core problem, it's always the same. So I stopped the individual meetings very quickly.[42]

Gangaji soon attracted a loyal following of students who see her as a guru or realized master. In 1993, volunteers in Boulder, Colorado, founded the Gangaji Foundation, which supports her teaching mission by sponsoring workshops, retreats, lectures, and the publication of her books and tapes. Followers in more than 40 U.S. cities and 100 cities around the world hold *satsangs* at their homes or in rented venues that feature video replays of live *satsangs* given by Gangaji since the early 1990s. A majority of these *satsangs* occurs in California, Oregon—where her foundation is headquartered—and Washington state, as well as in Germany, Canada, the United Kingdom, and Australia.[43]

Gangaji's website makes her connection with Ramana Maharshi very clear. Under "The Lineage," a picture of the Maharshi appears with a short synopsis of his life and teachings. Under that section is a picture of H. W. L. Poonja with a short biography, and on a related page is a picture and biography of Gangaji, "About Gangaji." In this section's discussion of her relationship to Poonja, the following paragraph appears:

Today, Gangaji travels the world speaking to seekers from all walks of life. A teacher and author, she shares her direct experience of the essential message she received from Poonjaji and offers it to all who want to discover true and lasting fulfillment. Through her life and words, she powerfully articulates how it is really possible to discover the truth of who you are and to be true to that discovery.[44]

The website offers various books and DVDs related to the life and teachings of the Maharshi. Gangaji has also visited Ramanashram in Tiruvannamalai with her students.

Gangaji's usual *satsang* begins with a period of silent meditation, followed by a question-and-answer session with students, who often come up on the stage and enter into an intimate dialogue with her. This method of *satsang*, we should note, is not unique to Gangaji in Neo-Advaitin circles. I have witnessed at least ten Neo-Advaitin teachers using this method in India and in North America. Many of my interviewees from Neo-Advaitin circles have indicated that many Osho (1931-1990) disciples became followers of Papaji after Osho's death. The method could have originated in *satsang* encounters and dialogues common in the Osho movement.[45] The method seems well suited to Western seekers, who often expect personal attention and intimacy from their spiritual teachers. It also reflects the public confessional approach found on daytime talk shows such as *Oprah* and *Dr. Phil*.

Gangaji's written works are direct, informal, and accessible to the unchurched seeker of the late twentieth and early twenty-first centuries. Like Ramana Maharshi, she asserts that the fundamental question of human existence is "Who am I?" Through the method of self-inquiry:

> the momentum and the power of the question direct the search for true Self. . . . When the question, Who? is followed. . . all the way back to its source, there is a huge, astounding realization: there is no entity here at all! There is only the indefinable, boundless recognition of oneself as the fullness of being found everywhere in everything. . . . You are endless. There is no bottom to you, no boundary to you. Any idea about yourself appears in the fullness and will disappear back into it. You are awareness, and awareness is consciousness, full beyond measure.[46]

Much of her method involves recognition that the endless narratives the ego creates about itself are fictions, pointing to nothing actually real: "The world is not as you think it is. You are not who you think you are. I am not who you think me to be. Your thoughts about the world, yourself, or me are based on perceptions. Whether they are inner or outer perceptions, they are limited."[47] This insight is classic Advaita and has its roots in the Upanishads and the teaching of the great Advaita sage, Shankara. It also resonates with various schools of Buddhist philosophy and reflects Gangaji's exposure to Buddhist teachings while in the San Francisco Bay Area.

Gangaji asserts that as identification with ephemeral thoughts, emotions, and bodily sensations drops away, and mental activity winds down, a crack opens in conditioned perception, and a state of silence appears within which recognizing one's deepest spiritual identity, beyond definition, thought, or words is possible. For Gangaji, as for most Neo-Advaitins, this supreme identity is eternal, permanent, and unaffected by the shadowy dreams of the ego. "The moment of recognizing what cannot be thought is the moment of recognizing who you are. It is a moment of the mind's surrender to silence. The only obstacle to realizing the truth of who you are is thinking who you are. It is really that simple."[48]

Gangaji's teachings, like those of Tolle, synthesize a lifetime of Western transpersonal therapies and spiritual practices with the basic insights of Advaitic spirituality. They demonstrate, in Csordas's formulation, the *transposability* of the Maharshi's teaching and the ease with which the teaching can be lifted out of its traditional Indian cultural setting and taken into other cultural ecologies. Gangaji does not require her students to accept all facets of Advaitic philosophy, nor does she ask them to participate in Hindu devotional practices and *puja*s. Her use of the Maharshi's method of self-inquiry also resonates with Csordas's theory of *portable practice* by showing how easily this meditative practice can be taken from its specifically Advaitic framework and adapted to contemporary Westerner seekers and their eclectic use of traditional spiritual methods. Thus, one can argue that the Maharshi's essential teaching and practice is preserved, but in a way that does not overly burden those inscribed with a Western cultural and religious outlook. Finally, her teachings fit well within the American liberal religious stream with their focus on interior awakening, open-ended spiritual seeking, cosmopolitan appreciation of the unity of the world's spiritual traditions, and the power of silence, solitude, and meditation.

Arunachala Ramana

A final example of Ramana Maharshi's influence is the American-born Neo-Advaitin teacher Arunachala Ramana (1929–2010). Born Dee Wayne Trammell in El Paso, Texas, A. Ramana grew up in a conservative Christian environment in East Texas.[49] Finding this early exposure to religion self-limiting and unsuited to his more esoteric spiritual inclinations, Trammell explored the teachings of Edgar Cayce (1877–1945) and Unity School of Christianity founders Charles (1854–1948) and Myrtle (1845–1931) Fillmore. After attending the Unity Institute in Lee's Summit, Missouri, and serving as an associate Unity minister, he decided Unity did not offer an effective method of meditation for the spiritual awakening he was seeking.[50] After leaving the Unity community in the late 1960s, Trammell lived in California and worked as co-owner of a franchised self-improvement school related to the teachings of Napoleon

Figure 7.3. Arunachala Ramana (Photo courtesy of AHAM, the Association of Happiness for All Mankind)

Hill (1883–1970), author of *Think and Grow Rich*. He studied esoteric Christianity and experienced his "final spiritual enlightenment" in 1973 "by the grace of Sri Bhagavan Ramana." Claiming the awakening of "an enlightened 'mastermind' " between Jesus, Sri Bhagavan Ramana, and himself, in 1978 he founded the Association of Happiness for All Mankind (AHAM), a nonprofit spiritual education organization.[51]

AHAM's stated mission is the "dissemination of Self-Inquiry, the Consciousness Transforming Process for realizing and abiding in the true Self, which is not different from conscious communion with Real God."[52] But before one can practice self-inquiry effectively, one must learn to apply the "Law of Conscious Assumption" so that one can complete all that is left unfinished in one's life. To teach how to complete one's unfinished business, A. Ramana developed the Power of Awareness Training (POA) as part of the more advanced Intensive Self-Inquiry Training. Using language adapted from New Thought and Unity, POA gave instructions in employing one's "inherent creative Power" to bring about suitable conditions in one's professional life, personal relationships, health, and family duties.[53] POA was later reframed as AHAM's "Completion Process," which is currently offered in the Intensive Self-Inquiry Training. The Completion Process "awakens one to the experience of completion now with regard to any area or aspect of one's life that he/ she feels is distracting from or impeding their spiritual awakening."[54] Clearly, A. Ramana's strategy was to combine New Thought teachings of self-empowerment and positive thinking with Ramana Maharshi's method of self-inquiry. The result is that the student can fulfill "worldly obligations and responsibilities and at the same time maintain a spiritual practice, without confusion or conflict between these opposing goals."[55]

Ramana's combination of pragmatism, self-empowerment, and advanced meditative practice resonates with Csordas's concept of *transposable message*, which allows a teaching or method to move into a new cultural milieu by synergizing currents from that culture and transforming a teaching so that it meets the needs of individuals in a specific cultural space without losing its original "nature." In this sense, one might say that A. Ramana was simply playing the Advaitic melody in a different key, with some variations based on his familiarity with metaphysical religious currents in North America.[56]

AHAM's teaching incorporates an additional dimension that amplifies its cultural continuity with North America, an Advaitic interpretation of the Christian Bible and the message of Christ. The organization represents Jesus as a great sage, a "spiritually enlightened being," who of necessity communicated the "Truth of Being" in parables, analogies, and allegories. Because later "unenlightened" theologians interpreted these symbolic communications literally, it became necessary to reinterpret Christian scriptures using the direct insights of an "Awakened master" such as A. Ramana. Like the Fillmores before him, A. Ramana advanced a "metaphysical" interpretation of Gospel texts. These interpretations consistently translated conventional Christian doctrines, such as being "born again" or the divine nature of Christ, into Advaitic teachings concerning awakening to the "One Reality, or true Self." In A. Ramana's vision of Christianity, Jesus became a human who awakened to his true Self—"like the Buddha before him and Bhagavan Sri Ramana more recently"—and attempted to teach this awakening to his disciples. To a remarkable degree, AHAM has woven together the three major strands of A. Ramana's spiritual biography—Christianity, Unity, and Ramana Maharshi—and created a syncretistic teaching well-adapted to the spiritual sensibilities of its North American audience.[57]

In contrast to Tolle or Gangaji, A. Ramana's appropriation of the Maharshi's "lineage" was much more direct and explicit. This extended from his name, which combines both Ramana and the title of Shiva's sacred mountain, to his choice of ashram sites. Although AHAM is headquartered at its forty-acre Meditation Retreat and Spiritual Training Center near Asheboro, North Carolina, A. Ramana in the last decade of his life spent November through February each year at Arunachala Ramana AHAM Ashram just outside Tiruvannamalai. Attendees at his meditation retreats in India mimicked the pattern of practices at Sri Ramanasramam. These included *pradakshina* (worshipful circumambulation) of Arunachala (especially on evenings of the full moon), meditation in two caves that the Maharshi once occupied, circling the Maharshi's *samadhi* (tomb) at Sri Ramanshram, and several other rites.[58]

A. Ramana claimed that his authority to share the Maharshi's "Conscious Process of Self-Inquiry" could be traced to a 1978 vision in which the Maharshi appeared in his subtle form to A. Ramana in deep meditation. During this visit, A. Ramana was telepathically given the idea and vision for AHAM, including the "unmistakable communication that he was to 'take this teaching to all the world.'"[59] A. Ramana understood from this encounter that it was his mission to present the Maharshi and his teaching to peoples of "all religions and cultures," so that they might "directly awaken to their own natural and true state of inner Peace, Freedom, Love and Happiness." From that day forward, A. Ramana dedicated his life to fulfilling this "commission" through workshops, retreats, and publication of books, pamphlets, and teaching manuals.[60]

A. Ramana's appropriation of the Maharshi's teaching included assertion of a traditional lineage linked directly to the great sage (a matter of some controversy for traditional Advaita followers), wholesale use of the Maharshi's writings and talks, and the claim to be Self-realized himself. In this sense, A. Ramana adopted some of the conventional tropes of a traditional guru in the Advaitic tradition, including a monastic lifestyle, close personal contact with students (including retreat and seminar attendees),[61] careful instruction according to a preset system of spiritual unfoldment, traditional devotional practices, pilgrimage to holy places, and a close-knit inner circle of followers and administrators. Interestingly, A. Ramana's strategy of identification with, and wholesale appropriation of, the Maharshi's teaching and transmission did not result in the same appeal to a mass audience as seen with Tolle and Gangaji. His adoption of a more traditional and demanding spiritual training and practice probably limited his appeal to Western spiritual seekers, who are often drawn more to teachings that promise immediate enlightenment experiences and that are shorn of traditional Hindu language, devotions, and organizational hierarchies.

Conclusion

This chapter interprets the growing influence of Ramana Maharshi on contemporary currents of American spirituality. That this long-deceased Hindu teacher has any influence at all is remarkable, given the fact that he started no organization, commissioned no missionaries, and showed no apparent interest in a mass movement in his name. Csordas's theoretical model for understanding the factors that allow for a successful transmission of a tradition's beliefs and practices into diverse cultural settings in the era of globalization proves helpful for understanding the "Ramana Effect."

First, Ramana's method of self-inquiry fits within Csordas's concept of *portable practice*. The method is simple, direct, requires no special knowledge or accoutrements, is not overtly tied to any particular cultural setting, and can be taught by numerous Neo-Advaitin teachers in the American context since no proprietary interest is exercised by a particular organization or "owner." Teachers can adapt the practice to their own teaching styles and promise to bring persons to an experience of their true nature or original identity as the Absolute Reality behind phenomenal appearances.

The Maharshi's teaching also fits within Csordas's second factor, *transposable message*, in that it has a universality and transformability that allows it to be transmitted in Western religious discourses or, alternatively, without any religious discourses at all. Authors such as Eckhart Tolle articulate this teaching using the discourses of New Age millennialism, Zen, self-empowerment and self-therapy, as well as the Jewish and Christian traditions. Gangaji transmits her teaching in the same self-empowerment and self-therapy discourses and also within a New Age spirituality frame, which foregrounds inner transformation through self-transcendence and a centering awareness that goes beyond conventional modes of thinking. One can read Tolle's or Gangaji's writings and *satsangs* and almost never see the traditional language or cultural frames of Advaita Vedanta. In A. Ramana's version of the Maharshi's teaching, a more conscious attempt is made to identify with Advaitic language and traditions, while at the same time finding common ground with America's tradition of liberal, metaphysical religion. The Maharshi embodied this transcendence of conventional religious identities in his acceptance of students from all religious backgrounds, his disinterest in converting Westerners away from their religious commitments, and his occasional use of biblical quotations in his teaching discourses.

Csordas's examination of the *means* by which religious traditions travel to diverse cultural settings also provides insights into the Ramana Effect. The increased *migration* of South Asians to the United States has brought people with ties to the Maharshi tradition into the North American religious milieu and provided a growing clientele for Advaitic spirituality and its various teachers. The *mobility* of individuals in the globalizing conditions of the contemporary era has allowed thousands of Americans to travel throughout a Neo-Advaitin subculture stretching from British Columbia to Nova Scotia, from California to North Carolina, from Australia to New Zealand, and from Western Europe to South Asia. These seekers can listen to a diverse cohort of Neo-Advaitin and Advaitin teachers at seminars, workshops, retreats, and *satsangs* on five continents. The center of gravity for this subculture appears to be Tiruvannamalai, India, where the Maharshi's ashram still hosts seekers by the thousands each year. Around this main ashram is a diverse array of teachers and gurus such as A. Ramana, who come to this midsize town in Tamil Nadu during the winter season to offer their variations on traditional Advaitic spirituality.

Finally, Csordas's factor of *mediatization* has arguably helped accelerate the visibility and accessibility of Advaita-based modes of spiritual practice and teaching in America. Most Neo-Advaitin teachers have their own websites and publishing enterprises, which provide students access to *satsangs* through video and audio streaming as well as the opportunity to order books and other publications. Neo-Advaitin teachers have rapidly employed these electronic media to reach a steadily growing audience of students and seekers. Perhaps the most influential (to date) of these media transmissions has been Tolle's 10-episode webcast in 2008 with Oprah Winfrey that garnered an estimated international audience of 11 million.

The teaching of Ramana Maharshi and his Neo-Advaitin interpreters fits well within a longstanding tradition of liberal religion in America both Leigh Schmidt and Catherine Albanese identified, particularly with its emphasis on meditative solitude, its aspiration to mystical experience, its belief in the deeper unity of the world's spiritual traditions, and its valorization of a serious and open-ended search for spiritual fulfillment.

Notes

Author's note: An earlier version of chapter 7 was originally published in *Nova Religio* 15, no. 2 (Nov. 2011): 93–114, as "When a Movement Is Not a Movement: Ramana Maharshi and Neo Advaita in North America."

1. See Ramana Maharshi, *Ramana, Shankara, and the Forty Verses: The Essential Teachings of Advaita*, foreword by Alan Jacobs (London: Watkins Publishing, 2002), 7–13. This ancient tradition of Hindu philosophical and spiritual thought was consolidated, rearticulated, and spread by the ninth-century sage Adi Shankara, who authored seminal commentaries on the *Brahma Sutras*, the *Bhagavad-Gita*, and the ten principal Upanishads. He is also said to have founded four monasteries in India, which continue to be acknowledged as authentic transmitters of Advaita Vedanta. Strictly speaking, *Vedanta* means the end of the Vedas, and refers to the Upanishads (ca. 600–300 BCE), the final portion of the Vedic corpus. Although several teachers created philosophical systems based on their readings of the Upanishads, Shankara articulated the system of thought known today as Advaita, the school that focuses on the nondual nature of *Brahman*.

2. Ramana Maharshi, *Ramana, Shankara*. Also see James Swartz, "What Is Neo-Advaita?" http://www.shiningworld.com/Satsang%20Pages/HTML%20Satsangs%20by%20Topic/Neo Advaita/What%20is%20Neo Advaita.htm (accessed June 9, 2011).

3. Dakshinamurthi is described as being the form the Hindu god Shiva takes to teach the mysteries of existence to humanity. Hindu tradition relates that Shiva took the form of an ascetic to teach the four sons of Brahma how to attain truth. He sat in the lotus position under a banyan tree and communicated the truth to them in utter silence.

4. Ramana Maharshi, *Ramana, Shankara*, 7–13.

5. Chris Quilkey, interview with author, Tiruvannamalai, India, Dec. 24, 2007. See also Paramahansa Yogananda, *Autobiography of a Yogi* (Los Angeles: Self-Realization Fellowship, 1998), 455. The interviews for this chapter were conducted in Tiruvannamalai, Tamil Nadu, India, in December 2005 and 2007, and at various Neo-Advaitin centers in North America between 2005 and 2009. The interviews were open-ended and sought to probe the influence of Ramana Maharshi on American currents of Hindu-oriented spiritual practice between 1940 and 2009, as well as the ways Neo-Advaitin groups and teachers have attempted to adapt the Maharshi's teachings to the American cultural context.

6. Ramana Maharshi, *Talks with Sri Ramana Maharshi* (Tiruvannamalai, Tamil Nadu: Sri Ramanasramam, 1996), iii.

7. This estimate is based on various Neo-Advaitin websites, for example, "Advaita Vedanta: Current, http://www.dmoz.org/Society/Religion_and_Spirituality/Advaita_Vedanta/Current_Teachers/ (accessed June 14, 2011); and Guru Ratings, http://gururatings.org/ (accessed June 14, 2011). Another helpful website is http://www.satsangteachers.com/ (accessed Jan. 28, 2013).

8. Eckhart Tolle, *The Power of Now* (Mumbai, India: Yogi Impressions, 2001); Eckhart Tolle, *A New Earth: Awakening to Your Life's Purpose* (New York: Plume, 2005).

9. See Francis Lucille, http://www.francislucille.com/advaita_non-duality_meditation_retreats.html (accessed Apr. 27, 2012); and "Types of Events," Gangaji, http://www.gangaji.org/index.php?modules=content&op=typeofevent (accessed May 29, 2011).

10. Sri Ramanasramam, http://www.sriramanamaharshi.org/ (accessed May 29, 2011).

11. Arthur Osborne, *Ramana Maharshi and the Path of Self-Knowledge* (New York: Samuel Weiser, 1970), 15–19.

12. Carl T. Jackson, *Vedanta for the West: The Ramakrishna Movement in the United States* (Bloomington: Indiana University Press, 1994), 25; see also Catherine Wessinger, "Hinduism Arrives in America," in *America's Alternative Religions*, ed. Timothy Miller, 173–190 (Albany, NY: SUNY Press, 1995).

13. "Mission Statement," Chinmaya Mission West, http://www.chinmayamission.org/aboutus.php (accessed May 29, 2011).

14. James Swartz, email *satsang*, http://www.shiningworld.com/Satsang%20Pages/HTML%20Satsangs%20by%20Topic/Neo-Advaita/Teaching%20enlightenment.htm (accessed June 9, 2011); Swami Sadasivananda, email correspondence, Oct. 25, 2009.

15. Ramana Maharshi, *Talks with Sri Ramana Maharshi*, v.

16. Thomas J. Csordas, *Transnational Transcendence: Essays on Religion and Globalization* (Berkeley: University of California Press, 2009), 4.

17. Ibid., 5.

18. T. M. P. Mahadevan, quoted in Ramana Maharshi, *Talks with Sri Ramana Maharshi*, v.

19. David Godman reports that Papaji never claimed to be a disciple of the Maharshi and that he was never commissioned to teach on the Maharshi's behalf. Thus, Neo-Advaitins' claims to be in the "lineage" of Ramana Maharshi through Papaji have to be understood in a nontraditional sense. David Godman, interview with author, Tiruvannamalai, India, Jan. 3, 2008.

20. Csordas, *Transnational Transcendence*, 5.

21. Ibid., 6.

22. Audio and video downloads of these broadcasts can be accessed at "Oprah's Book Club Collection: Download and Take It with You," Oprah, July 11, 2008, http://www.oprah.com/oprahsbookclub/Download-the-A-New-Earth-Web-Classes.

23. Leigh Schmidt, *Restless Souls: The Making of American Spirituality* (New York: HarperOne, 2006), 12; Catherine L. Albanese, *A Republic of Mind and Spirit: A Cultural History of American Metaphysical Religion* (New Haven, CT: Yale University Press, 2008).

24. Schmidt, *Restless Souls*, 12.

25. Paul Brunton, *A Search in Secret India* (London: Ebury Press, 2003).

26. Dennis Hartel, "Sri Ramana Maharshi: An American Perspective," *The Mountain Path* (Winter 2003): 52.

27. See Arunachala Ashrama—Nova Scotia, http://www.arunachala.org/ashrama/nova_scotia, (accessed May 29, 2011).

28. Hartel, "Sri Ramana Maharshi," 52–53.

29. John W. Parker, "Interview with Eckhart Tolle," http://www.inner-growth.info/power_of_now_tolle/eckhart_tolle_interview_parker.htm (accessed July 13, 2009).

30. David Godman, *Be as You Are: The Teachings of Sri Ramana Maharshi* (New York: Penguin Books, 1992), 1–2.

31. Parker, "Interview with Eckhart Tolle." Jiddu Krishnamurti was a famed writer and teacher on spiritual and philosophical subjects. He was born into a Telugu-speaking Brahmin family in Tamil Nadu, India, and in early adolescence came under the tutelage of Theosophical leaders Annie Besant and Charles W. Leadbeater. Besant proclaimed him as the next "World Teacher," but Krishnamurti distanced himself from this role (at least publicly) and became an independent teacher and author with a worldwide audience. Among his teachings is the cultivation of "choiceless awareness," a practice that in some ways resembles the Maharshi's practice of self-inquiry. For more details on Krishnamurti's status as a world teacher, see Radha Rajagopal Sloss, *Lives in the Shadow with Krishnamurti* (London: Bloomsbury Publishing, 1991); and Catherine Lowman Wessinger, *Annie Besant and Progressive Messianism* (Lewiston, NY: Edwin Mellen, 1988). The blending of Ramana Maharshi's Advaitic perspective with Krishnamurti's nontraditional practice of choiceless awareness occurs not only in the teachings of Eckhart Tolle, but also in other Advaitin teachers such as Sri V. Ganesan, Ramana Maharshi's great-nephew. Sri Ganesan lives in Tiruvannamalai but has taught throughout North America. His written teachings include extensive selections from Krishnamurti's writings.

32. Tolle, *Power of Now*, 10.

33. Parker, "Interview with Eckhart Tolle."

34. Colleen Smith, "Finding Peace with the 'Power of Now,'" denverpost.com, May 18, 2008, http://www.denverpost.com/ci_9273807?source=rss (accessed Jan. 20, 2013). *A New Earth* was originally published by Namaste Publishing in Canada in 1997 and in the United States in 1999. The book had a growing readership and was well distributed before Tolle's appearance on the Winfrey "class" in spring 2008. The most well-known version of *A New Earth: Awakening to Your Life's Purpose* is published by the Penguin Group with a 2005 copyright.

35. Deepak Chopra, endorsement at "The Power of Now: Reviews," Eckhart Tolle: A Fan Site, http://www.inner-growth.info/power_of_now_tolle/eckhart_tolle_pon_reviews.htm (accessed May 29, 2011).

36. Tolle, *New Earth*, 17–18.

37. Ibid., 21.

38. Ibid., 21–22.

39. Eckhart Tolle, "The One Thing," http://www.godlikeproductions.com/forum1/message535437/pg1 (accessed June 9, 2011).

40. Alexandra Hart, "Gangaji: Interview with Alexandra Hart for AHP," http://www.ahpweb.org/pub/perspective/gangaji.html (accessed May 29, 2011).

41. We should note that other Papaji disciples, such as David Godman, dispute these claims, but they are generally accepted as valid by Neo-Advaitins in the United States. The alternative view is that Gangaji and others were given permission to "invite people over to tea and talk about what they had experienced

with Papaji." This permission allegedly did not include a commission to establish themselves as gurus with their own disciples. Godman, interview with author, Tiruvannamalai, India, Jan. 3, 2008. Correspondence between Gangaji and Papaji that reveals the extent of their relationship can be found at http://www.gangaji.org/index.php?modules=content&op=letters.

42. Hart, "Gangaji: Interview."

43. Gangaji, "Types of Events," http://www.gangaji.org/index.php?modules=community&op=videogroup (accessed June 9, 2011). Perhaps because of criticism of the *satsang* format, Gangaji has stopped using the word "*satsang*" to describe her public meetings. She now refers to them as "open" or "public" meetings.

44. Gangaji, "About Gangaji," http://www.gangaji.org/index.php?modules=content&op=about; and "The Lineage," at http://www.gangaji.org/index.php?modules=content&op=lineage (both accessed June 9, 2011).

45. See also Liselotte Frisk, "The Satsang Network: A Growing Post-Osho Phenomenon," *Nova Religio* 6, no. 1 (Oct. 2002): 64–85.

46. Gangaji and Eli, "The Awakening Power of Two Simple Questions," *Pathways Magazine*, Apr. 2004, Leela Foundation, http://www.leela.org/library/interviews-and-articles-/two-simple-questions.html (accessed June 9, 2011).

47. Gangaji, "Gangaji Satsang," http://www.gangaji.org/satsang/library/inspired/sacred.htm (accessed Aug. 8, 2008; now defunct).

48. Ibid.

49. AHAM, "AHAM's Lineage: Arunachala Ramana, AHAM's Spiritual Director," http://www.aham.com/Original/enlightenment/lineagepages/aramana.html (accessed Oct. 23, 2009; now defunct).

50. Stanley Davis Jr., email correspondence with author, Aug. 15, 2011.

51. AHAM, "On Ramana's Life," http://www.aham.com/Original/enlightenment/ (accessed Oct. 23, 2009; now defunct).

52. AHAM, "Our Name Is Our Purpose," http://www.aham.com/Original/retreat/purpose.html (accessed Oct. 23, 2009; now defunct).

53. Ibid.

54. Davis, email correspondence. Davis is a current official with AHAM.

55. AHAM, "Our Name Is Our Purpose," http://www.aham.com/Original/retreat/purpose.html (accessed Oct. 23, 2009; now defunct).

56. Csordas, *Transnational Transcendence*, 5.

57. AHAM, "Jesus' Role in AHAM's Lineage," http://www.aham.com/Original/enlightenment/ (accessed Oct.24, 2009; now defunct).

58. AHAM, "AHAM's Retreat Centers," http://www.aham.com/Original/retreat/index.html (accessed Oct. 29, 2009; now defunct).

59. AHAM, "How AHAM Came into Being," http://www.aham.com/Original/enlightenment/index.html (accessed Oct. 23, 2009; now defunct).

60. Ibid.

61. Stanley Davis Jr., an AHAM official writing after A. Ramana's death, contends that "those who are involved in AHAM's Teaching and the practice of Self-Inquiry are not considered to be disciples or devotees of A. Ramana. We can be considered his students and students of the AHAM Teaching, which is

also Bhagavan Ramana Maharshi's pure teaching of Self-Inquiry. A. Ramana always emphasized that one should be devoted to the Source within or to the true Self, Pure I AM and a disciple of Truth." The focus of AHAM following A. Ramana's death appears to be shifting away from A. Ramana as a gurulike figure and toward his version of Neo-Advaitic teaching—with a clear emphasis on the teaching's antecedents in Ramana Maharshi (email correspondence).

8

From Being to Becoming, Transcending to Transforming

Andrew Cohen and the Evolution of Enlightenment

Ann Gleig

Several Asian religious and philosophical articulations of nonduality exist. One of the most fundamental contrasts is between a nonduality that affirms the identity of absolute and relative phenomena, and consequently embraces the material world as an expression of the absolute, as found within the pan–Asian Tantric traditions, and a nonduality that denies the reality of all phenomena except the absolute, and which devalues the material world, as found within Advaita Vedanta. This chapter considers which forms of nonduality have been embraced in America and under what conditions by tracing the American guru Andrew Cohen's reinvention from a Neo-Advaita teacher to a leading proponent of "evolutionary enlightenment," an essentially Tantric rendering of nonduality in an evolutionary context.

Following Cohen's own evolution affords some instructive insights into the transformation of Hindu concepts in America. His early period shows the further deinstitutionalization of traditional Advaita Vedanta within the radically decontextualized Neo-Advaitin network, and his current teaching engages another less-known but increasingly influential Hindu lineage, namely that of Sri Aurobindo's Integral Yoga. Cohen has also been the subject of much controversy over the efficacy of importing a traditional Indian hierarchical guru-disciple relationship into a modern American democratic and individualistic culture. While Cohen's current metaphysics shows a clear Americanization of Hinduism, his role as guru has opposed that very same process and, as such, he both repeats and reacts against the modernization of traditional Indian religions.

Methodologically, I employ both discourse analysis and ethnography. In addition to several books and articles, textual analysis includes a significant amount of Internet material. As much of contemporary spirituality is deinstitutionalized and decentralized, the Internet functions as a central forum for information and participation. This is true for the three main communities engaged in this chapter: Neo-Advaita, Cohen's evolutionary enlightenment, and integral networks. Numerous websites are devoted to the topic of *advaita* or nonduality that provide discussions of current debates and controversies engaging the nondual community.[1] This textual analysis is supplemented with participant observation and oral interviews and written correspondence with Cohen's former and current students.

My Master Is My Self: Cohen, Poonja, and Neo-Advaita

Born in New York City on October 23, 1955, the second son of upper-middle-class Jewish parents, Cohen's childhood was somewhat bohemian. He attended a progressive elementary school; began psychoanalysis at age five; read Freud, Laing, and Jung as a teenager; and was expelled from a Swiss boarding school for smoking marijuana. At age sixteen, a year after the death of his father, Cohen was talking with his mother when he suddenly had a spontaneous spiritual awakening:

> I suddenly knew without any doubt that there was no such thing as death and that life itself had no beginning and no end. I saw that all of life was intimately connected and inseparable. It became clear that there was no such thing as individuality separate from that one Self that was all of life. The glory and majesty in the cosmic unity that was revealing itself to me was completely overwhelming.[2]

Six years later, Cohen resolved to devote his life to the rediscovery of this experience, which he identified simply as "THAT."[3] His early years as a spiritual seeker were eclectic; he explored several Eastern and Western religious traditions, and traveled around the spiritual retreat circuit in Europe and India. During this period, three teachers particularly influenced him: an American martial arts master, an Indian *kundalini* yogi, and a British *vipassana* teacher. Following an initial period of idealization, however, Cohen became deeply disillusioned with each of these figures. He became dismayed by what he described as the discrepancy between the teaching and behavior of these teachers. After this pattern occurred for the third time, Cohen swore never to submit to spiritual authority again. Yet, earlier on hearing about H. W. L. Poonja (1913–1997), a little-known disciple of Ramana Maharshi, Cohen had been instantly compelled to visit him, and he decided to do so before leaving for Japan where he planned to undertake Zen Buddhist and martial arts training.[4]

Poonja, or Papaji as he was often called, was born into a devout Brahmin family in the Punjab in 1910 (according to him) or 1913 (according to official documents). Accounts of his life are inconsistent and unreliable, but some key events can be sketched.[5] While visiting relatives in Lahore in 1919, Poonja became absorbed in what he describes as an extremely still, peaceful, and blissful state and, although completely aware of what was happening around him, was effectively paralyzed for two days. In 1944 on meeting the Indian guru Ramana Maharshi, Poonja immediately recognized that this childhood state was the *atman* or Self and, shortly after, he claimed to have fully realized the Self in Maharshi's presence.[6] Poonja spent the next forty years alternating between family obligations, holding *satsangs* (spiritual gatherings), and undertaking pilgrimages. He attracted a small group of Indian and foreign devotees and visited students in Europe and South America, but was relatively unknown, however, until Cohen's first book, *My Master Is My Self*, introduced him to a larger Western audience.[7]

A word here is necessary on the type of Advaita that Poonja taught. Many scholars have noted the difference between the traditional Advaita Vedanta of Shankara and the deinstitionalized and experiential Advaita of Ramana Maharshi.[8] The term *advaita* means "nondual" and refers to the tradition's absolute monism, which, put simply, maintains that reality consists of one substance. This one absolute essence is referred to as *Brahman* and described as pure subjectivity characterized as eternal, unchanging consciousness. The phenomenal world of changing multiplicity is explained as *maya*, an illusion that appears due to ignorance. The most famous Advaitin philosopher is Shankara, who has been dated between 788 and 820 CE. Shankara stated that realization of Brahman is to be achieved through the correct interpretation of the *Upanishads* and the refutation of what are regarded as false views. He founded a socially conservative and elite scholastic tradition in which only male Brahmin renouncers are fully qualified to study the scriptures.

Born in 1879, Ramana Maharshi was a South Indian guru who advocated a direct experiential realization of *Brahman* and initiated a deinstitutionalized strand of Advaita. When he was a teenager, Maharshi had a spontaneous realization of the Self and, although he became a celibate ascetic renunciate, was never part of institutional Advaita. Maharshi insisted that true renunciation is being free of the illusory separate sense of "I" and that one did not have to renounce the world to experience *Brahman*. He was indifferent to intellectual and scriptural training and taught that Self-realization could be attained by Self-inquiry, a meditation on the question, "Who am I?" Moreover, he offered his teaching to all people without caste, ethnicity, or gender restrictions. Although Poonja and his students align themselves with Maharshi, he never appointed any successors, so claims to lineage are contentious. Poonja is better approached as a father of a further decontextualized and experiential Advaita, which has since been dubbed as Western or Neo-Advaita. He further radicalized Maharshi's approach in claiming that no methods or effort are necessary to attain enlightenment because it is merely the realization of what one already is.[9]

This teaching profoundly affected Cohen. At their first meeting in Lucknow, North India, on March 25, 1986, Cohen asked Poonja a question about effort. Poonja's response, "You don't have to make any effort to be free," was catalytic. "In that instant," Cohen reports, "I realized that I had always been free."[10] As recorded in Cohen's diary, revelation after revelation followed in the next three weeks that the newfound master and disciple spent together. "The universe is *samsara*," Cohen marveled, "It has no substance and is unreal. Creation itself is an illusion. What is beyond time cannot be born and cannot die. It is uncreated and timeless."[11] On their first parting, Poonja declared that Cohen was his spiritual heir and should take responsibility for the teaching.[12]

Predicted by Poonja to "start a revolution among the young," Cohen began his first teaching incarnation as a Neo-Advaita guru. With a small group of students, including his future Indian wife, Cohen moved to Cornwall, England, in September 1986 and would spend the next two years giving *satsangs* in various locations across Europe and in Israel. Reports commonly depict this as an idyllic period during which Cohen was accessible to his students, living and traveling with them. By all accounts, he was a charismatic teacher who was successful in transmitting his states of consciousness. In my interviews with former and current students, all reported having dramatic spiritual experiences on their first encounter with Cohen, whether through meeting him in person, being in the company of his students, or reading one of his books. An international community of devotees began to form spontaneously around him and in 1988, when the community relocated to Amherst, Massachusetts, it had grown to around 150 students.[13]

Thematically, Cohen's initial teachings were consistent with Poonja's and typify the Neo-Advaita perspective: enlightenment requires no effort because one is and always has been liberated. Time, the world, and the individual self are an illusion. Only the unchanging, eternal, and pure consciousness Self is real. Enlightenment can be attained instantly; a gradual approach only reinforces the illusory concept of time. No methods are necessary because practice and effort assume a dualistic framework: a separate self attempting to achieve a future goal of enlightenment. To realize the Self all that is necessary is to surrender to the Self, which can be achieved in the presence of the teacher who is identical to the Self.[14] Cohen's message was simple: nothing has to change because everything is perfect as it is.[15]

From Experience to Ethics:
The Split from Poonja and Neo-Advaita

After a few years, however, Cohen began to question Poonja's perspective on the nature of enlightenment. He observed that despite many powerful enlightenment experiences, his students had not been fundamentally transformed:

> My Teacher always said someone was "Enlightened" after this initial glimpse into their true nature. I soon realized this wasn't true. If a person was "Enlightened," to me that meant they [sic] had to be able to manifest and express that Enlightenment consistently in their [sic] behavior. I had observed so many people who had experienced profound awakenings and yet still would be unable to manifest and express that realization in their outer lives. It seemed that in spite of "Enlightenment," much neurotic and conditioned behavior usually remained.[16]

Cohen began, therefore, to realize the limitations of the ecstatic experiences his students were having in his presence. While he was convinced he had been fully liberated from his "karmic chains," he declared that his students were still immersed in their self-centered egoic behavior.[17] Framing this as a gap between the experience and expression of enlightenment, Cohen began to demand more commitment from them. His focus shifted from enlightenment experiences to the purification of karmic conditioning and the transcendence of the ego, which Cohen declared was the primary obstacle to the perfect expression of enlightenment.

To eradicate the ego, Cohen introduced new teaching methods, including separate groups for male and female students where they would meet twice a week to discuss his teachings and determine to what extent they had been followed. The main objective of such groups was what Cohen called, "facing it," namely, exposing the root of one's egoic motivations, admitting guilt, expressing regret, and resolving to change. In addition, Cohen implemented many traditional ascetic practices such as intensive meditation, prostrations, celibacy, and head shaving. He became much more removed from his students and took an increasingly authoritative role in their lives, declaring whom they could have relationships with and where they should live. The early days of blissful *satsang* and effortless enlightenment were over. Sangha became, as one former student put it, a "spiritual boot camp."[18]

Cohen's role as a traditional guru with his adoring devotees was already problematic for many of his more egalitarian-inclined American contemporaries, and complaints against him grew as he began to demand more renunciation from his students. Most troublingly, however, was dissent from inside the community. Rumors began to circulate that Poonja was also criticizing Cohen, claiming his teaching was "off" and advising Cohen's students to come directly to him.[19] In 1989 the strained relationship between the once beloved father and son irrevocably broke down and much acrimony ensued between their two communities.

What had caused the breakdown of what Cohen had once referred to as "the fairytale" between himself and Poonja? The main point of contention was the relationship between enlightenment and ethics or, put differently, the relationship between absolute and relative reality and how this played out in the guru-disciple relationship. According to Cohen, Poonja insisted that the realization of the Self had nothing to do with worldly behavior, and he did not believe fully transcending the ego was possible. Poonja's perspective was that although karmic tendencies remained after enlightenment, the enlightened person was no longer identified with them and, therefore, did not accrue any further karmic consequences.[20] Moreover, ethical standards, being based in a dualistic understanding of reality and assuming an individual agent, could never be used to measure nondual enlightenment. For Poonja, the goal was the realization of the Self; the illusory realm of relative reality was ultimately irrelevant.[21]

Cohen, on the other hand, was adamant that the experience of enlightenment must manifest in flawless behavior. He insisted that one could be fully liberated from karmic conditioning in order to perfectly express nondual realization in the world. It soon became clear that his and Poonja's view of enlightenment were "diametrically opposed"[22] and that this opposition extended to their respective teaching methods. As

Cohen saw it, he was not willing to compromise and those students who failed to meet his standards were subject to intense reparative measures, such as public humiliations, compulsory ascetic practices, and being demoted in or thrown out of the community. Some of these students went directly to Poonja and found, in contrast, "unconditional love," sympathy, and acceptance from him. One of these was American Antoinette Roberson Varner, whom Poonja apparently declared to be enlightened, gave her the new name "Gangaji," and sent her back to America to "clean up after Andrew" and restore the proper understanding of Advaita Vedanta.[23]

Cohen's attempts to convince Poonja of his perspective were unsuccessful and he eventually concluded that he had surpassed his teacher and painted a final portrait of Poonja as an immoral, power-mad hypocrite. Similarly, he pointed to gurus such as Bhagwan Rajneesh, Da Free John, and Swami Muktananda, all of whom, despite being "enlightened to an extraordinary degree," had been implicated in various sexual, drug, and power scandals. Such failings, Cohen claimed, had produced a prevalent cultural cynicism about the "possibility of perfection," and he stood alone as a spiritual pioneer who had the courage to live the truth at whatever cost.[24] Insisting that complete ego-transcendence was possible, he set impersonal enlightenment as the aim of his new teaching.

Impersonal Enlightenment and the War against the Ego

The split with Poonja led Cohen to rethink the entire nature of spiritual liberation and, in 1991 he began the aptly titled in-house journal *What Is Enlightenment?* to investigate the nature of enlightenment. *What Is Enlightenment?* soon grew into an international magazine with a broad readership. Tackling topics such as the nature of the ego and the relationship between spirituality and sex, it featured many well-known Asian and Western spiritual teachers and established Cohen as a major contemporary spiritual figure.

This period saw the further development of the second major stage of Cohen's evolution: his teaching of impersonal enlightenment and the war against the ego. Pointing to the number of guru scandals, Cohen declared that the fundamental self-concern of the individual ego all too often motivated and corrupted the search for personal enlightenment. His community, however, had begun to manifest something beyond individual enlightenment—what he called impersonal enlightenment—in which enlightenment was realized for its own sake and not for the sake of the individual.

The aim of impersonal enlightenment is the perfect expression of the absolute Self on the relative level. Cohen now described spiritual life as consisting of two aspects: meditation and contemplation.[25] Through meditation one realizes one's true identity—the eternal, unchanging, nondual Self—and through contemplation one fully manifests that Self in enlightened action in the world. With the aspect of meditation, Cohen remained more or less faithful to the Neo-Advaitin perspective, to just *"let everything be as it is."*[26] For contemplation, however, he produced a new methodology called "the five fundamental tenets of enlightenment" that stressed complete dedication, total renunciation, taking full responsibility for one's actions, and not personalizing any experience.[27] The target of these tenets was the ego, which Cohen defined as "the compulsive need to remain separate at all times."[28] Such egoic individuality prevented the perfect expression of the impersonal absolute on the relative level, and he insisted that the "compulsion with the personal" must be completely severed.[29]

Framing spiritual life as a battle between good and evil, enlightenment and the ego, Cohen intensely pushed his students to eradicate the many layers of conditioning that comprise the ego.[30] He implemented several new practices to aid in what he called the "heroic battle" against the ego, and, in 1996, after the community moved back to Massachusetts to an estate called Foxhollow, measures became even more extreme. Cohen introduced several dramatic, some would later claim abusive, teaching methods designed to ruthlessly expose and annihilate the ego.

While interpretations of these methods greatly differ, both critics and supporters of Cohen have corroborated most of the reported incidents. They include the use of physical force, verbal abuse, and intense psychological pressure against students. Cohen instructed certain students to deliver "messages" to fellow students by slapping them hard in the face. The men's group was ordered to "rough up" certain male students. Cohen devised methods to encourage what he called "healthy shame," exposing students' egoic traits giving them names such as Mad Dog, Raging Bull, and the Clown. One student had paint poured over her head; another had a bag of garbage emptied on her bed. Bedrooms and the spa at Foxhollow were smeared with red paint to signify that students were spilling Cohen's blood by not fully living up to his teachings, and student letters that had offended Cohen were blown up, splattered with fake blood, or publicly posted. Another feature of this period was Cohen's targeting of gender-specific egoic traits or conditioning. One of his tactics against "women's ego" was having the basement walls covered with caricatures of female students as devils tearing out Cohen's intestines and dancing around a fire while burning his books. Another was having groups of female students listen to Bob Dylan's "Just Like a Woman" nonstop for twenty-four hours.[31]

WHAT Enlightenment??!
Spiritual Authoritarianism and Breaking the Code of Silence

> Bottom line, I experienced so much that was truly profound and transformative—and that I will ever be grateful for—and also so much that was really abusive and twisted—and that still deeply saddens me. The lightest light and the darkest dark. Both. All tangled together like miles of black and white yarn entwined in a big ball at the pit of my stomach.[32]

The biggest causality of Cohen's war against the ego, however, might well have been himself. Just as his Neo-Advaitin period had ended with a critique of the guru, in that case Poonja, this period closed with numerous assaults on Cohen. The first strike came from his mother and former student, the novelist Luna Tarlo, who in 1997 published the ironically titled *The Mother of God,* in which she portrayed Cohen as a spiritual tyrant controlling his community through fear and domination. According to Tarlo, Cohen had become increasingly narcissistic and his teaching methods encouraged students to be abusive to each other. After a decisive meeting with the antiguru teacher, U. G. Krishnamurti, Tarlo concluded that her son had become lost in self-delusion and compared his community to a dysfunctional family. Her relationship with Cohen was completely severed, and they have had no contact since 1995. A similar although more nuanced account of life with Cohen appeared in Andre van der Braak's thought-provoking 2003 memoir, *Enlightenment Blues.* A senior student of Cohen's for eleven years, van der Braak details his initial adoration, progressive disillusionment, and acrimonious split with him. He suggests that the main problem was that Cohen imported the traditional authoritarian Eastern guru system into a modern Western culture that respects individual difference and autonomy; rather than attempt to annihilate such individuality, Cohen, he believes, should integrate it.

Reviews of these two texts spurred a series of critical press articles against Cohen but the heaviest blow came with the appearance of *WHAT Enlightenment??!*, a website started by former *What Is Enlightenment?* editor Hal Blacker.[33] Since 2004, the site has functioned as a public forum for discussion of Cohen's controversial teaching methods and includes both critical and supportive postings as well as general reflections on the guru-disciple relationship. The main flavor of the site, however, is critical: several former senior students accuse him of things such as presiding autocratically over a shame-based community, narcissism, financial extortion, and physical and psychological abuse.

For some former students, Cohen is depicted as a power-hungry narcissistic fraud on whom the community projected their own collective experiences and longings. According to William Yenner, for example, Cohen's students were engaged in a collective transference and little other than the comradeship between them is salvageable.[34] The majority of critiques, however, are more measured; they acknowledge that Cohen is spiritually accomplished but severely limited in psychological and pedagogical areas. One common perspective is that because Cohen did not belong to a spiritual lineage he had no peer support or checks on his authority. Another is that Cohen was untrained as a teacher, "absolutized" his understanding, and forced a one-size-fits-all model on his students. His teaching methods, they insist, were heavy-handed and unskilled at best, delusional and abusive at worst. Some of these students declare that they still value much of their time with him and, to some extent, even appreciate his intentions. A few also take responsibility for their part in the "creation of the painful mix of enlightenment and insanity, of hope and fear, of bondage and ecstasy that he and his community embody."[35]

Crazy Wisdom, Rude Boys, and the Shadow Sangha

Andrew Cohen is a Rude Boy. He is not here to offer comfort. . . . He is here to tear you into approximately a thousand pieces . . . so that Infinity can reassemble you. . . . Every deeply enlightened teacher I have known has been a Rude Boy. . . . Rude Boys are on your case in the worst way, they breathe fire, eat hot coals, will roast your ass in a screaming second and fry your ego before you know what hit it.[36]

Cohen and his supporters have countered critiques by what he has referred to as his "shadow sangha" in numerous ways. First, they have completely denied some of the allegations and claimed that other incidents have been exaggerated and taken out of context. Second, they have launched character attacks on and questioned the motives of the people who have made these allegations. They claim that critiques can be attributed to a few malicious students whose sole aim is to destroy Cohen's reputation. Cohen declares that these former students have "failed miserably" on the spiritual path and need to justify why they have abandoned that which gave their life higher meaning.[37] Third, in his *Defense of the Guru Principle*, Cohen delivers an impassioned defense of the guru principal as a force of love and evolution whose primary purpose is to destroy the ego. Complaints against him, Cohen claims, are the voices of wounded and manipulative egos and signal a profound lack of understanding of the traditional guru-disciple relationship.[38] According to him, the guru scandals have made people cynical about the possibility of an authentic teacher and this has been further accentuated in a postmodern culture that is deeply suspicious of authority and hierarchy.

In a related vein, Cohen's supporters have used the crazy wisdom hermeneutic to legitimate what they see as Cohen's innovative teaching strategies.[39] Populating Buddhist and Hindu traditions, crazy wisdom teachers are enlightened gurus who use shocking methods, including physical force and breaking religious ethics, to awaken their students. Ken Wilber, for example, has celebrated Cohen as an authentic modern day crazy wisdom teacher and compared him to the early antinomian Zen masters.[40] One former supportive student of Cohen has also attempted to counter *WHAT Enlightenment??!* by hosting a website called *Guru Talk* that promotes positive testimonies of Cohen including ones from both agents and recipients of some of the controversial incidents. These students express gratitude for what they experienced as a challenging but truly transformative pedagogy.[41]

One notable characteristic of defenses is that they are unequivocally affirmative of Cohen and aim at thoroughly discrediting his critics. In doing so they focus solely on the most caustic portraits and ignore the more complex ones, with Cohen complaining, for example, that critiques have reduced him to a "two-dimensional caricature of a cultural stereotype: the charismatic and corrupt guru."[42] Many of the accounts, however, depict a more ambivalent picture:

> I find Andrew Cohen one of the great mysteries of the dharma. He had a profound enlightenment experience and has a passionate commitment to the dharma; these have enabled him to inspire many people to plunge wholeheartedly into the spiritual path. That is no small thing. At the same time, I believe he has a number of blind spots that make him in many ways an ineffective, immature spiritual teacher.[43]

Whatever hermeneutic one is ultimately convinced by—spiritual authoritarianism or crazy wisdom—the considerable complexities around the guru-disciple relationship deserve a more considerate and nuanced response than Cohen and his supporters have afforded them. This is where the latter have fallen short. In contrast to those former students who have struggled to make sense of and take some responsibility for the conflicting elements of life in the community, Cohen has failed to do either. His harsh vilification of students, many of whom dedicated their lives to him for over a decade, is questionable. It is also somewhat ironic that Cohen's supporters draw on the crazy wisdom narrative to legitimate his approach, as undergirding this is the doctrine of skillful means, which, in brief, argues that an enlightened master must use skill and flexibility in teaching different individual students.[44] Such flexibility has been notably absent in Cohen who has continually affirmed that no concessions must be made to individual needs in the "black-and-white" battle against the ego.[45]

Despite his completely unapologetic public stance, however, Cohen has affected numerous changes that suggest that critiques have had an impact, even if only in terms of self-marketing. For example, Cohen now presents himself as spiritual mentor, as well as guru, and asks for spiritual partners rather than followers. He has also declared that in the future the guru principle will not function through an individual teacher but through a collective body of realized individuals.[46] This refashioning of the guru has occurred within a larger remodeling of his community with the development of his third and current teaching of "evolutionary enlightenment."

From Being to Becoming:
Evolutionary Enlightenment and the Integral Alliance

Cohen states that the ongoing question his teaching has revolved around is "what is the relationship between the unchanging, unmanifest, primordial Self and the ever-changing manifest world of time and space?"[47] Whereas impersonal enlightenment explored this question through an emphasis on the ethical expression of enlightenment, in his current manifestation as a "pioneer of evolutionary enlightenment," Cohen has shifted his focus to the relationship between enlightenment and evolution.

At the base of evolutionary enlightenment is a critique of the limitations of both postmodern Western secular culture and premodern Eastern spiritual traditions. While the West has attained material sophistication, Cohen believes that the majority of its citizens are adrift without any moral compass or existential purpose.[48] Although many have turned to Eastern religions in search of meaning, Cohen cautions against such a response. He argues that one cannot find authentic solutions in premodern Eastern enlightenment traditions that perpetuate super-stitious myths, lack scientific knowledge, and aim at transcendence of the world.[49] The answer, rather, is to develop a new "post-traditional" spirituality that unites the contemplative wisdom of the East with the scientific achievements of the West and thereby renders enlightenment relevant for the twenty-first century. This is how Cohen frames evo-lutionary enlightenment, which, as the name indicates, has two com-ponents: "enlightenment" refers to the nondual realization revealed by Indian enlightenment traditions and "evolution" signifies the deep time developmental perspective discovered by Western science.

Putting these two perspectives into dialogue, Cohen posits a spir-itual hermeneutic of evolution and an evolutionary interpretation of enlightenment. He follows a lineage of mainly Western thinkers, who have interpreted evolution as the progressive unfolding of Spirit and identified human self-awareness as instrumental to the process. Cohen's specific take on this spiritual evolutionary narrative is that the evolving universe is created from the unmanifest or "empty ground of being" that is realized in enlightenment. From unmanifest Being emerged an evolu-tionary impulse or creative principle, which initiated the leap from being to becoming, nothing to something, or the One to the many. Shifting into a Western religious register, Cohen explains the creation process through "a theological fantasy" in which God, abiding as perfectly blissful and peaceful unmanifest consciousness, chose to manifest in and through form. God's ultimate purpose is the awakening of all matter, a "seem-ingly impossible task," that is dependent upon the conscious evolution of the enlightened human being.[50]

According to Cohen, traditional understandings of enlightenment must be updated in wake of the evolutionary knowledge that has been discovered in the last 150 years. Evolution theory, he argues, has prov-en—contra to the beliefs of Indian enlightenment traditions—that time is not cyclic, but linear and developing. Ego transcendence must now be pursued not to escape the cycle of becoming, as in traditional Eastern paths, but rather to enable one to fully participate in the evolution-ary process. Only through the transcendence of the inherently narcis-sistic ego, Cohen states, will individuals be able to intentionally work in service of evolution and "literally create the future."[51] Enlightenment, therefore, must not only be expressed in perfect ethical behavior, but becomes itself an ethical imperative to further evolution.

Presenting his teaching as a shift "from Being to Becoming or from Transcending to Transforming," Cohen reconfigures enlightenment from a world-negating and utterly transcendent state to a unique form of con-sciousness that both embraces and extends the universe. This remodeling is achieved primarily by the introduction of a new dimension of consciousness or subjectivity called the "authentic self," which functions as a bridge between the unmanifest absolute and the world. The absolute Self is aligned with the classical Advaita Vedanta concept of the *Brahman*. It is the unborn, unmanifest Self, which is characterized by ultimate peace and bliss.[52] Unlike the absolute Self, which is utterly transcendent from the world, the authentic self is fully engaged and involved with the world. Drawing from Western theology, philosophy, and science, Cohen uses several terms to describe the authentic self. It is the "First Cause," "Eros, the creative principle," or the "evolutionary impulse," the energy and intelligence that created the universe that manifests on numerous hierarchical levels spanning from the procreative instinct to the evolution of consciousness.

Whereas the absolute Self exists beyond time as pure Being, the authentic self is the future-directed principle of becoming. Yet, while it is life embracing and "cares passionately" about evolution, it is an impersonal function of consciousness that exists in a dimension beyond form and is not subject to or affected by its limitations.[53] Somewhat vague on the specific mechanics, Cohen claims that the authentic self is triggered when one realizes the absolute Self, or as he puts it, the "realization of Being catalyzes the evolutionary process of becoming." The authentic self, in short, enables Cohen to reconcile a traditional Indian transcendent understanding of enlightenment, such as found in Advaita Vedanta, with a world-embracing evolutionary ethos and, at the same time, remain faithful to his impersonal perspective.

Along with his metaphysics, Cohen's teaching mediums and community have also had evolutionary makeovers. *What Is Enlightenment?* has been relaunched as *EnlightenNext: The Magazine for Evolutionaries,* his Impersonal Enlightenment Fellowship has been revamped as *Enlighten-Next,* and his students renamed as evolutionaries.[54] Such future-oriented remodeling strongly characterizes the evolutionary discourse, which is laden with terms such as *innovation, radicalism, revolutionary, pioneering,* the *leading edge,* and the *cutting edge.* Cohen has fully engaged innovative multimedia methods of teaching, including a sophisticated interactive website that hosts regular podcasts and virtual discussions, weekly webcasts and telephone conference calls, and monthly virtual workshops and seminars. In February 2010, he taught his first virtual weekend retreat, and a virtual conference followed in May 2010.[55] Cohen has also extended his teaching format to four types of events: lectures, seminars, daylong retreats, and intensive retreats.[56] Another significant development is the appearance of an educational and training program in which sixty qualified EnlightenNext instructors offer a variety of live and virtual events.[57] This collective model of teaching marks a notable shift from the traditional guru-student model that previously character-ized Cohen's community.

Through these new teaching methods, Cohen is ambitiously attempting to "create a global movement" and a "worldwide learning community." This global outreach initiative is linked to Cohen's new focus on the relationship between consciousness and culture. Declaring that the two are inextricably linked, he wants to pioneer new forms of "enlightened culture" that support and stabilize the newly emerging higher levels of human development revealed in evolutionary enlighten-ment.[58] To this end, *EnlightenNext* sponsors both live and media forums that host debates between leading spiritual and culture figures, and has developed programs such as authentic leadership for the business world and enlightened cultural activism. Particularly significant here is Cohen's alliance with the Integral community of thinkers such as Ken Wilber, Duane Elgin, and Don Beck, an alliance that has been at the forefront of many of his theoretical, pedagogical, and organizational innovations.

Experiential and Historic Legitimating Strategies

One can identify two main strategies by which Cohen legitimates his new evolutionary teaching: an experiential narrative that validates the teaching as spontaneously emerged and a historic narrative that locates it in a distinguished lineage of thinkers who have proposed a spiritual dimension to evolution. These dual narratives function to give historical credence and philosophical weight to evolutionary enlightenment while maintaining its uniqueness and perpetuating Cohen's status as spiri-tual pioneer. According to Cohen, the primary source for evolutionary enlightenment is experiential; he claims that the teaching spontaneously unfolded in his own awakening and as a result of his concerted efforts later began to emerge in his students. The turning point came on July 30, 2001, a date the community now celebrates as "the birth of evolutionary enlightenment" when a group of ten male students experienced what is now referred to as collective or intersubjective enlightenment during an intensive retreat. In my interview with one of these students, he described it as "an explosion, a ring of fire whirled around the room, and we saw that everyone was enlightened . . . [it was] a simultaneous expe-rience of autonomy and communion. A higher intelligence revealed itself through all of us." Cohen declared this event as the fulfillment of what he had been intuiting with impersonal enlightenment. He now explains intersubjective enlightenment as a new higher level of consciousness in which enlightenment emerges through a collective and reveals our evolutionary potential; "it is literally the birth of a new form of subjectivity, one that transcends and includes individuality and will enable the creation of a new world."[59]

The next significant emergence of collective enlightenment occurred in early November 2005. Shortly after, Cohen appeared before an audience of several hundred students to declare that his two decades of teaching were finally starting to show their intended results.[60] He claimed that a shared experience of enlightenment had occurred across his entire student body and, unlike previous temporary bursts, was sustained for more than a month.[61] This stabilization signified a "ground-shift" in his community in their shared attempts to lay a foundation for a higher stage of development for the human species.[62]

In addition to completing the unfoldment of impersonal enlightenment, evolutionary enlightenment also effectively functions to legitimate Cohen's controversial teaching methods because he claims that it was only able to emerge as a result of his "momentous efforts" to push his students beyond their egoic selves.[63] Similarly, Pete Bampton, founder of *Guru Talk,* argues that the intense pressure Cohen inflicted on his students is understandable only in light of intersubjective enlightenment. He points out that critical former students left the community before this occurred and so do not appreciate the higher purpose of such severe pressure.[64] The end, in others words, justifies the means. For all of Cohen's attempts to link impersonal and evolutionary enlightenment, however, the latter is clearly distinguished by several new terms and concepts, many of which can be traced to his second legitimating strategy, the historical narrative.

After the collective awakening in his community, Cohen claims he was astonished to discover similar insights in numerous other thinkers. He locates evolutionary enlightenment in a historic, mainly Western, lineage of "evolutionary spirituality" that begins with the German idealists such as Friedrich Schelling and includes figures such as the French philosopher Henri Bergson, the Catholic priest and paleontologist Pierre Teilhard de Chardin, transcendentalist Ralph Waldo Emerson, and philosopher Jean Gebser. Most notable, however, and deserving some special attention are the twentieth-century Indian revolutionary turned mystic, Sri Aurobindo, and contemporary integral theorist, Ken Wilber.[65]

Reinterpreting the Vedas through an evolutionary lens, Aurobindo rejected both traditional Indian renouncer paths and Western scientific materialism in favor of an all-encompassing or "integral" metaphysics that recognized the truths of both "spirit and nature" and aimed at divinization of rather than liberation from the world. To catalyze the transformation of not only the individual but also cultural life, Aurobindo developed a system of "Integral Yoga."[66] The foundation of Integral Yoga is a dialectical metaphysics that advances a bipolar model of ultimate reality. Aurobindo refers to ultimate reality as *Brahman* and explains that it has both static and dynamic aspects: it is both the unmoving and moving, the unmanifest and manifest, transcendent and immanent, spirit and nature. Whereas Indian renunciate traditions have exclusively focused on the unmanifest aspect of *Brahman* and rejected the manifest as an illusion, Aurobindo attempts to reunite the two through the use of an involution-evolution or descent-ascent narrative. Involution refers to the descent of spirit into nature and the progressive emergence of "matter, life and mind," and evolution signifies the reascent of the latter to their spiritual origin, a process that results in a spiritualization of matter or "the divine life."

The similarities between Aurobindo and Cohen should be apparent: both thinkers share a bipolar ontology of an unmanifest and manifest absolute; both reinterpret nonduality through an evolutionary lens; both understand their spiritual awakening as instrumental to the evolutionary process and describe their spiritual communities as evolutionary "laboratories"; both recast the goal of spiritual realization from transcendence to the divinization of the world; both posit the birth of a "new being"; and both aim at the spiritualization of culture as well as the transmutation of the individual.

The most striking parallel, however, is between Aurobindo's concept of "psychic being" and Cohen's authentic self. Both are described as an evolving higher level of consciousness that acts as an intermediary between the unmanifest and manifest realms and whose realization is pivotal to the spiritual evolutionary process.[67] Cohen claims he discovered Aurobindo's work after the emergence of evolutionary enlightenment and was astonished to find that the psychic being clearly defined that which he had earlier intuited.[68] His mother, however, records visiting the Sri Aurobindo ashram in Pondicherry with Cohen before he met Poonja and, given Cohen's familiarity with Eastern spirituality, it is surprising that he had not encountered Aurobindo before.

One would assume, for example, that he was familiar with Aurobindo through the work of Ken Wilber, who has been absolutely instrumental in the development of evolutionary enlightenment. In a corpus spanning more than thirty years, Wilber has attempted to update "the Great Chain of Being" presented by the perennial philosophers with the insights of modern and postmodern epistemologies in order to construct an inclusive model of human development.[69] His theoretical signature is the integration of Western developmental structural models with the different cartographies of consciousness charted by Asian religious traditions. Wilber's earlier transpersonal model, "the spectrum of consciousness," refracted the Great Chain through Western psychological developmental models and an evolutionary framework, and he has continued this refashioning by adding more recent developmental schemas to develop the "four quadrants model" and "integral map."

Cohen and his students have also claimed they were amazed to discover a precise articulation of their experiences in Wilber's work. Wilber's evolutionary developmental model, Cohen enthuses, gave him the language to better express and more fully understand the significance of his own spontaneous realizations. Former students, however, have countered that Cohen had been reading Wilber since his Neo-Advaita days and spent considerable time and energy courting a relationship with him.[70] Critics view his relationship with Wilber as a strategic alliance that has been highly beneficial for both parties.

Whatever the origin of the relationship, it clearly has been a mutually rewarding one. In 2002 *What Is Enlightenment?* announced a new regular feature, "The Guru and Pandit," a dialogue between Cohen and Wilber devoted mainly to developing evolutionary enlightenment with Cohen incorporating many of Wilber's theoretical concepts into his teaching. Wilber has been an influential vocal supporter of Cohen, endorsing many of his books and promoting his status as a crazy wisdom teacher. Cohen, for his part, has brought an experiential legitimacy to Wilber's largely theoretical achievements. The two are also collaborating on numerous spiritual empire-building projects. Cohen is one of the founding members of the Integral Institute, a "global think-tank" Wilber established in 1998; *EnlightenNext* has become a leading forum for integral theory; and the two organizations have cosponsored numerous events.[71] The integral alliance may also be credited with helping revitalize Cohen's community in the wake of the guru scandals. In some ways, Cohen is more influential than ever; he was a well-received guest speaker at the World Parliament of Religion in 2004 and 2009 and has exposure to a new and larger audience through joint integral and evolutionary events.

Cohen in Context: Beyond Experience, the Tantric Turn, and Revisioning the Guru

In conclusion, I offer some reflections on how we might locate Cohen's evolution in the wider context of the contemporary American assimilation of Indian contemplation traditions, focusing on three areas: (1) a move away from the modern rhetoric of experience; (2) the privileging of a Tantric nondual metaphysics; and (3) a revisioning of the traditional guru-disciple relationship. Cohen's development shows a move away from the privileging of experience that scholars such as Robert Sharf have shown to be characteristic of the modern Western understanding of Asian mysticism. In an influential analysis of the status of experience in modern representations of Asian religions and the modern academic study of religion, Sharf has targeted the privileging of meditative experience. He traces the modern understanding of the essence of spirituality as an individual inner experience to Friedrich Schleiermacher's attempt to protect religion from Enlightenment critiques. This experiential model is adopted and applied to Asian religions by a handful of twentieth-century Asian religious leaders and apologists such Swami Vivekananda and Sarvepalli Radhakrishna who, in sustained dialogue with their intellectual counterparts in the West, promoted the experiential narrative in service of their own neo-Hindu agendas. Extending Sharf, one can further trace this experiential thread through the popular work of figures such as Houston Smith and Aldous Huxley who further disseminated an experiential model of Asian religions to the counterculture. Sharf, however, questions the assumption that meditation experience is central to traditional Asian religious practice and redraws attention to the indispensable aspects of ethical training, ritual, and scripture.[72]

Cohen's struggle with Poonja and his subsequent attempts to create a context for enlightenment experiences is a perfect example of the modern experiential legacy. Many of their issues would simply never have arisen in traditional Advaita Vedanta in which ethics and training are essential aspects in a complete religious matrix. Similarly, although Cohen poses his question about the relationship between enlightenment and karma as if it is a revolutionary one, there is a long-running debate in traditional Advaita about the relationship between liberation and embodiment.[73]

Cohen's dissatisfaction with the experiential vision and attempt to create a stable context for mystical experiences is also characteristic of the wider contemporary American assimilation of Asian spirituality. Jorge Ferrer, for example, has critiqued the centrality of the experiential legacy in the field of transpersonal psychology, which has been a central landscape for East-West integrations.[74] I have delineated two main contemporary responses to the limitations of the experiential legacy: recovery of tradition or the creation of new contemporary context. In the first instance, some communities have called for a return to tradition or have, at least, developed a renewed interest in elements of tradition religion that were discarded or neglected by the modern experiential emphasis, such as scripture and ritual. For example, critiques of the Neo-Advaitin sole focus on experiences of the Self and its neglect of ethical and scriptural training by both Ramana Maharshi's community and the proponents of traditional Advaitin Vedanta show this revalorization of tradition. David McMahan and Jeff Wilson have noted similar trends in their respective studies of American Buddhism and have revealed that the American adaptation of Buddhism is not a progressive linear movement away from traditional Asian elements toward modern phenomena, but increasingly demonstrates an interest in more traditional elements discarded in the initial modernization process.[75]

Rather than return to tradition, however, Cohen's solution to the limitations of the modern experiential emphasis has been to create a new religious context, a "post-traditional spirituality" that is relevant to the present cultural moment. In this way, Cohen appears to support Jeffrey J. Kripal's recent claim that we are witnessing the emergence of new forms of American mysticism that draw on both the ontological revelations of Asian religions and the democratic, pluralistic, and scientific revolutions of modernity. Such mysticism operates with democratic principles, individualist values, and socially liberal agendas, all of which in turn attempt to liberalize the limitations of Asian spiritualities. Central to such integrative traditions, Kripal argues, is the embrace of world-affirming Tantric forms of Asian spirituality over world-negating renouncer traditions such as Advaita Vedanta. By Tantra, Kripal adopts Andre Padoux's classic definitions that Tantra is "an attempt to place *kama*, desire, in every sense of the word, in the service of liberation, . . . not to sacrifice the world for liberation's sake but to reinstate it, in varying ways within the perspective of salvation." As Kripal notes, whereas ascetic Asian traditions such as Advaita Vedanta privilege the transcendent Absolute and renounce the everyday world as illusory, the Tantric traditions insist of the essential unity of the transcendent and immanent.[76] It should be stressed, however, that the new American spiritualities do not adopt the traditional Asian Tantric traditions wholesale but rather use a Tantric metaphysics to legitimate the development of more integral forms of spirituality that value both the absolute and relative dimensions of reality.

At first glance, Cohen's evolutionary enlightenment seems a perfect fit with Kripal's modern American mystical traditions. Cohen's posttraditional spirituality combines aspects of the ontological revelations of Asian religions and the evolutionary revelations of Western science and metaphysically accords with Kripal's Tantric hermeneutic. Both Cohen and Wilber have explicitly identified evolutionary enlightenment with a Tantric metaphysics, declaring that it is the evolutionary updating and fulfillment of traditional Asian Tantric articulations of nonduality.[77]

However, while Cohen metaphysically resonates with the contemporary integrative East-West spiritualities that Kripal analyzes, there are also significant differences. According to Kripal, a definitive mark of these new world-embracing traditions is that they are suspicious of hierarchy and authority, and they affirm the value of the individual over tradition. The traditional Indian guru-disciple relationship, in particular, has been the source of much controversy in America with numerous tensions arising from attempts to transport what is essentially a premodern Eastern hierarchical model into a modern American culture that values individualism, democracy, and pluralism. As Kripal notes, the guru institution has many problems, but foremost among them are the guru's absolute authority, his or her claims of a divine infallibility, and the theocratic structure of the guru-disciple relationship. These tensions erupted in the now well-documented "fall of the guru" the series of sexual, financial, and alcohol scandals that rocked several North American religious communities in the 1980s.[78]

Such scandals significantly contributed to the traditional guru-disciple model being subject to several modifications that are seen as making it more suitable for the contemporary American cultural climate. Many Hindu-inspired and Buddhist communities, for example, have developed more democratic models of authority that promote multiple mentors, presented as "spiritual friends," rather than a single authoritative guru.[79] Much attention has also been drawn to the myriad psychological dynamics that occur within guru communities, and many groups have invited psychotherapists to work with them.[80] Similarly, numerous figures have argued persuasively for the need to discriminate between spiritual realization and psychological development and suggested supplementing spiritual discipline with psychotherapy.[81] In a related vein, therapist and Tibetan Buddhist John Welwood advocates more dialogue between the traditional Eastern model of surrender and the Western model of individuation. Welwood suggests that individuality should not be viewed as an obstacle to spiritual awakening but rather as a precious vehicle for embodying it more fully.[82]

Cohen, however, forms a notable counterpoint to contemporary American trends regarding the guru-disciple model and the value of the personal individual. Since his Neo-Advaitin days Cohen has been very comfortable in a traditional authoritative guru role. He has been a vocal supporter of what he calls the guru principle and has strongly criticized the Western democratization and psychologization of the guru-disciple relationship. Cohen and his students claim that spiritual individualism and psychological dilution motivates contemporary guru revisionings and lament what they view as a prevalent postmodern cultural distrust and cynicism about spiritual authority.[83] Cohen also significantly departs with his contemporaries on the issue of how integration between the absolute and relative is to be attained. Dismissing common attempts to integrate Asian spirituality with Western depth psychology, for example, Cohen has insisted that psychology consolidates the ego and that incorporating the personal into spiritual practice always sacrifices the perspective of the absolute.[84] Holding strong to his impersonal approach, he has attempted to erase rather than include personal individuality.

In Cohen, therefore, we find an American guru who both radicalizes and reacts against the modernization of Indian religions. As noted earlier, for example, in spite of Cohen's protests he is clearly aligning his teaching with more common trends. In addition to his collective revisioning of the guru, in what could be interpreted as a concession to individuality, he includes autonomy as a characteristic of collective enlightenment, and I was surprised to recently hear him recommend psychological work to a participant at a virtual retreat. Such discrepancies and the mix of traditional, modern, and now postmodern elements that characterize his teaching, however, are what ultimately make Cohen such an interesting if sometimes troubling figure in the study of contemporary American Hinduism.

⟨⟩

Since this chapter was written, Cohen has stepped down as guru and leader of EnlightenNext and has issued a public apology for his inability to confront his own ego, and his mistreatment of students. Andrew Cohen, "An Apology," June 26, 2013 *AndrewCohen.org*, http://andrewcohen.org/blog/apology (accessed Jun. 26, 2013). EnlightenNext will continue to be run by his senior students with no change, at this time, in the teaching of evolutionary enlightenment. For a critical perspective see Hal Blacker, "Andrew Cohen and the Fall of the Mythic Guru in the Age of PR-Spin," June 21, 2013, *WHAT Enlightenment??!* http://whatenlightenment.blogspot.co.uk/ (accessed Jun. 22, 2013). Also of note is that in 2011, due to financial challenges, EnlightenNext magazine folded. *EnlightenNext Magazine*, http://andrewcohen.org/about/ENMag (accessed Jun. 22, 2013).

Notes

1. For example, *Jerry Katz's Non-Dual Salon*, http://www.nonduality.com/ (accessed Apr. 28, 2010).
2. Andrew Cohen, *Autobiography of an Awakening* (Corte Madera, CA: Moksha Foundation, 1992), 5–6.

3. Ibid., 13.

4. Ibid., 22.

5. The major source of information comes from David Godman, *Nothing Ever Happened*, vols. 1–3 (Boulder, CO: Avadhuta Foundation, 1998). Despite Godman's attempts to verify information, the biography is written as an act of homage and must be treated cautiously as a hagiographic portrait.

6. Ibid., 121–122. I follow common practice in capitalizing the *atman* Self in order to distinguish it from the illusory ego self.

7. Andrew Cohen, *My Master Is My Self* (Corte Madera, CA: Moksha Foundation, 1989).

8. Andrew Fort, *Jivanmukti in Transformation* (Albany, NY: SUNY Press, 1998); and Arvind Sharma, *Experiential Dimensions of Advaita Vedanta* (Arvind Delhi, India: Motil Banarsidass Publishers, 1993).

9. For details of Poonja's teaching, see H. W. L. Poonja, *Wake Up and Roar* (Boulder, CO: Sounds True, 2007).

10. Cohen, *Autobiography*, 30.

11. Cohen, *My Master*, 12.

12. Cohen, *Autobiography*, 35–36.

13. Ibid., 22–32

14. Andrew Cohen, *Enlightenment Is a Secret* (Larkspur, CA: Moksha Press, 1991).

15. Andre van der Braak, *Enlightenment Blues: My Years with an American Guru* (New York: Monkfish Books, 2003), 37.

16. Cohen, *Autobiography*, 56–57.

17. Ibid., 124.

18. For an account of this shift in Cohen's community see, van der Braak, *Enlightenment Blues*, 56–62.

19. For van der Braak's description of this period see *Enlightenment Blues*, 99–109.

20. Ibid., 106–108.

21. There is no mention of Cohen in Godman's biography of Poonja, but there are places in which Poonja is dismissive of relative reality. Godman, *Nothing Ever Happened*, 127, 317.

22. Cohen, *Autobiography*, 106.

23. Van der Braak, *Enlightenment Blues*, 101–102. Gangaji is one of the most famous and well-respected Western Advaita teachers, http://www.gangaji.org/ (accessed Apr. 16, 2010).

24. Cohen, *Autobiography*, 126.

25. Andrew Cohen, *Who Am I? & How Shall I Live?* (Lenox, MA: Moksha Press, 1998).

26. Ibid., 6.

27. Ibid., 14–29.

28. Andrew Cohen, *Embracing Heaven and Earth* (Lenox, MA: Moksha Press, 2000).

29. Cohen, *Enlightenment Is a Secret*, 85–86.

30. Van der Braak, *Enlightenment Blues*, 157

31. See accounts of these and related incidents at *WHAT Enlightenment??! An Uncensored Look at Self-Styled American Guru Andrew Cohen,* http://whatenlightenment.blogspot.com/ (accessed between Apr. 2009 and May 2010).

32. Susan Bridle, "A Legacy of Scorched Earth" posted Feb. 2, 2005, *WHAT Enlightenment??!,* http://whatenlightenment.blogspot.com/2005/02/legacy-of-scorched-earth.html (accessed Apr. 2009).

33. *WHAT Enlightenment??!,* http://whatenlightenment.blogspot.com/ (accessed between Apr. 2009 and May 2010).

34. William Yenner and contributors, *American Guru* (Rhinebeck, NY: Epigraph Books, 2009).

35. Anonymous, "Letter to a Seeker," posted Friday, Oct. 29, 2004; see also Stas M "Letter from a Senior Student," posted Feb. 7, 2005; and Susan Bridle "A Legacy of Scorched Earth," posted Feb. 2, 2005. All posted on *WHAT Enlightenment??!*

36. Ken Wilber's foreword to Andrew Cohen, *Living Enlightenment: Evolution beyond the Ego* (Lenox, MA: Moksha Press, 2002), xvi.

37. Andrew Cohen, "A Declaration of Integrity," http://www.andrewcohen.org/blog/index.php?/blog/post/declaration-of-integrity/ (accessed on May 9, 2010).

38. Andrew Cohen, *In Defense of the Guru Principle.*

39. For a thoughtful account of the crazy wisdom tradition see Michael Stoeber, "Amoral Trickster or Mystic-Saint? Spiritual Teachers and the Transmoral Narrative," in *Crossing Boundaries: Essays on the Ethical Status of Mysticism,* ed. Jeffrey J. Kripal and William B. Barnard, 381–405 (New York: Seven Bridges Press, 2002).

40. Ken Wilber's foreword to Cohen, *Living Enlightenment,* xiii–xviii.

41. *Guru Talk: American Guru Andrew Cohen: Former Students Speak Out,* http://www.guru-talk.com/ (accessed May 9, 2010).

42. Ibid.

43. Susan Bridle's response to Yonatan Levy's questions regarding Andrew Cohen and EnlightenNext at Yonatan Levy, at *WHAT Enlightenment??!,* http://whatenlightenment.blogspot.com/search?q=levy (accessed May 9, 2010).

44. For a description of skillful means see Paul Williams, *Mahayana Buddhism* (London: Routledge, 1989), 197–204.

45. "Why Are You So Controversial? Part Six of a Multimedia Interview with Andrew Cohen," *AndrewCohen.org,* https://www.andrewcohen.org/interview/controversial.asp (accessed May 9, 2010).

46. "Do We Still Need Gurus? Part Five of a Multimedia Interview with Andrew Cohen." *AndrewCohen.org,* https://www.andrewcohen.org/interview/guru.asp (accessed May 9, 2010).

47. Andrew Cohen, *Living Enlightenment,* 16.

48. "What Is Your Vision?" http://www.andrewcohen.org/interview/default.asp (accessed Apr. 23, 2010).

49. "What Is Evolutionary Enlightenment?" http://www.andrewcohen.org/interview/evolutionary-enlightenment.asp (accessed Apr. 23, 2010).

50. "When Nothing becomes Something and Being and Becoming: The Philosophy and Vision of Evolutionary Enlightenment," *Andrew Cohen.org* (accessed Apr. 17, 2010).

51. "A Revolution in Consciousness and Culture," http://www.andrewcohen.org/andrew/revolution-consciousness-culture.asp (accessed Apr. 18, 2010).

52. The absolute self is often capitalized to differentiate it from the false ego-self. "The Self Absolute," http://www.andrewcohen.org/teachings/model-viewer.asp (accessed Apr. 23, 2010).

53. "The Authentic Self and the Ego: Two Different Parts of the Self," http://www.andrewcohen.org/teachings/authentic-self-ego.asp (accessed Apr. 23, 2010).

54. "About EnlightenNext," http://www.enlightennext.org/about/ (accessed Apr. 17, 2010).

55. The virtual retreat was attended by 450 participants whereas the virtual conference was attended by 13,000 people, which shows that the integral alliance is giving Cohen exposure to a much larger audience.

56. http://www.andrewcohen.org/events/ (accessed Apr. 17, 2010).

57. "Evolutionary Enlightenment courses," *EnlightenNext*, http://www.eecourse.org/index.php?q=en/index (accessed Apr. 17, 2010).

58. "A Revolution in Consciousness and Culture," http://www.andrewcohen.org/andrew/revolution-consciousness-culture.asp (accessed Apr. 18, 2010).

59. Ibid.

60. Tom Houston, "Declaration Day: The Emergence of Evolutionary Enlightenment," http://www.andrewcohen.org/notes/index.php?/weblog/blog/declaration_day/ (accessed Apr. 5, 2010).

61. For student testimonies see Tom Houston's "Conferencing in Consciousness," http://www.andrewcohen.org/notes/index.php?/blog/conferencing_in_consciousness/ (accessed Apr. 25, 2010).

62. "Victory!" http://www.andrewcohen.org/notes/index.php?/weblog/blog/victory/ (accessed Apr. 25, 2010).

63. Ibid.

64. Phone interview with author, Dec. 7, 2009.

65. The Evolution of Enlightenment: The Guru and the Pandit, Ken Wilber and Andrew Cohen in Dialogue," *What Is Enlightenment?* (Spring–Summer 2002), http://www.enlightennext.org/magazine/j21/gurupandit.asp (accessed Apr. 27, 2010).

66. See Sri Aurobindo, *The Life Divine* (Pondicherry, India: Sri Aurobindo Ashram, 2009); and Peter Heehs, *The Lives of Sri Aurobindo* (New York: Columbia University Press, 2008).

67. Craig Hamilton, "Why Sri Aurobindo Is so Cool," *What Is Enlightenment?* Spring–Summer 2002, http://www.enlightennext.org/magazine/j21/aurobindo.asp?page=1 (accessed Apr. 25, 2009).

68. "Following the Grain of the Kosmos. The Guru and the Pandit: Ken Wilber and Andrew Cohen in Dialogue," *What Is Enlightenment?* (May–July 2004), http://www.enlightennext.org/magazine/j25/guruPandit.asp (accessed Apr. 25, 2009).

69. Ken Wilber, *Integral Psychology: Consciousness, Spirit, Psychology, Therapy* (Boston: Shambhala Publications, 2000), and *Integral Spirituality: A Startling New Role for Religion in the Modern and Postmodern World* (Boston: Integral Books, 2006).

70. Van der Braak, *Enlightenment Blues,* 66–67.

71. Integral Institute at http://www.integralinstitute.org/ Integral Life at http://integrallife.com/ and Integral Naked at http://in.integralinstitute.org/ (all three accessed Apr. 27, 2010).

72. Robert Sharf, "Experience," in *Critical Terms for Religious Studies,* ed. Mark C. Taylor (Chicago: University of Chicago Press, 1998), 94–116.

73. Fort, *Jivanmukti in Transformation.*

74. Jorge Ferrer, *Revisioning Transpersonal Psychology* (Albany, NY: SUNY Press, 2002), 15–40.

75. Jeff Wilson, *Mourning the Unborn Dead* (Oxford, Eng.: Oxford University Press, 2009); and David McMahan, *The Making of Buddhist Modernism* (Oxford, Eng.: Oxford University Press, 2009).

76. Jeffrey J. Kripal, *Esalen: America and the Religion of No Religion* (Chicago: Chicago University Press, 2007), 16–24.

77. "The Evolution of Enlightenment. The Guru and the Pandit, Ken Wilber and Andrew Cohen in Dialogue," *What Is Enlightenment?* (Spring–Summer 2002), http://www.enlightennext.org/magazine/j21/gurupandit.asp (accessed Apr. 27, 2010).

78. Jeffrey J. Kripal, "Debating the Mystical as the Ethical: An Indological Map," in *Crossing Boundaries,* 53–55.

79. Mariana Caplan, *Do You Need a Guru?* (London: Thorsons, 2002).

80. Kathy Butler, "Encountering the Shadow in Buddhist America," in *Meeting the Shadow,* ed. Connie Zweig and Jeremiah Abrams, 137–147 (New York: Tarcher/Putnam).

81. Georg Feuerstein, "The Shadow of the Enlightened Guru," in *Meeting the Shadow,* ed. Connie Zweig and Jeremiah Abrams, xxx–xxx (New York: Tarcher/Putnam), 148–150.

82. John Welwood, "East Meets West—The Psychology of the Student-Teacher Relationship," in *Do You Need a Guru?* 20.

83. Deborah Debold, "The Future of the Student-Teacher Relationship: Definitely NOT Just a Book Review of Mariana Caplan's *Do You Need a Guru?*" *What Is Enlightenment?* (Spring–Summer 2003).

84. "What Is Ego? Friend or Foe," *What Is Enlightenment?* (Spring–Summer 2000).

Conclusion

On Reason, Religion, and the Real

Jeffrey J. Kripal

An old master says the soul is created in the middle between one
and two. The one is eternity, which maintains itself ever alone and
without variation. The two is time, which is changeable and given
to multiplication.

—Meister Eckhart, Sermon Fifty-Two

There are two in here.

—Sri Ramakrishna

How does one conclude such rich and diverse chapters on such a col-
orful cast of characters—and in just a few pages?[1] One certainly does
not try to summarize the individual chapters, nor is dwelling on the
particulars particularly helpful. Better instead to try to isolate a few core
arguments of the book as a whole. This is always tricky, though, as these
"core arguments" may turn out to be my core arguments instead of those
of the authors. Still, an obvious consensus appears to be forming around
key issues and concerns in the community of scholarship expressed in
volumes like this one, so our risk is somewhat mooted here. With this
trickiness and growing consensus in mind, let me frame my concluding
comments around a series of questions something like this. . . .

How does one put into an English-language framework a complex set of Euroamerican spiritual teachers whose central doctrines
originated well outside of Europe or America, that is, in South Asian

cultures and languages? How does one understand historical subjects undergoing enlightenment events whose central implications appear to be that (1) the historically conditioned subject does not constitute the deepest nature of the human being; and (2) this deeper human nature can directly access the real beyond space and time since it is the real? Presumably, such a claim pertains as much to the historian of religions as the religious subject and is as true at 80° West longitude as it is at 80° East longitude. Or does the real discriminate according to profession as well as longitude and latitude? Is the real less real in some people and places?

The Historian, the Believer, and the Knower

Therein lies the rub. And it rubs as much against the reason of the traditional historian as the religion of the traditional believer. This double rub constitutes the deepest challenge of the present volume. The topic of Western subjects becoming authoritative spiritual teachers of nondual systems that originated in Hindu India, after all, strikes at the very core of a whole set of assumptions commonly made by both the believer and the historian or humanist, if in very different modes. Allow me, for the sake of discussion, to exaggerate both positions.

I am referring here, of course, to Western scholarship and modern Hindu guru traditions, as that is the focus of the present volume, but my observations could just as easily be applied to historical scholarship on any other traveling religious tradition, with different nuances and effects. The point remains the same: the historical study of religion, that is, the historical study of systems that claim to transcend history is a paradox through and through. One can remove this paradox only by removing one of its two poles: the historical method or the presumed experience of transcendence. Religious believers deny the former; traditional scholars the latter. Neither can really stomach the coincidentia at the heart of the professional study of religion.

Beyond belief and beyond reason, however, the fundamental paradox remains: The traditional historian or humanist—bound to a reigning materialist ontology that recognizes no form of transcendence and a reigning epistemology that is dualist, Kantian, and objectivist (with an internal subject perceiving external objects through the medium of the brain and senses)—generally insists that all human experience is local, relative, socially constructed, and, in the end, reducible to social, political, psychological, neurological, chemical, and, finally, physical processes. Oddly, the traditional believer makes an analogous move, if in a very different religious register now. He or she generally insists that the very particular and very local form of belief and practice that just happened to be in place where he or she was born (or has since adopted) is the ultimate or final truth of human existence, that there is, in the end, no real difference between ultimate reality and "my" cultural framing of it. We might accurately say, then, that the historian and the believer both absolutize the local.

From the perspective of at least some of the nondual knowers featured herein (in particular Ramana Maharshi, Andrew Cohen, and Eckhart Tolle and, to a lesser extent, Ram Dass and Rudi), this materialist ontology, dualist epistemology, and absolutization of the local are at best obvious half-truths and at worst patent and dangerous nonsense. From what we might call a culturally liberated nondual gnosis, both the historian and the believer (and too often the guru) are always making the same epistemological and ontological mistake: they are conflating and confusing culture with consciousness.[2]

In effect, they are mistaking the historical context of a particular revelation with the revelation itself. In the present context, they are turning what have every appearance of being genuine enlightenment experiences—which happen all the time and to all sorts of people—into a long, depressing, and ultimately silly series of relativisms, narcissisms, cultural chauvinisms, nationalisms, and fundamentalisms. Such conflations, of course, are not unimportant historically. Quite the opposite. Indeed, these conflations drive and determine the politics of ethnicity, religion building, identity politics, elections, the control and flow of wealth, social structure, real-world violence, and all sorts of other very practical and very important things. But, if we are to take seriously the claims of the nondual traditions, these things have absolutely nothing to do with knowing reality as it really is. Neither the reason of the historians nor the belief of the believers constitute a gnosis, that is, an immediate and direct knowing of the real as real. The Buddhists were right, then: there is a difference between conventional truth and ultimate truth (what I have invoked in my own work as the Human as Two). Followers of various American Hindu groups often commit the error of equating the conventional level of religious egos (especially that of the guru), community, and tradition with the ultimate truth itself.[3] They may indeed experience something of the ultimate truth through these conventional structures, egos, and historical traditions (all of our authors seem open to this possibility), but they then conflate these two levels, alas, at the cost of immeasurable confusion and, too often, immoral, if not downright criminal, behavior. Anything, after all, can be justified if your guru is the ultimate truth of things, as opposed to a historical human being channeling a culturally filtered form of the real in an always relative and limited fashion.

This is why I love the study of North American guru traditions. It forces these paradoxes and moral questions. It provokes these double thoughts, and on all sorts of levels, including those of race and ethnicity. Even when the "white guy" or "white gal" gurus behave badly—and they often do—their very presence, their very existence cuts through the rationalist's and believer's conflation of consciousness and culture and witnesses to the possibility of a deeply human truth beyond all skin color or ethnicity and beyond all the academic materialism and religious bigotry. We need these nondual knowers, these modern gnostics, desperately.

But we also need real scholars, truly sympathetic and truly critical thinkers who are not afraid to study these teachers and their communities with all the tools of the humanities and social sciences, to interact with them, to be moved, maybe even enlightened, by them, but also to argue with them and make some historical sense of the riotous and often troubling facts of their biographies and community narratives. This is what we finally have in the present volume: a collection of courageous intellectuals struggling to make historical and philosophical sense of some of the most interesting, most provocative, and most important religious figures teaching today.

Today. This raises another provocation of this volume: its implicit location of enlightenment in the present. Here too the academic study of religion and the traditional believer share something in common: they generally assume that religious truth is somehow always a thing of the past; that the "real" (or at least the most prestigious) study of religion is the study of ancient languages and very dead cultures; or that "real" religion (or at least the most authoritative) lies in the distant past; that we live in an age of ignorance and darkness, and that our job is to somehow approximate the past revelation, accurately describe it, get back to it, or, if all else fails, simply to "believe" it.

This is most definitely not the teaching of the most radical of these homegrown gurus. The full religious truth lies in the present, right here, right now. And even if this form of consciousness is always known within a particular cultural and historical context, its truths lie—paradoxically—beyond every culture and context. A culture of no culture (or what we once called a counterculture). A religion of no religion. The results are stunning, and deliciously unpredictable. A gay Jewish psychologist from Harvard, a New York oriental art dealer, a sexually promiscuous Indian yoga teacher, an energy healer and spiritual teacher in a small Pennsylvania town, a white orthodox Hindu in Hawaii, a pot-smoking gay hippie, even—God forbid—professional Indologists can know the true nature of consciousness as directly and as surely as the Buddha knew it in north India 2,500 years ago, or Ramana Maharshi knew it in South India 50 years ago.

This is not to claim, of course, that such individuals have known it; only that, by the logic of these traditions, they can. Enlightenment is possible, here and now. Of course, such a claim is not always quite articulated in this way (and sometimes it is actively denied in figures like Swami Prabhupada Bhaktivedanta, who was not technically a home-grown guru and whose constant invocation of "Krishna Consciousness" put the accent squarely on the "Krishna" part), but that is the impli-cation, for sure, of the more consistent and radical nondual teachings outlined herein. And why not? Is not this the natural, logical end of the nondual position? Short of this, we are left with an absurdity—that the real is not equally real everywhere at all times, that wearing certain clothes or eating certain foods or possessing a particular kind of skin or language gives one access to the true nature of consciousness and human being. This cannot be the truth. Unfortunately, this type of spiri-tual pathology accurately describes most of what we also call "religion."

American Hinduism and the Tantric Transmission

Oddly, this refusal to idolize localism and ethnic identity is not only the logical end of nondualism, but it is also potentially resonant with the deepest philosophical currents of democracy, which insist on a very dif-ferent kind of human equality (one historically based on Western mono-theism and the biblical doctrine of the *imago dei* or "image of God"), but one nevertheless that can be synchronized with these same Asian nondualisms. There is nothing, of course, inherently "democratic" about nondualism. Its doctrines can be aligned with highly authoritarian and hierarchical socioreligious systems as well (like the Indian caste system). Indeed, such authoritarian systems have been the norm, a fact that cre-ated untold human suffering in the "fall of the guru" of the 1970s and 1980s, because authoritarian, often caste-based guru systems clashed with basic American values like freedom of expression and individuality. I do not personally think it is possible to overestimate the impact that American democracy and individualism, and all the civil liberties that these carry, have had on the American transformation of Hindu nondual traditions and the whole subject of the American guru.

Admittedly, there were South Asian precedents and analogues, particularly in the bhakti traditions that valorized a deeply personal relationship of love and devotion over the rituals and scriptures of ortho-doxy and ended up divinizing the guru as an "incarnation" or avatar of the divine. But something else and something more happened when these traditions came to America. The particulars of the Hindu traditions, including the gods themselves, often dropped away and the philosophi-cal underpinnings came increasingly to the fore. This is a theme, often framed as a turn to personal "experience," that the authors return to constantly and rightly. Hence the deeply personal autobiography of Ram Dass in *Be Here Now* as studied by F. X. Charet; the nontraditional, cul-turally "transposable" Advaita Vedanta of Ramana Maharshi analyzed by Philip Charles Lucas; or the energy-mysticism and "soul building" of Rudi as mapped by Helen Crovetto. In the latter case, the very raison d'être of the teaching is to construct a kind of occult individual that can survive the physical dissolution of death!

This is another way of saying that what the editors call American Hinduism is not the same thing Hinduism in America, much less Hindu-ism in India. The authors map these differences in all sorts of detailed ways. There are too many differences to list here, but one seems especial-ly worth flagging: what the authors call Tantra and what I have referred to repeatedly in my own work as the Tantric transmission, a theme Ann Gleig picks up with her usual precision and verve in her chapter on Andrew Cohen. By Tantra, authors like Helen Crovetto, Lola Willi32m-son, and Gleig refer, each in their own ways and accents, to a particular deep worldview that understands the divine as both immanent to and transcendent of the physical material world, including and especially the human body, whose esoteric physiology becomes the instrument or subtle technology through which the aspirant seeks to realize the divine. Countless variants appear across Asia, as recent scholarship has shown in abundance, but most work through some kind of double move that insists that the real is temporally polarized in human experience but exists on its own noumenal level beyond every difference or dualism. This overarching both-and, then spins out into a whole series of "unit-ed pairs" in myth, symbol, and doctrine: Male and Female (hence the famous sexual symbolism and rituals of some of these traditions), God and Goddess, Ultimate and Conventional, Nirvana and World, Purity and Pollution, Consciousness and Energy, Spirit and Sex, and so on.

Every missionary or homegrown guru in the States has by no means taught a form of Tantra, however we choose to define the abstraction. The Neo-Advaitic version of Shaiva Siddhanta of Sivaya Subramuniyaswami and the fundamentalist Gaudiya Vaisnava teaching of Swami Prabhupada Bhaktivedanta come to mind, as does the more Westernizing Maharishi Mahesh Yogi.[4] A figure like Amrit Desai does not quite fit the model either, although his signature concentration on esoteric physiology, kriyas, and prana fuse effortlessly with the Tantric focus on the body as the material site of transcendent gnosis. Exceptions aside, one could argue that the Tantric traditions came to the fore of the American appropriation of Asian religions in the second half of the twentieth century. Hence the Beat embrace of Zen Buddhism and the countercultural efflorescence of Tibetan Buddhism, Chinese Taoism, the *chakras* and esoteric physiology of kundalini yoga, Muktanananda's Kashmir Shaivism, Chogyam Trungpa's Naropa community, Da Free John's "Enlightenment of the Whole Body," and so on. These movements all fed in turn into what E. Burke Rochford Jr. so aptly calls the "new countercultural epistemology," which was Romantic, antinomian, ecstatic, and psychedelic in orientation. And, I would argue, "Tantric."

What the American countercultural actors and enthusiasts did not understand was that these Tantric traditions were, more often than not, essentially Asia's countercultures and, as such, were widely and systematically rejected—if not actively repressed and denied—by the orthodox social systems. They did not understand that the American Hinduisms and Buddhisms that they were adopting, adapting, and creating were not generally representative of the Hindu and Buddhist traditions of Asia. I am not passing any moral judgment here. I am simply making an historical observation toward some measure of cultural understanding. This is why, for example, the Hindu diaspora community reacted so strongly, and so negatively, to the prominence of these same Tantric traditions in the academy in the 1990s and into the new millennium. Tantra, whether in nineteenth-century Calcutta or twenty-first-century California, after all, is not orthodox Hinduism. Indeed, in many ways it is a deconstruction of the brahmanical or orthodox Hindu identity.[5]

But so what? Why on earth should Euro-Americans create an American Hinduism or Buddhism that looks and acts like those of Asia? Does, say, Vajrayana Buddhism in Tibet look anything like Theravada Buddhism in Sri Lanka? Does Bostonian Transcendentalism look anything like thirteenth-century French Catholicism? This is how the history of religions works, has always worked, and will always work. "Moving forward we see no end to proliferation," Williamson concludes. Exactly.

Abandon All Assumptions Ye Who Enter Here

A final feature that makes the study of North American guru traditions so special and that is very much on display in these chapters is the fact that we are much closer to them in space and time and so have access to more details about how they form and develop. The closer we look, the more anomalous and mind-boggling things become. I have referred elsewhere in my history of the human potential movement to these special moments as the "altered states of history," by which I mean to signal the profound effect altered states of consciousness have on the shape, direction, and "feel" of a tradition's history.[6] Far from some modernist sense of objectivity, simple causality, and linear time, we are plunged here into a maze of space-bending, time-bending experiences and subsequent altered histories.

And so we encounter, for example, the story of Neem Karoli reading Richard Alpert's mind, a telepathic event that played a crucial role in Alpert's metamorphosis into the charismatic and influential Ram Dass.[7] We read of Sandra Barnard seeing Nityananda in a vision before she had ever heard of him or seen him (this is an especially common narrative that I have heard numerous times in my own interviews with devotees, particularly those of Sai Baba). We hear of Rudi as a child receiving, like some young shaman or alien abductee, a kind of implant as two "knowledge jars" are placed in his abdomen by two visionary Tibetan monks. We encounter esoteric models of breath and life-energy or *prana*, as in the case of Amrit Desai. We read of electric-like plasmic energies zapping, illuminating, and rewiring devotees (I should add that I have been told of the same energies sexually arousing devotees, sometimes for days). We watch as these vital energies are interpreted and advanced through various para-scientific models, be it the "entrainment" of the two hemispheres of the brain, as we see in Master Charles, or vitalistic embraces of evolutionary biology, as we see in Andrew Cohen (a metatheme if ever there was one apparent in the nineteenth-century British psychical research tradition, Sri Aurobindo's evolving gnostic Superman, Gopi Krishna's reframing of kundalini yoga as the "evolutionary energy in man," and Michael Murphy's the Future of the Body, with its "evolutionary buds" as universal human potentials intuited in mystical and psychical phenomena).

We also struggle again and again with charismatic gurus preaching celibacy but having sex with their disciples, often in the context of occult models of semen, sexual energies, and sublimation. We meet a finally honest homosexual guru (Ram Dass) proposing a "Devotional Tantra," describing himself becoming "both the lingam, the phallus, and the yoni, the vagina," and relating this homoerotic Tantra to the figure of Ramakrishna. We hear painful stories of a Vaishnava community exposing tolerated children to all sorts of physical, emotional, and sexual abuse in its own religious schools via a dysfunctional ascetic worldview. Finally, and perhaps most of all, we encounter various forms of emotional and psychological abuse at the hands of enlightened gurus and their authoritarian institutions, as we see, for example, in the case of Andrew Cohen.

I resist the temptation to explain or expand on my own positions about all of these subjects and figures. It is enough to end here with my admiration for the courage, honesty, and integrity with which all of these difficult questions have been treated herein. I congratulate the editors and authors. The discussion is now moving beyond the earlier dead ends of a flatland rationalism, devotional denial, and orthodox censorship. This in itself is reason to celebrate.

Notes

1. This chapter extends a thread of thinking that I introduced in my earlier essay on Adi Da in Gurus in America and expressed again in my Foreword to Prem Saran's book on the anthropology of Indian Tantra. Both of these books are fine companions to this volume. See Jeffrey J. Kripal, "Riding the Dawn Horse: Adi Da and the Eros of Nonduality," in *Gurus in America*, ed. Thomas Forsthoefel and Cynthia Anne Humes, 193–217 (Albany, NY: SUNY Press, 2005); and "Consciousness as Counterculture," Foreword to *Prem Saran, Yoga, Bhoga and Ardhanareswara: Individuality, Wellbeing and Gender in Tantra* (London: Routledge, 2008).

2. And here they are not so different from that new fetishized figure, the cognitive scientist, who is always making yet another epistemological and ontological mistake: confusing and conflating cognition and consciousness.

3. Dick Anthony, Bruce Ecker, and Ken Wilber, eds., *Spiritual Choices: The Problem of Recognizing Paths to Inner Transformation* (New York: Paragon, 1987). Academics tend to make the opposite mistake: they are always conflating a historically mediated experience of ultimacy with its conventional context or container.

4. The most fundamentalist of all the gurus treated herein seems to be the one who spent the least amount of time in the United States and so was in no real sense "homegrown"—Prabhupada. Still, his ISKCON movement was definitely "homegrown" in the sense that it first flourished and took root in the American counterculture.

5. For more on this, see Jeffrey J. Kripal, "Re-membering Ourselves: Some Countercultural Echoes of Contemporary Tantric Studies," lead essay of inaugural issue, *Journal of South Asian Religion* 1 no. 1 (Summer 2007): 11–28.

6. See Jeffrey J. Kripal, *Esalen: America and the Religion of No Religion* (Chicago: University of Chicago Press, 2007).

7. It takes a special kind of historian to highlight these moments, hence F. X. Charet's early work produced a most remarkable study of the occult and psychical influences on the life and work of a major Western intellectual. See F. X. Charet, *Spiritualism and the Foundations of C. G. Jung's Psychology* (Albany, NY: SUNY Press, 1993).

Contributors

F. X. Charet is a faculty member at Goddard College and coordinates the graduate concentration in Consciousness Studies. His research interests are in the psychology of religious experiences and contemporary spirituality, and he is the author of *Spiritualism and the Foundations of C. G. Jung's Psychology* (SUNY Press, 1993).

Helen Crovetto is an Independent Scholar of New Religious Movements within Hinduism. She holds a master of arts in Religious Studies from the University of South Florida and a master of science in teaching from Rochester Institute of Technology. A list of her publications on new religious movements that engage Tantra is available at www.Tantricmysticism.com.

Henry Doktorski lived at the New Vrindaban Hare Krishna community from 1978 to 1994 where he served in various capacities including artist during the design and construction of Prabhupada's Palace of Gold, schoolteacher, fund-raiser, codirector of Palace Publishing, and minister of music. Since leaving the community he has published articles and letters in journals and magazines including *Musical Performance; Music Theory: Explorations and Applications; Pittsburgh Catholic; USA Today;* and *Playboy*. He is currently working on a three-volume biographical history titled *Gold, Guns and God: Swami Bhaktipada and the West Virginia Hare Krishnas*. Doktorski currently serves on the faculty of the City Music Center at Duquesne University in Pittsburgh.

Ann Gleig is Assistant Professor of Religious Studies at the University of Central Florida, Orlando. She is also an editor for *Religious Studies Review*. She has published several book reviews, encyclopedia entries, journal articles, and book chapters in the fields of Asian religions in America, and religion and psychology.

Ellen Goldberg is Associate Professor of South Asian Religions in the Department of Religious Studies at Queen's University in Kingston, Ontario. She is currently working on a book with Mark Singleton titled *Gurus of Modern Yoga*. Her publications include *The Lord Who Is Half Woman: Ardhanarisvara in Indian and Feminist Perspective* (SUNY Press, 2002) as well as several articles on yoga and cognitive science.

Jeffrey J. Kripal holds the J. Newton Rayzor Chair in Philosophy and Religious Thought at Rice University in Houston, Texas, where he is also chair of the Department of Religious Studies. He is the author of numerous books including *Authors of the Impossible: The Paranormal and the Sacred* (University of Chicago Press, 2010), *Esalen: America and the Religion of No Religion* (University of Chicago Press, 2007), and *Kali's Child: The Mystical and the Erotic in the Life and Teachings of Ramakrishna* (University of Chicago Press, 1995).

Phillip Charles Lucas is Professor of Religious Studies at Stetson University in DeLand, Florida. He is the founding general editor of *Nova Religio: The Journal of Alternative and Emergent Religions* and author of *New Religious Movements in the Twenty-First Century: Legal, Political and Social Challenges in Global Perspective,* co-edited with Thomas Robbins (Routledge, 2004); *Cassadaga: The South's Oldest Spiritualist Community,* co-edited with John J. Guthrie (University Press of Florida, Florida History and Culture Series, 2000); *Prime Time Religion: An Encyclopedic Guide to Religious Broadcasting,* principal author, with J. Gordon Melton and Jon R. Stone (Oryx Press, 1997); and *The Odyssey of a New Religion: The Holy Order of MANS from New Age to Orthodoxy* (Indiana University Press, Religion in North America Series, 1995).

Richard D. Mann is Assistant Professor of Religion at Carleton University in Ottawa, Canada. He has researched and published on the Shaiva tradition and in particular developments in the early traditions of Skanda-Karttikeya and is the author of *The Rise of Mahāsena: The Transformation of Skanda-Kārttikeya in North India from the Kuṣāṇa to Gupta Empires* (Brill, 2012).

E. Burke Rochford Jr. is Professor of Sociology and Religion at Middlebury College in Vermont. He has researched the Hare Krishna movement for thirty-five years and is the author of *Hare Krishna in America* (Rutgers University Press, 1985) and *Hare Krishna Transformed* (New York University Press, 2007) as well as numerous articles on the movement and new religions.

Lola Williamson is Associate Professor of Religious Studies and Director of Peace Studies at Millsaps College in Jackson, Mississippi. Articles and contributions to edited books and encyclopedias focus on the transmission of Hinduism to the United States through immigration as well as through yoga and meditation movements. She is the author of *Transcendent in America: Hindu-Inspired Meditation Movements as New Religion* (New York University Press, 2010).

Index